VANISHING VANCOUVER

VANISHING
MICHAEL
Watercolour.

WHITECA

A typical scene in Vancouver during the 1980s — a row of forlorn little houses, gutted, boarded up, and awaiting demolition. These houses stood on the north side of 16th Avenue east of Laurel Street until their demolition in August, 1989, to make way for the southward march of townhouses and apartments near Vancouver General Hospital. At the time the houses were built, 16th Avenue was the city's southern boundary. The oldest house on the street was the tall, blue-grey one third in from the corner; built in 1907 by a carpenter named W.H. Patterson, it was the only house on the block, and the farthest one west of Cambie Street and the comparatively settled Mount Pleasant area. The sixth gable along was the second one on the block, built in 1911. Streetcar service began on 16th Avenue between Oak and Main streets in October, 1912, on the same day that the Connaught Bridge opened. These two houses had the block to themselves until 1923, when the other houses visible in the water-colour were built. South of 16th Avenue was the Municipality of Point Grey, which amalgamated with the city in 1929.

16TH +LAUREL, VANCOUVER

VANCOUVER

KLUCKNER

by the author

BOOKS LTD.

M. KLUCKNER
1989

Published by Whitecap Books Ltd., 1086 West 3rd Street, North Vancouver, B.C. Telephone (604) 980-9852.

Second Printing, 1991

Canadian Cataloguing in Publication Data

Kluckner, Michael
    Vanishing Vancouver

1. Historic buildings – British Columbia – Vancouver, 2. Vancouver (B.C.) – Buildings, structures, etc. 3. Vancouver (B.C.) – History. I. Title.
FC 3847.7.K68 1990   971.1'33   C90-091335-5
F1089.5.V22K68 1990

Includes index.
ISBN 1-895099-24-2

Typography by CompuType Inc., Vancouver, B.C.

Printed and bound in Canada by Friesen Printers, Altona, Manitoba

There's a little side street at the edge of the town,
That slopes from the brow of the hill,
Where the shadows lie deep from the sun going down,
And the harsh city noises are still.
The white wings of peace seem to brood in the air
Of this little side street that I know,
And Phyllis so fair is awaiting me there,
In our own little bungalow.

—anonymous, from ''Representative California Homes,''
Los Angeles, California, 1912.

And on the pedestal these words appear:
'My name is Ozymandias, king of kings:
Look on my works, ye Mighty, and despair!'
Nothing beside remains. Round the decay
Of that colossal wreck, boundless and bare
The lone and level sands stretch far away.

—Percy Bysshe Shelley, ''Ozymandias.''

All creative art must rise out of a specific soil, and flicker with a
sense of place.

—D.H. Lawrence

CONTENTS

LIST OF MAPS

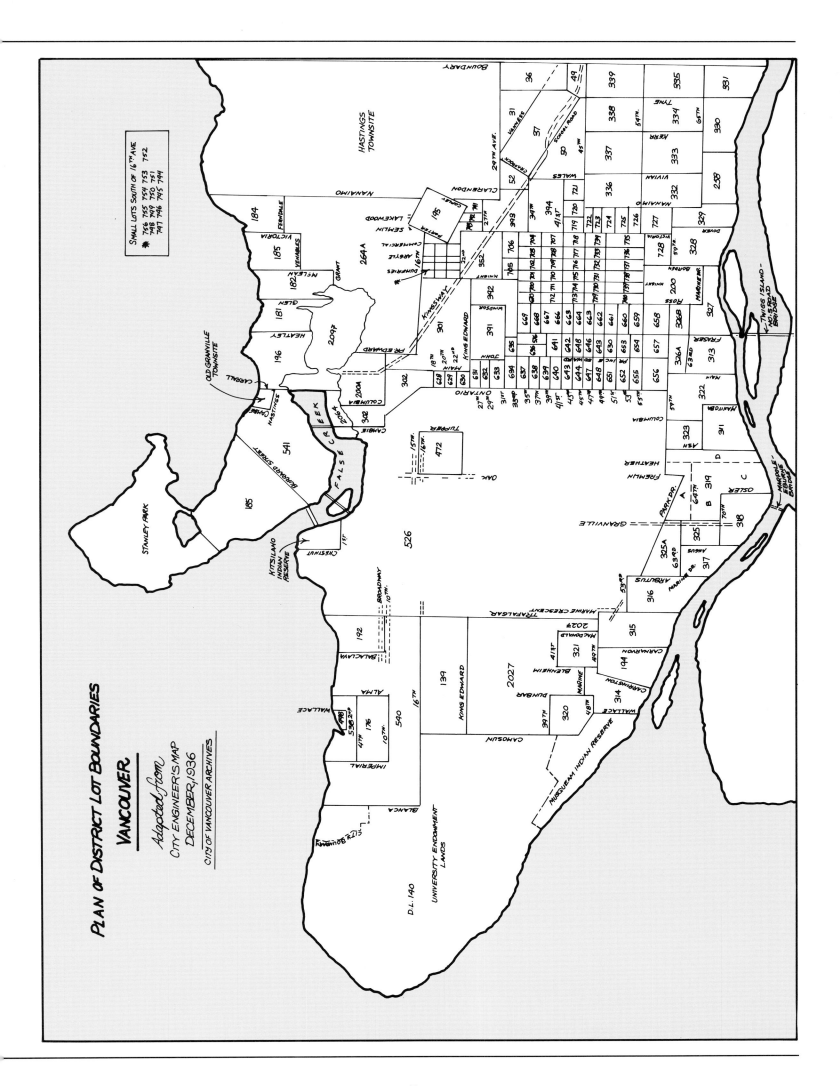

PLAN OF DISTRICT LOT BOUNDARIES

VANCOUVER

Adopted from
CITY ENGINEER'S MAP
DECEMBER, 1936

CITY OF VANCOUVER ARCHIVES

Glory be to God for dappled things—
—*Gerard Manley Hopkins, "Pied Beauty"*

*Horse chestnut trees on the boulevard in October — a house built in 1922 at the
northwest corner of 37th Avenue and Larch in Kerrisdale.*

There are places I remember,
All my life, though some have changed,
Some forever not for better,
Some have gone, and some remain.

All these places have their moments,
With lovers and friends, I still can recall,
Some are dead and some are living,
In my life, I've loved them all.

"IN MY LIFE" by John Lennon and Paul McCartney

PREFACE

One day in the summer of 1986 — the Expo summer — I was walking through downtown on my way to the old James Inglis Reid shop, which I wanted to paint before it ceased business to make way for an expansion of the Pacific Centre shopping mall. I heard the bell in the clock tower of the old post office at Hastings and Granville sounding the hour, and the cry of seagulls disturbed by its tolling, and was suddenly struck by a wave of nostalgia for all the old times, and all the years that I had been in the city, and a recognition that many pieces of my past were slowly disappearing. For better or worse, I thought, the city is changing irrevocably, and some of the things that have been landmarks in my life will soon be gone.

I did not then think of that impending change as a negative thing, but in the years since Expo, as the redevelopment steamroller has gathered speed and audacity, it has seemed to me that the record of an entire way of life is being threatened. It is ironic to reflect that in 1986, when I was considering painting this series of watercolours of the distinctive and disappearing aspects of Vancouver, I thought I would be able to choose my subjects with some sort of repose and detachment, and wallow in the bittersweet nostalgia of the John Lennon lyrics reproduced on the previous page. But the building boom of the past few years has not allowed for detachment and repose.

Of course we must have change, and of course we must have development and employment, but this current orgy of destruction is wasting the good things from the past, which have not worn out or broken down, but are simply disposed of like so much of the detritus of our junky, overpackaged, throwaway culture. Every time a fine downtown building is razed, or an elegant old house and garden is smashed and dug up and hauled away on the back of a truck, or a healthy tree is bulldozed to clear a lot, a piece of me goes with it. Every time a historically significant Vancouver building is needlessly demolished, a crime is committed against both this city's past and its future.

If we, the residents and owners of Vancouver, are to develop a pride in the city's distinctive old neighbourhoods, and its fine downtown buildings, and make the leap of faith necessary to ensure the preservation of our surviving heritage, we must first love the old Vancouver houses, in the way that owners in Toronto's neighbourhoods love their "bay & gable" rowhouses and "Annex houses," and owners in San Francisco love their "painted lady" Victorians, and Sydneysiders love their terrace-houses and "Federation houses." We have, in our Vancouver Boxes and Craftsman bungalows and Tudors, houses that are every bit as significant architecturally, and as adaptable to the 1990s, as are the old houses elsewhere in the world. We must change our attitudes towards the city, and stop taking refuge in the thought that no matter what happens, it will still be Vancouver because there will always be the mountains and the sea.

The majority of the development that has recently occurred in the city may be good, and well designed, and even an improvement over what was there before, but in the few years since Expo I have managed with little difficulty to fill this large book with fragments of the Lower Mainland's roots, now lost. In most cases, they could have been preserved and adapted to the needs of the present, without affecting the local economy's level of growth. But I did not want *Vanishing Vancouver* to be just a collection of ghosts from the 1980s, so a number of the watercolours are of buildings and streetscapes that still exist, and the text accompanying them sets out the historical and architectural case for their preservation.

Painting many of the watercolours in this book was a singularly intense experience. As I sat by the hour in front of my subjects, knowing they were doomed, I could imagine the long-forgotten dreams that went into them, and almost palpably feel their forlorn decay. The watercolours were painted out of doors, or at the very least from inside a car looking out over rolled-down windows, during the months from the summer of 1988 until the spring of 1990. A few were painted from sketches I made in the early 1980s. The inclusion of a set of "after" photographs in the appendix is perhaps unfair, as the new houses have not in many cases been landscaped (although there is no certainty that they ever will be), but it lends credence to the argument that the mellow character is disappearing from our neighbourhoods, and that the cheaply built, quickly profitable "new" is less worthy than was the "old."

Part of the reason for this city's indifference to its surviving architectural heritage is the citizenry's ignorance of the city's history. For most people, architecture without historical context is meaningless and uninteresting; likewise, history without the visible evidence of the past is often boring. But a combination of the two — the surviving architecture and an understanding of its historical context — adds a dimension to life in a cosmopolitan city that no amount of new architecture and civic progress can provide.

M.K.
May, 1990.

INTRODUCTION

The city of Vancouver is at a crossroads. Owing largely to good luck and an often-sluggish economy, it has managed to stagger into its second century with some traces of its past still intact. But politics and economics in the late 1980s have speeded up the pace of redevelopment, threatening the city's ability to perceive its roots and preserve the physical evidence of its past — the buildings and historic streetscapes of the old parts of the city.

Whether your memory of Vancouver goes back five years, or twenty, or fifty, you cannot help but realize that the look and feel of the city is changing drastically. In the downtown, fine buildings have always shared space with parking lots, dilapidated shops and rooming houses, and a forest of power poles. Long-term land speculation having paid off, these neglected gaps are finally being filled. Vancouver's downtown has always needed character and "depth," for lack of a better word, and thus many of the new development plans are cause for some optimism. Conflict only arises when the spreading bulk of the new towers threatens to engulf the best of an earlier generation, along with the worst. Fortunately, in a few recent cases, distinctive heritage buildings that by conventional logic had outlived their time have been incorporated by enlightened developers into modern schemes.[1] There appears to be a dawning realization that if the best buildings from earlier eras are not preserved and adapted to future use, Vancouver's downtown will be a characterless expanse of constantly changing newness, fueled by the land speculation that is destroying the evidence of the city's business history and its architectural roots.

However, there is as yet no such realization of the value of the city's established residential neighbourhoods and their streetscapes, and it is there that Vancouver's true character is expressed and that redevelopment is changing the very nature of the city.[2] There is a unique quality to Vancouver neighbourhoods — an overgrown, ramshackle look to the unpaved back lanes, the yards like a series of individual outdoor rooms with an eccentric and diverse mixture of trees, flowers and shrubs, and an almost overwhelming greenness. It is vanishing under the onslaught of red roofs, blazing outdoor nightlights, pavement, huge garages, and professional lawncutters with noisy power tools. The neighbourliness which used to be such a part of life in Vancouver is being lost in a tide of developers and owners exercising their right to build houses and apartments with no sense of local context. Long-time residents are reluctant to walk through their old neighbourhoods because all the familiar landmarks have been razed. So little physical evidence remains of some old parts of town that it is fair to ask the question: did we actually have a past here, or did we just imagine it?

Except perhaps for Los Angeles, there has never been a major North American city with such an indifference to the value of preserving heritage and architectural diversity. Neither Vancouver nor Los Angeles really existed as an established community before its "invention" by the railway;[3] in the case of Vancouver, the arrival of the Canadian Pacific Railway in the mid-1880s spawned a property-speculation mentality that has never left the city. Whether structures were expensively or cheaply built, all were disposable as the city grew and lifestyles changed.

The conventional wisdom here has always been that, because the city has such a glorious and dramatic natural setting, buildings are a secondary concern. It has been a different case in cities such as Toronto, where character had to be created with buildings and streets and fine trees. Admittedly, some of the buildings erected in Vancouver in the early years were poorly built and thus ripe for replacement, but this was by no means the norm. The West End, for example, until its redevelopment in the fifties and sixties with highrise apartments, was a beautifully balanced, landscaped and settled neighbourhood, full of houses built with a level of craftsmanship and quality of materials almost unknown today. Its fate did not come about because it was cheaply built — it was discarded when times changed, and the same blight destroyed much of Fairview, Mount Pleasant, and Kitsilano in the 1960s and 1970s. By contrast, in cities such as Toronto, Boston, San Francisco, Sydney or Melbourne, during the same time period, tired old neighbourhoods have been rejuvenated by the actions of individual owners, supported in spirit by their civic administrations, who saw in the old neighbourhoods a potential character and prestige unattainable in new housing.

Part of the problem is that Vancouver has been unable to grasp the essential nature of its past — that it was a residential city of small houses amid gardens — and make the leap of faith and political action necessary to preserve the best of it. Vancouver was not a

1 The first such example in Vancouver was probably the Christ Church Cathedral density transfer; see page 48. See also the Sinclair Centre on page 40, and the Toronto-Dominion Bank building on page 54. There were also successful adaptations of old buildings to new uses in Chinatown and Gastown, and the SeaBus terminal, formerly the Canadian Pacific Railway station. At this writing, there are other proposals for the downtown area that will incorporate old buildings into substantial new developments, and the city decision to adopt the "lowrise model" for Granville Street south of Nelson. The recent "heritage" developments, including Tudor Manor and City Square (the Normal and Model schools) by the architect Paul Merrick, are more controversial among heritage advocates and architects: although the buildings were saved from demolition, some people feel they were not incorporated into the new developments in an especially sympathetic manner. Another questionable heritage development was the conversion of the Ledingham house, at Brunswick and East 8th Avenue in Mount Pleasant, into a seniors' housing complex. Little remains of that stylish old home other than its turret.

2 The few exceptions are West Mount Pleasant, First Shaughnessy, and the Talton Place area bounded by Burrard, Arbutus, 13th, and 16th, where a combination of zoning and very creative renovations are preserving the heritage character. City council agreed in April, 1990, to consider specific zoning for the Third Shaughnessy area; see page 114.

3 In the case of Los Angeles, the Southern Pacific Railway's arrival in the city in 1876 accelerated the sporadic progress made in the city over the previous twenty-five years. The frenzied land boom, prompted by the Southern Pacific, and subsequently by the Atchison, Topeka & Santa Fe, lasted until 1888, by which time Los Angeles was well established and had begun to take on elements of "The Promised Land" for American suburbanites. See page 24.

city, in the sense that eastern North Americans or Europeans think of the word; it lacked the urbanity of larger centres, but compensated for that by its gentle climate, proximity to water and wilderness, and clean, garden-city atmosphere. Before the Second World War, the downtown was like a bumptious sawmill town, with a few sophisticated touches exemplified by the old Hotel Vancouver, the *Empress* ocean liners, and the first-class trains of the Canadian Pacific Railway. Both the rough and the refined aspects of the old downtown have largely disappeared, but the established neighbourhoods and their surviving streetscapes still reflect the grace and serenity of life in this old residential city.[4] Demolition and redevelopment, whether for townhouses and apartments or for new single-family houses, is tearing the character out of the city.[5] As described and illustrated in the pages of this book, it is a rare occasion when a heritage building has to be demolished, whether to make way for the higher densities of a growing city, or to make more intensive use of a single-family lot; usually, old buildings are simply discarded, victims of the difficulty that this city has always had with cherishing its history.[6]

• • •

If the communities of the Lower Mainland are going to continue to permit the unrestrained demolition of heritage buildings and old neighbourhoods, they must turn their collective backs on the historical, architectural, financial, ecological, social, and aesthetic values inherent in preservation. The historical legacy in Vancouver has often been dismissed with the argument that Vancouver isn't old enough to have any history. Yet there is no absolute age at which something becomes valuable. In Vancouver, the buildings and streetscapes surviving from the past — whether the 1957 B.C. Electric office tower or a row of turn-of-the-century houses — are intrinsically valuable as the record of the generations who came before. They are our roots, and are no more disposable than are the values of the people who built this province and these buildings. As the Prince of Wales recently wrote, "when a man loses contact with the past, he loses his soul."[7]

The communities that make up Greater Vancouver have not yet lost a unique opportunity to preserve the physical evidence of all the stages of the Lower Mainland's growth: archaeological sites; networks of commercial buildings and houses whose interrelationships could be developed into attractions for sophisticated tourists (see page 177); little houses that have survived in the downtown and can be converted into offices and fitted like postage-stamp parks into contemporary redevelopments (see page 87); the office buildings of earlier generations that can be redeveloped and adapted to modern use (see page 54); the streetscapes in residential neighbourhoods that are the bones of our city (see pages 26-29 and elsewhere); and individual buildings scattered throughout the city that have specific historical meaning, such as the house in Marpole that served as the city's first Children's Hospital (see page 143). To this end, the city has been fortunate to have retained, by a combination of sheer good luck and some private initiative, the Gastown and Chinatown areas, which are protected by provincial heritage legislation.[8]

The development *vs.* preservation challenge in this city should be to prove that an old building *cannot* be adapted to and incorporated into a modern development, rather than to prove that an old building is so valuable that it must be saved. Heritage is perhaps the only issue in the city that, if ignored, cannot be rectified later — the city can replace worn-out pavement, or build new community centres after years of neglect, but it cannot replace its vanished buildings. However, Vancouverites have not yet acquired the sophistication to realize that we of the current generation are just temporary residents of the city, and that ownership should not automatically carry with it the right of demolition.[9]

While the city should not be an unchanging museum, neither should it be just a commodity that is bought and sold and traded and knocked down and built back up — that is not a city. As long as property owners retain the unfettered right to demolish historic buildings, Vancouver will never achieve the character and texture of a major city.

Partly because so many Vancouverites have come here from older and bigger cities, it has been difficult to achieve public and political consensus on the architectural merit of many of Vancouver's heritage buildings. From a purely architectural standpoint, few buildings in this city — or in most other cities, for that matter — are such design classics that a majority of people and politicians would rally around the cause of their preservation. In Vancouver, perhaps only the Marine building and Hotel Vancouver would automatically receive that broad support.[10] The city's inferiority complex is, however, based on pseudo-architectural judgements: we do not have buildings as impressive and monumental as other

4 The old neighbourhoods include the surviving parts of New Westminster, the ring of suburbs that were part of the pre-1929 City of Vancouver (the West End, Strathcona, Grandview, Mount Pleasant, Fairview, and Kitsilano), and the old residential areas such as Shaughnessy, Kerrisdale, and parts of North and West Vancouver.

5 There are other areas in the city, built up in the 1930s and later, that are also being redeveloped and losing their neighbourhood character, but the neighbourhoods referred to here are specifically losing their heritage character.

6 During the 1980s, the City of Vancouver planning department developed a heritage inventory, containing nearly three thousand buildings built before 1940. They were ranked either as "A," "B," or "C" according to their heritage value and character. Inclusion on this list does not protect a building from demolition. *Designated* heritage buildings, under either municipal or provincial law, have their exteriors protected from change, and proposed modifications to provincial heritage law will allow for the protection of heritage interiors and landscape features such as trees. Designation is a process negotiated between the building's owner and the city or province; the City of Vancouver has not designated properties without the owner's concurrence since 1977, when the provincial government amended its laws so that any imposed designation might oblige a city to pay compensation to the owner. Other municipalities and cities within the Lower Mainland have heritage inventories, too, but as is the case in Vancouver, a building's inclusion on an inventory does not necessarily give it any protection. In April, 1990, city council endorsed the proposed changes to provincial heritage legislation that would make restoration and ownership of old buildings more viable economically. By no means all of the buildings illustrated in this book are on the heritage inventories of Lower Mainland communities.

7 H.R.H. The Prince of Wales, *A Vision of Britain*, page 10. The comment is perhaps more true for the preservation of heritage than it is for the continuation of old architectural styles, which is the part of his thesis that has prompted such agitated controversy. The Prince maintains that contemporary architects have lost sight of basic principles and humanism, and should be designing in quasi-historical styles the better to incorporate their works into the existing British architectural fabric.

cities. This is a premise that subordinates the importance of historical context to some imaginary scale of absolute architectural value.

The old houses that make up Vancouver's "character neighbourhoods" are local variations on architectural themes, such as the Queen Anne and the California Bungalow, that were erected throughout North America between the 1880s and the 1930s. Although the individual houses have their own architectural value, it is when they are located on a period streetscape, or set within a lush west-coast garden, that they have irreplaceable value to the city's character. These house styles are described on pages 17 through 34 of this book.

Not only do Vancouver's old houses get in the way of "progress" — in many cases they are old-fashioned and smaller than what can be built under current zoning — but they are also threatened by the choice of materials that went into them. The vast majority of them are built of wood, and many Vancouver residents seem to feel that houses built of so-called permanent materials, such as brick and stone, are the only ones of long-term value.[11] Ironically, houses here are still being built of wood — beautiful, old wood-shingle-covered houses are being demolished and replaced by wood-*framed* houses with brick and stone veneers, or, worse, with vinyl or aluminum siding, and even with brick-look or stone-look styrofoam stabilized with a coat of acrylic and glued to the wooden frame![12] These new houses are the equivalent of the planned obsolescence seen elsewhere in society in cars and appliances.

An era of wooden houses, built with a quality of timber that scarcely exists any more, and with craftsmanship affordable today only by the richest citizens, is being torn down and replaced by cheaply built boxes, sheathed with chipboard, wrapped in plastic, stuccoed, veneered, and finished with mediocre detailing and paintwork, which are then marketed

Eccentric landscaping and the unsympathetic modification of fine wooden buildings are not new realities in the city, as witnessed by this photograph from the 1920s of the shell-encrusted house at 4393 Victoria Drive (demolished), with the designer/occupant and his loyal pet.

8 The provincial protection of Gastown and Chinatown has had its own share of problems, including the legislation's inability to save one of the main-floor interiors of the Wing Sang building at 61 East Pender — the oldest intact interior space in the city — which has been converted into a clothing boutique. The provincial government will likely soon pass heritage legislation with more teeth, but the proposed legislation contains a review clause that will expose designated buildings and sites in the province to a review process that could threaten their protected status.

as gracious and elegant on the basis of their size, their numbers of bathrooms, and their abundance of technological "toys" such as media rooms, security systems, power garage doors, and automatic lawn sprinklers. The mature landscaping surrounding the old houses, including some of the classic gardens in the city, is disappearing, too.

The question of building materials has particular relevance because of the inevitability here of a major earthquake. When built on solid ground, Greater Vancouver's wooden houses, regardless of their age, will perform quite well, although the brick veneers on the new houses will likely end up in a heap on their front lawns. Wooden buildings, such as the multi-family dwellings built by the city in the 1970s along the south shore of False Creek, might go the way of the wooden houses and apartments in San Francisco's Marina district during the 1989 earthquake there; like the Marina, False Creek is filled land (as is the Municipality of Richmond). Old downtown buildings of brick or reinforced concrete are in greater danger of collapse, or of losing bits of their decoration, during a strong earthquake, and the likelihood of this is often advanced as an argument for the razing of heritage buildings and their replacement by new ones. However, the evidence is by no means conclusive that, firstly, old buildings always perform badly in earthquakes, and, secondly, old buildings are uneconomic to upgrade seismically. The restoration and seismic upgrade of the old post office (see the Sinclair Centre, page 40) was done for less money per square foot than the cost of new construction;[13] by contrast, the restoration and seismic upgrade of the old Kelly-Douglas warehouse on Water Street, now The Landing, cost more per square foot. Other brick buildings, such as The Homer (see page 61), would be difficult to upgrade seismically because of their shape.[14] The seismic upgrading of the old Convent of the Sacred Heart would be less expensive than the construction of a new school building (see page 157). But regardless of the specifics of individual projects, the science and engineering of upgrading old buildings to current earthquake standards is a new one, and the cost per unit will inevitably drop as more are retrofitted and new techniques are developed.[15]

The financial argument against the preservation of heritage is based on two theories: new construction is cheaper than renovation; and the marketplace demands new buildings, rather than old ones. It has been true in Vancouver until recently that both the renters of downtown office space and the purchasers of housing attach no prestige and thus no dollar value to the venerability of old buildings, as illustrated by the developer's arguments in favour of demolition of the Georgia Medical-Dental Building (see page 48). A similar situation existed in Toronto and Sydney, Australia, to name two cities, until the mid-1960s, when adventurous home buyers recognized the character of old neighbourhoods such as Cabbagetown and Paddington to be worth preserving; real-estate values in those areas are now among the highest in those cities.[16]

As for the cost of renovation versus new construction, it is fair comment that the development permit system in the City of Vancouver is geared to the latter rather than to the former. If time is money, then the difficulty of getting city permits to renovate and restore makes new construction much easier.[17] Regardless, comparing new construction with high-quality renovation of old construction is like comparing apples with oranges — if the goal of a builder is simply to enclose volumes of air within walls, then certainly new construction can be done less expensively. But creative developers *can* make money on renovations, and can put their efforts competitively onto the market, as witnessed by the recent achievements in West Mount Pleasant (page 94).

The ecological issue in the preservation of heritage concerns the responsible use of resources. Our willingness to allow developers and property owners to ride roughshod over the city's old neighbourhoods, and to haul its perfectly useable houses, topsoil and mature shrubs and trees[18] in huge trucks to the dump, casts doubt on our collective ability to preserve wilderness, to manage resources, or to reduce pollution in a way that will sustain the environment into the future. What of recycling, when we do not recycle our buildings?

There is much that old houses, and the lifestyles of their original residents, can teach the current generation: with the exception of the *Titanic*-era houses of the rich in Shaughnessy and elsewhere, people lived modestly and frugally in small houses and — admittedly because they had little choice — depended on public transit. Each house had a clothesline, vented cupboards for cool storage in the kitchen, and meat safes and root cellars in the basement; cooking scraps and dead plants and leaves went into the compost, not into the garbage can. Many backyards contained a vegetable plot. It is possible to see in the wide porches and extensive gardens of many old houses a focus on simple pleasures and the outdoors. By contrast, many modern houses present a fortress-like façade to the street, have no

9 Countering this view is the one that holds the right to the unfettered use of private property as fundamental to our society; an upholder of this view is the Real Estate Board of Greater Vancouver, through its president Brian Calder, who feels that "a heritage designation is in many ways an expropriation of private property" (quoted in *Real Estate Weekly*, January 19, 1990). However, the public right to zone property for specific types of uses, to demand the inclusion of public amenities in large developments, and even to insist that a portion of a single-family lot be "garden" (meaning unpaved) has become part of the accepted trade off in society between private rights and the public good. Unless heritage preservation is to be dismissed by society as of no public or social value, the rights of an owner to unfettered use of private property will have to bend yet again.

10 Opinions of architecture are apt to be subjective: one wonders whether, if the Georgia Medical-Dental Building had been the same light brick colour as the Marine Building, a consensus would have emerged to save it.

11 Although eastern North American buildings are constructed of brick and stone, they have not yet lasted nearly as long as the typical half-timbered, thatch-roofed Elizabethan cottage of rural England, a place with the same climate as Vancouver.

12 In its ongoing battle with the monster houses that it effectively created by its *laissez-faire* zoning, city council in the spring of 1990 banned "phoney stone and brick on façades" as part of a package of amendments to its single-family zoning by-laws.

13 Information from Jacquie Murfitt, City of Vancouver planning department, 1990.

14 Ibid.

15 In the aftermath of the 1989 San Francisco earthquake, a number of experts were quoted to the effect that the predicted subduction earthquake in Vancouver would cause windows to shatter or burst away from modern highrise buildings, showering the streets below. A pane of glass will kill as surely as a piece of a cornice, but there have been few calls for the demolition of modern office buildings because they pose a hazard in the event of an earthquake.

significant garden or even lawn, and emphasize the great indoors, where owners indulge their passive preoccupation with media rooms and sprawling, luxurious, and plentiful bathrooms. A brief inspection tour of a representative sample of new houses in the Lower Mainland would convince an alien creature that the new west-coast lifestyle is absorbed with the bathroom, the television, and the automobile.[19]

The social issue of heritage often becomes an argument about "gentrification" — old buildings frequently provide affordable rental housing, and restoration usually pushes the rent out of the reach of the former tenants. But without massive government intervention in the real-estate market, the poor will remain dependent on the status quo, regardless of whether buildings are restored or demolished. The hippies and urban poor in old buildings and old neighbourhoods, such as Kitsilano in the sixties and seventies and Grandview in the eighties, and in low-rent and avant-garde parts of downtown, such as Pender Street around Victory Square, depend on their landlords' willingness to continue as long-term land speculators, and on the ability of their dwellings to deteriorate slowly while requiring little maintenance. When old buildings become decrepit, as is the case now with much of the "affordable housing" in the old neighbourhoods of the city, there are two possibilities: either the old houses will be removed or they will be saved. Neither option necessarily offers tenants any hope, and there is no guarantee that accommodation in a renovated old building will be any less affordable than accommodation in a new rental building.

Our throwaway attitude towards our buildings is in philosophical opposition to our old idea of home. The meaning of the word "home" seems to have changed in cities like Vancouver, and the continuity of a home from generation to generation of the same family has all but disappeared from the modern North American lifestyle. A "home" is now a

This sort of sculpture in a back-garden landscape is often an indication that the neighbourhood is being destabilized by real-estate speculation. Along with nearly all the others on the block, this Tudor Revival-style house, at 5992 Trafalgar Street in Kerrisdale, was built in 1923-4. It was not a small house in its day but, in common with the other houses in the area, it sits on a large city lot. This is what makes established Vancouver neighbourhoods subject to so much speculation and redevelopment: the people who planned and settled neighbourhoods such as Kerrisdale wanted houses amid large gardens, submerging the house in the shrubbery. Thus, some of the density and house size that could be built on the lot under current zoning, which recognizes only the absolute proportion of the house's floor space to the lot's total area, is "wasted."

16 The Federation House, seen all over Australia, is another example. This was a style commonly built there around the time of federation in 1901. These are modest houses, not unlike California Bungalows, which have become so popular that they are sought after and restored by owners who slavishly follow the dicta in numerous books and articles devoted to authentic restoration techniques.

17 Architect Robert Lemon, chairman of the city's Heritage Advisory Committee, and the Housing Group of the Architectural Institute of B.C., speaking at a public hearing of Vancouver city council held on March 15, 1990, to discuss amendments to the city's RS-1 zoning by-law.

18 So many lanes and yards have been paved and so many trees removed that a 1989 City Engineering Department study expressed concern about the ability of the city sewers to handle the increased run-off.

19 In old houses, bathrooms were in short supply — some old, unrenovated but luxurious Shaughnessy and Kerrisdale houses have only one, as have the original architect's plans for the nine-bedroom "Fairweather" on Bowen Island (page 192). Recent warnings about global warming and energy depletion, and of the severe automobile-caused air pollution crisis in the Lower Mainland, have not prompted politicians to stop zoning and servicing land in areas with such low densities that they are completely dependent on the automobile.

20 Translations in Sherman Lee, A History of Far Eastern Art, Abrams, New York, page 396.

21 Boris, Art and Labor, pages 60-78.

house — yet another commodity in the complex investment strategy of a family — and is useful as long as it is in a good location. Society is changing so fast that people move house or redecorate as often as they used to buy a new pair of shoes. The piece of property that, for those families who possess it, continues to be passed from parent to child is now the summer cottage. There, removed from some of the inflationary pressures that so twist and discolour city neighbourhoods, little jerry-built cabins can evolve and mellow over generations, and become in a philosophical way the "home" that city life denies us (see pages 192-197).

The old wooden houses and the gardens of Vancouver have mellowed and aged in a serene and gentle manner; time and climate modify them, and in the process comes the gracefulness that is so lacking in the harshly assertive newness of the constantly changing residential landscape. The watercolour on page 8, showing dappled sunlight falling on the garden and wall of a fine old house, captures something of that feeling. Together, the best of the houses and gardens create a sheltered and timeless quality that insulates the city dweller from a few of the ravages of modern life.

Most mature cultures seem to cherish the transition from new to old: the English landscape, with its soft-edged vegetation and quaint architecture, becomes more valuable emotionally and intellectually the older and more quirky it becomes; the Japanese concepts of *wabi* and *sabi*, of "quiet simplicity" and "reticence and lacking the assertiveness of the new,"[20] were the basis of their tea ceremony, and profoundly influenced traditional Japanese house design. The designers of the Craftsman houses and California Bungalows that are such a feature of Vancouver's old neighbourhoods (see pages 24-29) were influenced by Japanese designs and philosophies; one sees in the best of these small, weathered, Vancouver houses the reticence, simplicity and "honesty of materials" of Japanese thought, and of the English Arts and Crafts Movement inspired by John Ruskin and William Morris.[21]

The aesthetic issue has been the most difficult to address in residential areas, because the city has been unwilling to codify taste, except in First Shaughnessy and West Mount Pleasant where zoning bonuses are used to ensure that new development conforms to the existing character of the neighbourhood. Although new designs for townhouses have in some cases been integrated fairly well into Kitsilano, for example, the city has refused to get involved in the issue of what new construction should look like in the single-family areas of the city — which form the majority of the city land-area — except to make half-hearted and repeated stabs at amending the zoning by-law (see footnote 12). The ideal situation is one where owners and speculative builders respect the existing character of the neighbourhood in their new designs, but the reality has more often been the disruption of the established atmosphere and the intrusion of a barren landscape of "Vancouver Specials," monster houses, and the "Developer Georgian Box."

The mellowing of old houses contrasts sharply with many new houses, especially those sheathed with vinyl, pseudobrick, or aluminum, and roofed with tiles — these materials have been designed to resist aging gracefully. Undoubtedly, they will, like the cheaply built "Vancouver Specials" of the 1960s, begin to look tawdry and mildewed, and their pastel stucco will become waterstained.

Of course, there are some very fine new houses in Vancouver, well designed and beautifully built, but there are a lot more of the other type, built to the minimal requirements of the city's *laissez-faire* single-family zoning by-laws and the National Building Code. They may be no uglier than the little 1930s and 1940s stucco boxes that some of them replaced, but they are in addition big and ostentatious — a formidable combination when combined with ugliness.

But an appreciation of the value of heritage cannot be imposed. The stories within this book illustrate some of the difficulties in preservation, and contrast the nostalgia of the Beatles' song on page 9 with the more intellectual and practical issues preservation raises. In the successful cases, where a building or a streetscape has been preserved, someone has made the effort — in the face of bureaucratic obstacles and financial and technical difficulties — to secure a future for some of the best elements of our collective past. This has been and should continue to be an individual and privately financed endeavour, rather than the effort of any level of government, but government — especially the city — has an important role to play. Good zoning and taxation policies that recognize the social values inherent in an architecturally diverse city can promote and sponsor preservation and reward the owners who contribute to these. To date, Vancouver's zoning and taxation policies have been far from neutral on this matter: they have favoured speculators and developers, in the mistaken view that this is better in the long term for the city.

HOUSE DESIGN

Vancouver has always been a city of single-family houses; like the other west-coast North American cities which grew up about a century ago, it was settled by migrants who sought the freedom and independence — no matter how illusory — offered by cheap land and a detached house in a new city. By the early years of this century, house designs inspired by the Arts and Crafts Movement's "simple life" and the so-called Pasadena lifestyle (see page 24) were dominating popular taste in much of North America;[1] Vancouver's versions of this movement are its distinctive, verdant residential areas.

Very few of the thousands of wooden houses built in the 1880s and 1890s survive in Vancouver. They were mainly built in Gothic Revival, Victorian, and Queen Anne styles, often by speculative builders who bought mail-order patterns from American architectural firms; these houses lined the streets of the downtown peninsula and the West End, and have long since been razed for the redevelopment of the growing city. The remaining houses from that period that are illustrated in this book are the Queen Anne houses on Comox Street (page 76), on East Pender Street (page 87), on West 7th Avenue in Fairview (page 98), and in New Westminster (page 171) — the last three of which contain elements of the Eastlake style. City houses on city lots, they lack the lush landscaping typical of later Vancouver suburbs, and would have looked much the same if built in San Francisco or Los Angeles. Typical of many of these old houses are their narrow eaves, tall windows, small porches and bay windows, for they were designed and built at a time before electric lighting was commonplace. The houses of later generations, most notably the California Bungalows, are warm-climate houses with deep porches and broad eaves, adaptable to Vancouver because of the ready availability here of electricity.

The earliest distinctive and surviving Vancouver neighbourhoods developed between the time of the Klondike gold rush of 1898 and the economic depression of 1913-14. That fifteen-year period saw the city's population more than quadruple to over 100,000 people. The frenzied residential building of those years coincided with the popularity of two types of houses, which have — until the recent rash of demolitions — dominated the *look* of the city's old neighbourhoods.

Firstly, and the subject of almost infinite variation, are the Edwardian Builder houses — the Vancouver Boxes illustrated on pages 18 through 21. Inspired by or copied from books of house plans published by enterprising architects in the United States, they were intended as efficient and practical housing, and were varied and modified to suit the ideas of the builder, the desires of the buyer, and the availability of different types of decorative woodwork.[2]

Secondly, reflecting the Arts and Crafts Movement and the craze for the Pasadena lifestyle, are the Craftsman houses and California Bungalows illustrated on pages 24 through 29. These houses, especially when set on a verdant suburban lot and framed by mature, deciduous boulevard trees, seem to epitomize the "garden city" ideal of old Vancouver and the west-coast utopia of the little verse on page 5 of this book.

The views of architects had little direct influence on the style of these neighbourhoods, as comparatively few houses in Vancouver — even in prestigious neighbourhoods such as Shaughnessy Heights — were custom-designed. Other styles had superseded the Craftsman houses by the early 1920s. A penchant for conservative "revival" building styles in Vancouver, especially in west-side areas like Kerrisdale, Dunbar, and Mackenzie Heights, which had been only sparsely settled by 1914, coincided with a renewed building boom in the city.[3] Tudor and Georgian Revival houses[4] shared the streets with Dutch Colonials; although they were generally quite substantial houses for the time, they did not dominate their lots, and in the decades since, many have been almost buried by their large gardens. It is often these which are the targets of developers who build "monster houses" on the large lots. The Craftsman and Edwardian Builder houses of previous generations are usually in older suburbs, such as Kitsilano, Grandview, and Mount Pleasant; they have often been converted into suites, and later demolished and replaced by townhouses or apartments.

1 Boris, *Art and Labor*, page 76.

2 As it was a style seen in various forms throughout North America, and most of the patternbook plans came from the United States, the name Edwardian Builder, although favoured by Vancouver-area heritage experts, seems inappropriate — Edward VII was not an influential figure in the United States, and the term "Edwardian era" rarely appears in American books. The alternative of calling these houses "Builders' Boxes" or "Vancouver Boxes" may be visually accurate, but could be construed to have a derogatory meaning. In the absence of other terms, I have used all three interchangeably.

3 In southern California, after the First World War, a wave of nostalgia for simpler times helped to promote the Spanish Colonial Revival (see Gebhard and Winter, *Architecture in Los Angeles*, page 17), which arrived in Vancouver in the late 1920s, complete with wrought-iron balconies and red-tile roofs; the two remarkable examples here are the Reifel brothers' "Casa Mia" and "Rio Vista" on Southwest Marine Drive, a far cry from the modest Spanish Colonial boxes in districts like Arbutus Ridge and Mackenzie Heights.

4 A good Tudor Revival house-and-garden combination stood at 2383 West 49th Avenue (see page 125); another was at 1609 West 29th (see page 115). The little Georgian Revival house which stood at 5669 Angus Drive (page 114) is the sort of house often called the "CPR Box," and is still quite common in the CPR subdivisions of Second and Third Shaughnessy, and in Kerrisdale.

VANCOUVER BOX NUMBER 1

The Vancouver Box appeared on suburban streets between about 1900 and 1915. The type illustrated below is one of two types of early Builders' Boxes, and is still a common sight and easily recognizable, whether it is one storey or two, because of the small dormer cut into the attic of the hipped roof. All of the houses built during this period have a front porch, usually extending across the full width, although many owners have had them filled in to provide additional indoor living space. The ones below, in contrast to the examples on the next page, were built from scratch.

CORNER OF 38TH & TRAFALGAR, KERRISDALE

15TH & PRINCE ALBERT, MOUNT PLEASANT

MAPLE NEAR 2ND KITSILANO

8TH AVENUE NEAR MAPLE KITSILANO

M.KLUCKNER 1990

THE B.C. MILLS PREFABS

As part of its range of prefabricated houses, the B.C. Mills, Timber & Trading Company offered variations on the Vancouver Box, utilizing its patented modular wall system.[1] BCMT&T was the largest forest products company in the province, an amalgamation in the 1890s by John Hendry of the Royal City Planing Mills with the Moodyville sawmill in North Vancouver and the Hastings Sawmill on the Vancouver waterfront; following Hendry's death in 1916, the company was run by his son-in-law, Eric Hamber. The prefabricated houses owed their success to E.C. Mahony, who invented and patented in 1904 a four-foot wall-panel system, composed of layers of veneer and building papers with horizontal shiplap on the exterior and a locking, weatherproof vertical joint, which allowed the houses to be built at the factory and shipped almost anywhere.[2] The prefabrication — and the excellent insulating qualities of the wall panels — made them especially useful for shipment to the prairies, where there was little readily available lumber, but many were erected in the City of Vancouver, and floated as kits to North Vancouver (page 179) and Bowen Island (page 196). All had the same eye-catching feature — the vertical battens separating the shiplap wall sections. Doors and windows were built into the panels at the factory. Illustrated below is the "Model J"; in the watercolours on pages 33 and 197 are other designs. The company ceased production of its prefabricated houses in 1910.

1 B.C. Mills, Timber, & Trading Company brochure, printed in 1905, of "Patented Ready-Made Houses," in CVA, pamphlet number Und-507.

2 Claude Douglas, "The Pre-Fabricated Search Is On," *Heritage West*, Winter 1983.

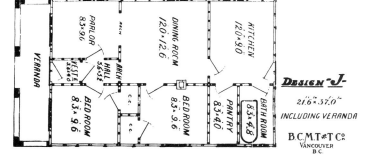

(Left) The page from the B.C. Mills, Timber & Trading Company brochure showing the ''Model J,'' its prefabricated version of the single-storey Vancouver Box: the 1905 price, FOB Vancouver, was $585. Note that the bathroom seems to be designed for a bath only — the water closet was intended to be outdoors.

(Right above) A ''Model J'' erected by the speculative builder J.J. Hanna somewhere on Comox Street in the West End.

(Right below) The ''Model J'' erected in Fairview by James Paul, whose testimonial letter, dated January 3, 1905, was printed in the above-mentioned brochure: ''Having just completed one of your Ready-made Houses, design 'J,' which I bought recently, I have much pleasure in stating my entire satisfaction therewith. As a practical carpenter, I consider the fact that all material is thoroughly seasoned of special merit, thereby avoiding open joints, settlements, shrinkage and consequent cracking of plaster. Another very important consideration which should commend itself to the buyer is that instead of months of waiting, as usually occurs under ordinary construction, it is only a question of days with the 'Ready-made.''' Signed, ''J.M. Paul, 5th Avenue near corner of Pine Street.''

The classic English cottage garden is a ramble of old-fashioned flowers and shrubs on both sides of the pathway leading from the front gate to the house. Most Vancouver city lots are not deep enough to achieve that effect, and most owners succumb to the convention — anathema to the ideal of the cottage garden — of a front lawn; however, the cottage-garden ideal of covering the building itself with flowers works well on the wooden houses of old Vancouver, such as this one, covered with wisteria, at 2775 West 42nd Avenue in Kerrisdale. It was built near the end of the great Vancouver boom of the early years of the century. Kerrisdale, then a part of the Municipality of Point Grey, had begun to open up to suburban development; early in 1912, the B.C. Electric Railway Company laid a single streetcar track west along Wilson Road (41st Avenue) from the interurban station at West Boulevard to Dunbar. The lots along 42nd Avenue, just west of the CPR land boundary at the uncleared right-of-way for Trafalgar Street, were subdivided and developed by speculative builders like Baynes & Horie, who built 2755 and 2765 West 42nd (see page 23).

The art nouveau cast-iron hot-air vents at 2775 West 42nd Avenue.

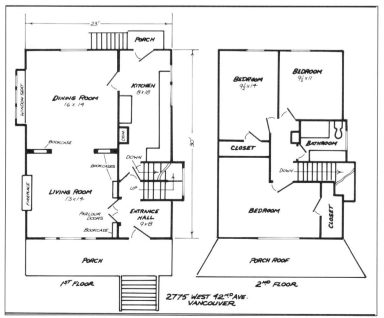

The house at 2775 West 42nd Avenue in Kerrisdale, built in 1912 by a carpenter named George W. Bissell, is a good example of the second type of Vancouver Box, and shows the influence of a variety of building styles, including the Craftsman. A gabled roof, large front porch, shingle siding, and decorative brackets are typical of the style,[1] while the use of the porch and the house itself as an extension of the garden is typical of the "garden city." There were many variations in this type of Vancouver Box, especially in the floor plans — 2775 has an entrance hallway, whereas the Vancouver Box next door at 2765, although built at exactly the same time (late 1912), has a den but no entrance hallway, and its front door opens directly into the living room. Both houses were probably adapted from a set of plans such as the ones illustrated below. The one at 2775 is also interesting because it has a more open floor plan — made possible in the northern climate by the technology of the hot-air furnace — than the warren of little parlours and fireplaces typical of earlier house styles;[2] it is quite small, 690 square feet on the main floor and 540 square feet above, but manages to convey a spacious feeling.

1 The second-floor wood-framed window visible in the watercolour on the adjoining page is not original — the house initially had two separated windows on the second floor (as in the Dustman plan below), but these have been replaced.

2 In addition to the living room fireplace, the house has a second chimney for the furnace and kitchen stove. A sleeve enters that chimney from the dining room, indicating that a parlour stove could have been added to the dining room.

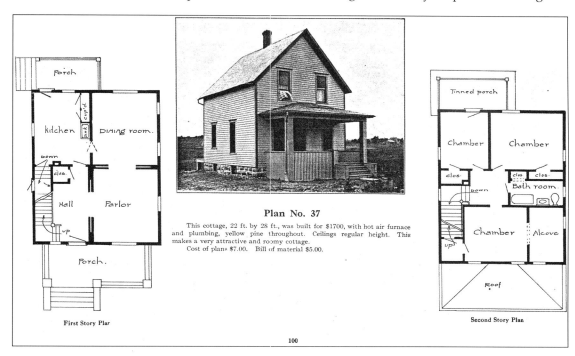

Plan No. 37

This cottage, 22 ft. by 28 ft., was built for $1700, with hot air furnace and plumbing, yellow pine throughout. Ceilings regular height. This makes a very attractive and roomy cottage.

Cost of plans $7.00.   Bill of material $5.00.

First Story Plan

Second Story Plan

100

A page from Dustman's Books of Plans and Building Construction, *by the architect U.M. Dustman of Freeport, Illinois, published in 1909, showing a "cottage" with a floor plan that is almost the mirror image of the one at 2775 West 42nd Avenue.*

The front porch of the house at 2775 West 42nd Avenue, painted in early October. Since the 1920s, most houses have been built without a front porch; the house is turned in upon itself, and the outdoor focus is on the privacy of the back garden. The front yard survives due to the obligatory Vancouver twenty-four-foot setback from the property line (in single-family RS-1 zones, about 70 percent of the city's land area), but as it and the street cannot be enjoyed from the comfort of a deck chair on a porch, it is abandoned and irrelevant, and usually landscaped with the boring monoculture of a front lawn.

INTERIORS

The builders' houses and California Bungalows described in these pages were probably erected from mail-order plans, which usually contained detailed drawings of interior cabinetry, bookcases, fireplaces and mantelpieces, colonnades, window seats, dining-room ceiling beams, and other "built-ins." The illustrations below are from old pattern books, and the watercolour on the adjoining page is the den of a 1912 shingled "Swiss cottage" — a variation on the Craftsman house.

 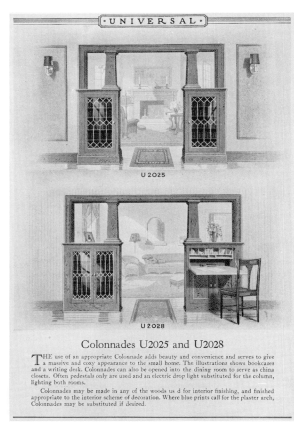

Colonnades U2025 and U2028

THE use of an appropriate Colonnade adds beauty and convenience and serves to give a massive and cozy appearance to the small home. The illustrations shows bookcases and a writing desk. Colonnades can also be opened into the dining room to serve as china closets. Often pedestals only are used and an electric drop light substituted for the column, lighting both rooms.

Colonnades may be made in any of the woods us d for interior finishing, and finished appropriate to the interior scheme of decoration. Where blue prints call for the plaster arch, Colonnades may be substituted if desired.

1 Both from *Dustman's Books of Plans and Building Construction*, Charles C. Thompson Company, 1909.

2 From *Craftsman Bungalows*, published in 1920 by Yoho & Merritt.

3 From *Practical Homes*, by Jens Pedersen.

(Left) Two interior views of a completed house by the Illinois architect and plan publisher U.M. Dustman, about 1909. The top view shows the colonnades separating the dining room from the parlour of a Dustman bungalow, "34' x 50', wood siding, concrete block foundation, wood shingle roof, hardwood floor, hot air furnace, built for $4,000 . . . . Complete plans for $15." The bottom view shows the staircase and hall seat in the small entranceway to a Dustman house.[1] (Top right) The dining room of a California Bungalow, built from the mail-order plans of Yoho & Merritt of Seattle. Note the wainscotting and plate rail, the ceiling beams, and the built-in china cabinet, all similar to the interiors of Vancouver houses on pages 130 and 155.[2] (Bottom right) Two of the Universal series of interior fittings, which included doorways, doors, windows, stairways, mantels and bookcases, sideboards, corner cupboards, breakfast nooks, kitchen cabinets, linen closets, bathroom cabinets, and the "Presto" Sliding Disappearing Stairway for reaching the attic.[3]

The watercolour shows the alcove, separated from the living room by colonnades, of the 1912 house at 2755 West 42nd Avenue. The built-in seat, wainscotting, colonnades, bookcases, mantelpiece and ceiling beams were all probably built on the spot by the contractor to the specifications of the mail-order plans.

The house, and the one next door to the west, were built by the firm of Baynes and Horie "on spec." Edgar George Baynes (1870-1956) was born in Bocking, Essex, apprenticed to a builder there at the age of fourteen, came to Vancouver when he was nineteen and was one of the first homesteaders in the Squamish River Valley, then organized his partnership with W.M. Horie two years later, in 1891.[1] William McCleod Horie (1858-1940) was a master-carpenter and craftsman from Quebec; he lived at 2396 York Avenue in Kitsilano.[2] Their firm also completed a number of major paving contracts, and was carried on after the founders' retirement by their two sons.

During the year that his firm was building the Craftsman house illustrated here, Baynes was also building the Hotel Grosvenor on Howe Street in downtown Vancouver, which he both owned and operated. It survived until the early 1980s (page 39). He was a member of the Vancouver Parks Commission from 1924 until 1940, and was Vancouver's "Good Citizen" of 1944. His reputation was tarnished by a highly publicized trial early in 1946, when the Grosvenor Hotel auditor filed charges against the hotel's accountant, Frederick Denis Whyte, charging that the latter had "converted for his own use" $28,600 in funds. In testimony on February 17, Whyte said that he falsified the books at Baynes's insistence and handed the money over to Baynes, allegedly so that the latter could avoid the wartime excess-profits tax. To cheers and handclapping from the gallery, Whyte was acquitted on February 20, but was rearrested as he stepped from the prisoner's box and charged, following an information sworn out by Baynes, with stealing $9,400 in 1938 and 1939. Those charges also failed to stick, and Whyte was acquitted on May 23.[3]

Baynes's own house at 1200 West Broadway was something of a landmark until its recent demolition. During the early 1960s, it was the Indian Social Centre.

Edgar George Baynes

1 *Who's Who in Canada*, 1930-31 edition, page 857. Advertisement from the booklet "Vancouver of Today Architecturally," circa 1900, pamphlet Und-506, CVA.
2 Obituary in Matthews news clippings, CVA.
3 News clippings in "Baynes" file, CVA.

THE CRAFTSMAN BUNGALOW

By the end of the First World War, Los Angeles had established itself in the public imagination as an Eldorado, a place where a person could live a prosperous life unfettered by the cares of the old world, under the always-shining sun, far from the soot and grime of the East, in "our own little bungalow." By the end of the War, "Hollywood" had become a household word, and "Pasadena" — the Los Angeles-region town that was the birthplace of the California, or Pasadena, Bungalow — became a synonym for the breezy, carefree American way of life, even in depressed postwar England.[1] "It was in Southern California that the bungalow, the apotheosis of William Morris's notion of a proletarian art that he could never himself attain, found its true home. . . . The California Bungalow, whatever its size or quality of workmanship, was the closest thing to a democratic art that has ever been produced. Even when it became a high-art product, as in the work of Charles and Henry Green of Pasadena, it was as much a tribute to the carpenters who lovingly put together the wood details as to the architects who designed them."[2] The California Bungalow — one manifestation of the Arts and Crafts or Craftsman style and "simple life" — came to be the dominant residential architectural style throughout North America, publicized by Gustav Stickley's *Craftsman* magazine, published between 1901 and 1915, by various architects' bungalow books, and by tracts such as Charles Keeler's 1902 *The Simple Home*.[3]

Firms all over the United States designed Craftsman houses, and their publications had a wide distribution. One such firm was Yoho & Merritt of Seattle, Washington, whose 1920

1 Interviews in "An Ocean Apart," Granada Television.

2 Gebhard and Winter, *Architecture in Los Angeles*, page 16.

3 Boris, *Art and Labor,* page 63. Copies of the *Craftsman* can be found in the Vancouver Public Library.

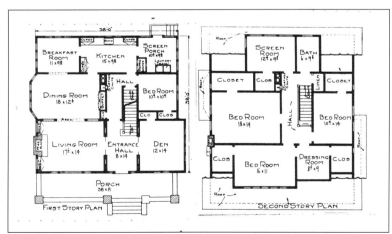

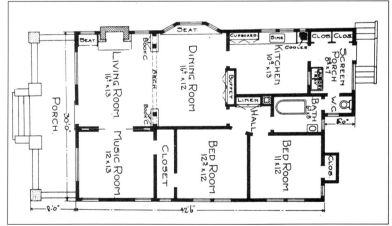

"It is a house of richness and elegance. The porch masonry and outside of the fireplace are hard burned and clinker brick laid rough. The walls are shingles. The porch floor and steps are concrete. The rooms of each plan are well connected and most of them easily accessible from a hall. The dining room and living room are separated by a wide open arch. These rooms have beamed ceilings and paneled wainscotting. A breakfast room is coming to be a necessity with many families. In this case it is conveniently located with reference to the kitchen and dining room. Provision is made in the working plans for the following conveniences: bookcases, fireplace, coat closet, kitchen cabinets, buffet, built-in refrigerator, laundry on screen porch, large closets on second floor and clothes chute." Estimated cost: $4,000 to $4,500. Plans: $20.

"This is a very conservative example of the Bungalow style and, where extremes are not desirable, it is best to build such a house as this. The walls are covered with alternate courses of rough wide and narrow siding. The porch gable is shingles laid irregularly. The stone work is cement blocks made in imitation of brown sandstone, laid broken ashlar style. The floor is concrete with steps in front and one end. The floor plan is different from several others only in details. The music room has a sliding door opening into the living room so that it may be converted into a bed room. The buffet is six feet wide inside and has leaded glass doors above an open counter shelf recess with a beveled plate mirror back. Other features of the plan are the seats, built-in bookcases, wide linen cabinet, kitchen cabinet with cupboards and cooler. The arrangement of the plumbing is especially good in this house. There is a cemented cellar with furnace connections." Estimated cost: $2,200. Plans: $10.

Craftsman Bungalows book was "a collection of the latest designs dedicated to The Lover of a Convenient Home." The firm sought to reassure buyers distant from balmy California that its plans were adaptable anywhere: "Designed to present to those interested in home building the very highest types of bungalows adapted to the cooler climates of the North and East. This book is unique in the fact that while every design or plan shown is a true bungalow, none of them is subject to the handicaps found in the California types, which make no provision for basements, heating plants, and other necessary utilities without which a Northern home is a failure."

The four Craftsman or California Bungalows below — the two on the left by Stillwell & Company of Los Angeles, the two on the right by Yoho & Merritt of Seattle — are indistinguishable from, and possibly are the originals of, ones built in the City of Vancouver between about 1910 and 1925. The captions are from the original plan books. Note the built-in interior features, and the inclusion of screened sleeping porches in all the designs; feeling that it was essential to good health and a long life, many west-coast residents slept in the outside air during all but the coldest weeks of the year. Note also that each house contains only one bathroom.

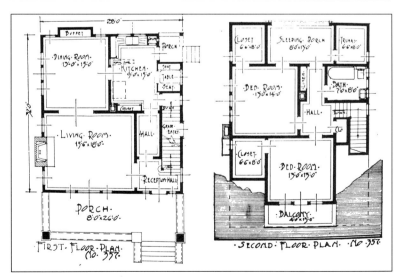

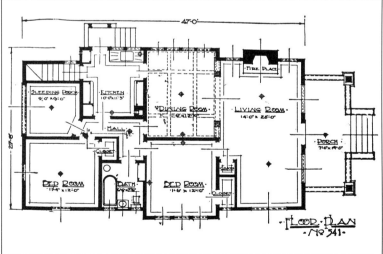

"A one-and-one-half storey home of unusual merit. Five splendid rooms and sleeping porch of good size, containing all the latest conveniences in the way of built-in features. Note the practical arrangement of breakfast nook, ironing board and cabinets; also the buffet and inviting fireplace. The downstairs hall will save steps. Fine roomy closets are provided in abundance. The open balcony makes a comfortable upstairs porch. The basement under the entire house is fitted up for laundry, furnace and fuel rooms and fruit storage. Four-inch cedar siding as the exterior wall covering lends a distinctive appearance to this attractive home."

"A very practical design of five rooms. The full width of the living room is fourteen feet, and it reaches from one side wall to the other. The dining room has beamed ceiling and paneled wainscot. A sleeping porch is included in the plan connected to either of the bedrooms by the hall. The kitchen is of the cabinet pattern; everything used in the kitchen may be kept out of sight here and kept spotlessly clean."

The Craftsman-style houses on the east side of Macdonald Street, looking south from 5th Avenue to about 7th.

With a few exceptions in the Strathcona area east of Chinatown, Vancouver has no surviving row housing of the types so typical in eastern North America, Europe, and Australia. Instead, detached houses were built on narrow suburban lots; in many cases, the houses are so close together that their roofs nearly touch, creating an almost lightless, six-foot-wide no-man's-land between them. This was suburban speculative development at its worst.

The Canadian Pacific Railway's land grant (see map, page 7) had as its western boundary Trafalgar Street, then called Boundary Road (although the city's western boundary was a mile to the west of there).[1] Development began in the CPR's new Kitsilano subdivision, so named in 1905, and picked up speed in the investor-owned land to the west in 1909, when the B.C. Electric Railway Company, responding to pressure from local landowners, agreed to extend the Fourth Avenue streetcar line west to Alma Street. The subdivision of that land, creating the tight blocks of builders' houses west of Trafalgar Street, date from that time.

The most distinctive of these builders' houses are the ones illustrated above, on Macdonald Street between 5th and 7th avenues. All of these houses were erected in 1911 by the builders Lockie and Miller. William Lockie was a carpenter, resident at 2246 West 2nd Avenue; his partner Miller was probably also a carpenter, but is untraceable. The men had no office other than their current jobsite, and they must have employed a large crew, as witnessed by the number of houses they built in a short time. Their first house completed was the one at 2146 Macdonald, the seventh one along in the row. The next three, for which water connection permits were signed on May 22, are numbers five, six and eight in the row, with street addresses of 2128, 2134, and 2150; the four houses on the left, at 2104, 2110, 2116 and 2122, had water connection permits signed on July 11. The four houses south of 6th Avenue were ready for water connections on December 28.[2]

No one of these houses on Macdonald Street is particularly special, although they all

M·KLUCKNER MARCH/90

demonstrate to varying degrees the hallmarks of the Craftsman style, as practiced by builders working in the superheated Vancouver building boom of 1910-1912: decorative brackets along the gable ends, wooden posts on the porch, exposed rafter ends, and shingle siding. They also illustrate the classic fate of all old Vancouver houses — they have been modified and altered, some of their porches filled in, some wooden windows replaced by cheap aluminum ones, and some extra doorways cut to effect the houses' transition from single-family use into the self-contained suites so typical of Kitsilano. There are few houses both pure of style and original of condition in Kitsilano.

In this case, as in the case of the California Bungalows on the next two pages, the whole is worth more than the sum of the individual parts; this group of houses, with its tightly packed, repetitive rooflines, forms a streetscape very evocative of old Vancouver. Part of the reason for this is the *lack* of boulevard trees, so that the houses stand out on their lots like the builders' subdivision that they really are — their hard edges have not been softened by gardens, as have the houses from the same period around the corner on Sixth Avenue. The lack of boulevard trees dates from a decision in the early 1930s — twenty years after these houses were built — to run a bus line from the corner of Broadway and Macdonald as a summer service to Kitsilano beach. In 1938, Dunbar Heights Realty opened up the area between 16th and 25th along Macdonald Street for "economical suburban homes," and offered building lots from $100 to $350.[3]

An article in the *Province* two years later noted that the new, mostly five-room houses that had been erected had corner windows and "magazine-picture kitchens," and cost between $2,750 and $3,800.[4] That same year, both the Town Planning Commission and the Traffic Commission recommended that the Macdonald bus line be extended through to downtown; this was accomplished in 1947, and resulted in the widening of the street and the removal of its trees.

1 Twenty-five years before the CPR was granted its District Lot 526, the land between Trafalgar Street and Balaclava, and the beach and Tenth Avenue — 161 acres — was purchased from the Crown for $388, as District Lot 192. It was bought in August, 1860, by Colonel R.C. Moody of the Royal Engineers, the namesake of Port Moody and the founder of New Westminster. DL 192 adjoined the Admiralty Reserve at Jericho.

2 City of Vancouver water records, CVA.

3 *Province*, April 4, 1938.

4 *Province*, August 17, 1940.

CALIFORNIA BUNGALOWS ON 5TH AVENUE, KITSILANO

1 Eventually the city will be faced with the question of whether to preserve rows of 1930s stucco boxes, "V.L.A. houses" (the little cottages built under the Veterans' Land Act after the Second World War for returned soldiers), and 1960s and 1970s "Vancouver Specials."

2 In cities such as San Francisco and Sydney, in districts such as the Western Addition and Paddington, owners seem to join enthusiastically in the spirit of reinforcing a neighbourhood's heritage character; if they are intent on expressing their individuality through a radical alteration of their house, they take their ideas elsewhere, often helped along by civic preservation legislation.

The south side of West Fifth Avenue, between Bayswater and Balaclava streets in Kitsilano, is the epitome of the early Vancouver subdivision. It is debatable at what point a bland builders' suburb becomes a period piece worth preserving,[1] but certainly this double-block-long row of California Bungalows is unique in the city. In the watercolour, I have exorcised the circa-1980 renovations at 2996 West 5th Avenue, which has been modified with a tall shed roof, destroying the consistency of the row.[2]

The style developed as an outgrowth of the Arts and Crafts Movement and the suburban development of the Los Angeles area — thus, this type of house was also called the Pasadena Bungalow. All of these bungalows on West Fifth Avenue adhere to the Craftsman ideal of a mixture of surfaces, including the rough clinker brick of porch posts and chimneys, and the wonderful use of wood in shingles and brackets and carved bargeboards. They all look the same at first glance, but many have individual touches, including the Japanese-inspired pointed peak and rounded brackets on 2970 West Fifth (second from the left in the watercolour), built in 1919 by the carpenter Fred Melton. It is the quality of their individual workmanship, and the adept mixing of surface

M·KLUCKNER 1990

textures such as brick and wood, that distinguishes these houses from the "bland suburban" moniker so easily attached to later generations of builders' houses.

These California Bungalows were erected by two groups of builders between 1919 and 1921. The five houses immediately to the west of the corner of Bayswater, numbered 2950 through 2978 (2950 is out of the picture to the left), were built in 1919 and 1920 by Fred Melton (1879-1956), an English-born contractor who arrived in Vancouver in 1906; he lived the last years of his life at Melton Court at 2310 Cornwall, one of the more interesting apartment buildings fronting Kitsilano Beach.[3] His wife was the "outstanding citizen of 1965," so named by the Kitsilano Chamber of Commerce. It appears likely, although there is no surviving city tax information to prove it, that Melton had to give number 2978 to the city in lieu of unpaid taxes, for the water permit for that house was signed in August, 1920, by the city comptroller, as owner.

Farther west on the block, the firm of Cook and Hawkins began construction around the beginning of 1921 on the group of six California Bungalows at numbers 2990 through 3030. Like Melton, W.J. Hawkins and C. Cook were carpenters, the latter living at 2210 Balaclava Street.[4]

3 Newspaper obituary January 11, 1956, in Matthews' news clippings, CVA.

4 Information from City of Vancouver water records, in CVA.

LOG HOUSES

With the exception of the occasional sturdy homesteader, such as the stump dweller in the wilds of the Municipality of South Vancouver (page 166), the early residents of the towns which now make up Greater Vancouver built their houses from *milled* lumber. The first businesses were sawmills (and saloons); the first houses, including the Gothic Revival 1862 Irving house on Royal Avenue in New Westminster, Fitzgerald McCleery's 1873 farmhouse at the south foot of Macdonald Street in Vancouver (see page 144), and "Navvy Jack" Thomas's 1873 Victorian cottage on the West Vancouver waterfront (since moved to 1768 Argyle Avenue), were built of boards and decorated with turned wood from the local sawmills. There were very few real log houses — where the logs form the structure of the house, rather than being a veneer over a stick frame — in the Lower Mainland. The log cabin below is probably the only one left that was built "casually" with the materials at hand. By contrast, the other old log houses in the Lower Mainland, including 4686 West 2nd Avenue, 1366 Inglewood Avenue in West Vancouver, "Spuraway" at 235 Keith Road in West Vancouver, and "Fairweather" on Bowen Island (page 192), used raw logs as an aesthetic statement.

The cabin illustrated below stands on 27th Avenue just west of Blenheim Street in Dunbar Heights. It dates from the purchase around 1913 of five acres of bush south of the corner of Blenheim and King Edward by Charles Henry Wilson. After arriving in Port Moody on July 4, 1886, on the first CPR train to reach the coast, Wilson laboured and saved and speculated on land, including twenty acres "in a swamp west of the old North Arm Road" (now Fraser Street), which he bought from the provincial government in 1900 for $2,000 and sold in the boom several years later for ten times as much. Wilson was a city alderman from 1902-5, and Wilson Avenue, now known as 41st Avenue, was named for him. "Prior to making a tour of Australia and New Zealand in 1913, Mr. and Mrs. Wilson acquired their estate of five acres, a delightful spot on the very crest of Dunbar Heights, and at a time when all that area was either forest or forest clearing," wrote city archivist J.S. Matthews in the 1930s. "One thousand dollars per acre was paid for the land, and during their absence in Australia on tour, a gardener was busy on the site of their future home (which stood at the corner of Balaclava and West King Edward, and has been demolished); the gardener lived in a hut of cedar shakes which had been the shack of an old logging camp at or near the corner of Balaclava and 25th Avenue, at the end of a corduroy skid road leading down by easy grades through the forest to salt water near the English Bay Cannery." Mrs. Wilson described the building of the log cabin: "The logs for this were hauled from our five acres of bush at the corner of the old Johnson Road, now Blenheim, and 25th Avenue, by our gardener. He used our driving horse, 'Daisy' . . . . There was a portable sawmill nearby, and the gardener asked could he have the empty kerosene tins and the wooden dynamite boxes. The mill was glad to get rid of them, of course. The tins were cut with my hubby's tin shears, and that made the roof of the cottage. The dove-tailed wooden boxes were straightened out, and that made the floor . . . ."[1] The house remains today as a little cottage, with a shed addition on the rear for a kitchen, wedged between more modern houses on a thirty-three-foot lot on its Dunbar-area street.

1 "Charles Henry Wilson" file, J.S. Matthews Add.Mss.54, CVA.

The little log house at 3344 West 27th Avenue, built about 1913.

STONE HOUSES

The Haigler house, on 30th Avenue near Dunbar.

There were and still are many houses in the city which have stone foundations and porch piers, such as the Craftsman house which stood on West 28th Avenue (page 156). Rarer are the stone houses, built at great expense and with painstaking craftsmanship, including Samuel Maclure's "Gabriola" in the West End (page 70), which is stone veneer over a wooden frame.

Not so well known is the Haigler house at 3537 West 30th Avenue in Dunbar, erected in 1918-19 by an unknown builder[1] in a Craftsman style, but with superb stonework on the house itself and on its surrounding wall. West 30th Avenue was opened through from Collingwood to Dunbar in 1918-19, and this house, built for a produce broker named George F. Haigler, was the first one built on the new block. It stands on a large double lot, with a superb cottage garden occupying its front yard. On the double lot adjoining this one on the east (right) was the house illustrated on page 160.

1 It is possible that the house was built by Grover Lloyd, who built the hexagonal-granite-faced house at 1979 West 19th Avenue, and probably built the almost-identical one at 1612 Cedar Crescent (page 110), in 1913.

BRICK HOUSES

The fable of the three little pigs was never given much credence in Vancouver. Although the Three Greenhorns — the Englishmen Morton, Brighouse, and Hailstone who purchased the future Vancouver West End in 1862 — initially hoped to make building bricks with the coal and clay along Burrard Inlet, they and their successors soon found that lumber was too available, too cheap, and simply too attractive as a building material. Another inducement to build frame houses with local lumber, instead of masonry houses, was the fashionability during Vancouver's boom years of the Arts and Crafts Movement, and the worldwide popularity of the California Bungalow. With the subsequent recognition of Vancouver's susceptibility to earthquakes, the ability of a frame house to withstand them is a fortunate postscript.

Brick never went out of fashion for commercial buildings, and the output from local brickworks found a ready market in the downtown area, in comparatively substantial buildings (for their time), such as the James Inglis Reid shop (page 45) and Victoria House (page 52). But it should be noted that many early downtown buildings, including the recently demolished Orillia Apartments (page 44), were built of wood.

With very few exceptions, mainly the lavish houses of the wealthy in the West End and Shaughnessy Heights, houses and small apartment buildings were built of wood. Many of the city's wealthy, who chose as their architect Samuel Maclure and his various partners, were enamoured of the English manor-house style and accordingly commissioned a number of magnificent wooden Tudor houses; these set a style in the city that resulted in the likes of the Hunter house (page 99), "Fairacres" (page 168), "Esmond" (page 170), and "Thorley Park" (Brock House) and "Aberthau" in Point Grey, the last four since converted to community purposes. The later Tudor Revival style, in apartments such as Tudor Manor (page 67) and the Knowles house (page 125), was usually a half-timbered façade affixed to the front of a building, and lacks the quality and visual impact of the big Tudors of the pre-World War I era.

Finding modest homes built of brick in the Vancouver area is like looking for needles in a haystack; *real* brick houses, where brick comprises the walls and is the support for floors and roof, are very different from the thousands of houses in the city — especially the variations on the "Vancouver Special" built in the past twenty-five years — which have a brick veneer over portions of the timber frame.

In the shadow of the enormous Metrotown development, just south of Kingsway at 6308 Willingdon Avenue in Burnaby, stands a classic brick Ontario cottage, with patterned brickwork and a frame bay window. The view in the watercolour looks south, to the SkyTrain crossing in the distance on the edge of Central Park; the watercolour was painted from the parking lot of the Dragon Inn, at the corner of Kingsway and Willingdon. It is impossible to tell when and by whom this house was built, although it probably dates from the early 1920s.

The two brick buildings on these pages are very similar in their design to the uncountable thousands of venerable brick structures in eastern North America. The notable feature of their construction is the arch of brick above each window, providing reinforcement for the window opening; more recent brick construction usually employs a straight iron beam — a lintel — instead of the arch. Four other *modest* brick houses in the city are at 1161 Keefer, 2343 East 6th Avenue, 4371 Victoria Drive, and 2593 East 18th Avenue.

The B.K. Grocery stands a few blocks south of Kingsway on Nanaimo Street, at East 34th Avenue. Built probably in 1917-18 by a bricklayer named Harry Bridge of 5131 Highgate Street, South Vancouver, it evidently was occupied by a laundryman named Howat in 1920, then by a Mr. Hatch and his "R Mfg Co" during the 1920s.[1] It appears as a grocery store late in the 1920s, operated by Charles J. Noel, but the "B.K." evidently has nothing to do with the B & K Grocery company that became ShopEasy. In the background of the watercolour, at 5042 Nanaimo Street, is even more of a rarity: a house built with the modular wall system patented by the B.C. Mills, Timber & Trading Company, but not in a style ever manufactured by the company.[2] This house was evidently built about 1914-15, several years after the BCMT&T ceased to manufacture its prefabricated buildings, so it is possible that the house was erected from left-over wall panels, by the aptly named Thomas H. Carpenter, who was the first listed resident on the property, in the 1916 city directory. This kind of suburban development became feasible because of the existence nearby of a streetcar line, and the upgrading of Westminster Road itself in 1913, when it was named Kingsway.

The B.K. Grocery at Nanaimo and 34th Avenue in East Vancouver.

1 It is hard to pin down exactly what was going on there, as the street numbers in that part of the Municipality of South Vancouver are inconsistent in various years of city directories. The building's water connection (SV0113) was signed in February, 1918, by Mrs. H. Bridge, whose husband was listed in city directories as a bricklayer.

2 At least, it was not in a style listed in their surviving 1906 catalogue — see page 19 and the footnote on page 197.

1545 W. 8TH VANCOUVER   M. KLUCKNER 1989

Built in 1907 for a machinist by the name of E. Lern, the picturesque "Swiss Cottage"-style builder's house at 1545 West 8th Avenue in Fairview, complete with rose garden, was the last one on the slope immediately west of Granville. After years of use as an office, it went on the market in the winter of 1988 as "C-3A site, hold or develop, 50' x 110', revenue $1,600 per month," and sold quickly. The house was moved to the Gulf Islands in October, 1989.

The love of wood and the textures and patterns that could be created with it were features of the carpenter-built houses of the early part of this century. Queen Anne and Stick-style houses often featured exceptionally detailed, finicky woodwork, including fish-scale shingles in the gables and complicated decorative brackets; Craftsman-style decoration was simpler and bolder, emphasizing wood as structure and *wood*, rather than as a medium for creating lacy patterns such as the late-Victorian art nouveau decorations in wrought iron. Patterned brick walls were common in eastern North America during the Victorian and Edwardian periods, when houses were built with multicoloured brick, usually in ochre and red.

All of these trends came together in a wooden house at 1545 West 8th Avenue, a half block west of Granville Street, in Fairview. Not only were its diamond-pattern shingles unique, it had excellent stained glass, by an unknown artist.

The noted stained glass artists of early Vancouver were Henry Bloomfield & Sons, whose work survives today in "Gabriola," St. Paul's Anglican Church on Pendrell Street in the West End, Holy Trinity Cathedral in New Westminster, and in the Parliament Buildings and Christ Church Cathedral in Victoria. The family firm consisted of father Henry and sons James and Charles — James was the artist, while Charles was the technician. The family moved from Maidenhead in England to Canada in 1887, and then to New Westminster in 1889. James, who had studied architecture and worked as a junior draftsman in his youth, illuminated an address for the governor general, the Earl of Aberdeen, who was so impressed that he sponsored James's formal training in stained glass in Chicago and later in Europe. In 1903, James designed the coat of arms of the City of Vancouver. Four years later, he and his wife left Vancouver for the United States, where they lived until 1920, when they moved to Toronto. The advertisement is from the circa 1900 publication Vancouver of Today Architecturally; *the Bloomfields' office and shop mentioned in the advertisement was on the site of a fine house just above Broadway, which has recently been restored by the Davis family (page 94). (Information in Add.Mss. 973, CVA.)*

DOWNTOWN VANCOUVER

Subservient to its natural setting, and chronically afflicted by land speculation, Vancouver's downtown has always had a half-baked, unfinished look. Many of its early arrivals were real-estate developers, such as James Welton Horne and Charles Dunbar (page 160), who viewed the vacant, recently logged site of the city of Vancouver as a commodity to be sold in pieces to whomever came off the next train; other early residents, such as Jonathan Rogers (pages 41 and 72), made their fortunes in real-estate development, but left a significant legacy in downtown buildings, parks, and civic service. None of these men achieved the dubious status of the notorious "boomers" of the Canadian Northern Railway period of 1908-1915, when communities such as Port Mann were promoted as pending metropolises, or of men like Alvo von Alvensleben, who won and lost fortunes on suburban land that had only a tenuous connection, via "Toonerville Trolleys" like the Oak Street tramline, with the established city. Regardless of the state of the economy, or the city's maturity or lack thereof, the business of Vancouver has always been real estate.

The greatest of all the Vancouver land developers was, and still is, the Canadian Pacific Railway Company. Compelled by its federal charter to build a line to tidewater at Port Moody, the company managed to negotiate a grant of more than 6,000 acres of public land from the province of British Columbia for extending its line the few miles to the community of Granville, which it would have had to do anyway to obtain enough land for railyards, maintenance facilities, and docks. It is debatable how Vancouver would have developed if the CPR had not received its land grant; certainly, the city did not lack rail transportation options, beginning with the Great Northern Railway's entry into the city in 1904, and the CNR's a decade later, while other companies competed strenuously for ocean-going freight and passenger business. But it was the CPR's land grant, formalized on February 28, 1885,[1] that created the city. The railway company was given District Lots 541 and 526 of the future City of Vancouver. The former, 480 acres, was all the land on the downtown peninsula between Burrard and Cambie; the latter, 5,795 acres, was the land between False Creek and the Fraser River farms of settlers such as Hugh Magee and Fitzgerald McCleery (see map, page 7). The company also received the unsold lots in the old Granville townsite, now the Gastown area; in addition, in return for the increase in land values that the railway would bring, the company obtained a number of privately owned lots in the old Brickmakers' Claim — District Lot 185, now the West End.

Never known as a sentimental corporation, the CPR has, over the years, demolished or sold to other developers many of the city's landmarks, some of which it had built, but disposed of when they outlived their purpose. Its real-estate activities established Granville Street as the heart of the city. Its first substantial railway station was at the foot of Granville Street; when the company built a larger one slightly to the east (the current SeaBus and SkyTrain terminal), it demolished the original one. Its Hotel Vancouver at Georgia and Granville made that corner the centre of the city, but in the most startling real-estate deal of the era, the CPR closed it in 1939 to allow pre-eminence to the Canadian National Railway's new hotel at Georgia and Burrard; the old Hotel Vancouver was demolished in 1949, following the sale of the property to Eaton's, and the land, which had anchored the most important corner in the city since the late 1880s, became a parking lot for twenty years (page 43). Such was city planning, and the indifference of the city's major absentee landowners to the notion of a significant downtown, in the decades before the 1970s.

Only part of the reason for Vancouver's unfinished, semi-established downtown can be traced to this sort of real-estate trading; another significant influence in the city's development has been its "boom and bust" economy. Poised for greatness, its downtown filling rapidly with fine Edwardian skyscrapers, the city and region fell into a deep slump in 1914, following the collapse of the realty- and railway-based B.C. economy. Recovering in the 1920s on the basis of trade through the Panama Canal, mining, and lumbering, the city began to develop again with fine structures such as the Hotel Georgia, the Georgia Medical-Dental Building, the new Hotel Vancouver, and the Marine Building. Plans were afoot in the late 1920s for a massive civic centre in a style like City Hall which would have made the city a "Moscow by the Mountains,"[2] but the Depression intervened with more severe consequences, because of the city's remote location and resource- and trade-based economy, than those experienced in the established manufacturing cities of the east. Then came the Second World War, followed first by a postwar depression, then by the economic problems of the late 1950s. Finally, in the 1960s, the city recommenced its development.

From a long-term city planning standpoint, these chronic economic uncertainties have been fortunate, because the city has matured to a point where its planning, architecture, and redevelopment is generally more sophisticated than was the case during the wholesale makeover of the West End and the creation of the Pacific Centre "black hole," during the fifties and sixties.

[1] Sessional Papers, page 460, 1886.

[2] The Harland Bartholomew city centre plan, CVA Map. P.62. The epithet is mine.

More of the CPR's property holdings, notably the railway lands along Coal Harbour and the north side of False Creek (the Expo lands), have recently been presented for redevelopment, and are receiving more scrutiny and sensitive handling than perhaps would otherwise have been the case. From a heritage standpoint, the long delay in the redevelopment of the north shore of False Creek is likewise fortunate, because with an increasing awareness of the city's history came a desire to preserve the CPR's 1888 roundhouse — one of the most historically significant buildings in the province — which the CPR was on the point of demolishing in the 1970s.

Other real-estate decisions have had profound impacts on the preservation of the city's heritage. When the B.C. Electric Railway Company decided in the mid-1950s to move its head office from the old downtown on Hastings Street to the residential West End southwest of Georgia and Granville, it abandoned the turn-of-the-century downtown area east of Victory Square, rather than building new office space there. Concurrently, and also a result of the B.C. Electric's decision to get out of the rapid transit and streetcar business in the face of competition from privately owned automobiles, the North Vancouver-to-downtown ferry service, with a terminus on the Gastown waterfront, ceased operation. Redevelopment pressure in this old part of downtown ceased, as firms such as B.C. Electric and Eaton's relocated or established themselves uptown, and so it sat in a sort of time warp, missing the breakneck redevelopment of the western downtown. Recognition of the historical significance of Gastown and Chinatown, which had survived more or less intact, followed in the late 1960s and early 1970s; both areas were then designated as provincial heritage areas, and have become, among other things, significant attractions to tourists. Hastings Street, and the adjoining blocks around B.C. Place stadium, have so far avoided both heritage designation and commercial desirability, but now stand on the threshhold of some sort of change due to their proximity to the former Expo site.

The CPR's real-estate activities to the south of False Creek, in its District Lot 526, were in the early days the only consistent planning applied to the residential parts of Vancouver. The fight between the residents of the west side of the city, most significant of whom were buyers in the CPR's DL 526 subdivisions, and those of the unplanned east side, resulted in the secession of the west side from South Vancouver and the creation of the Municipality of Point Grey (see page 166).

But all of the gestures in the direction of good planning, and the fortunate historical coincidences which have saved buildings and heritage districts, cannot compete with the constant randomness of real-estate speculation, the craving for "world-class" newness, and the inability of the citizenry and its politicians to grasp the historical significance of the city's fine buildings and the uniqueness of some of its residential neighbourhoods. The old city is vanishing, in some cases for the better, in many cases for the worse. During the 1980s, many of the links in the chain of the city's history have been broken, demolished and discarded. Some of the loss is unavoidable; many old businesses, landmarks, and quirky streetscapes have a nostalgic value, but little true historical importance. In other cases, areas are redeveloped to increase density, but at the needless expense of significant old landmarks, which are removed capriciously in the headlong Vancouver rush for the new at any cost.

Vancouver is a series of parking lots. It has always been possible to walk across the downtown, cutting through back lanes and across parking lots, and to see in the distance, in the gaps between the tall buildings, a landmark from another era a few streets away. This view, looking west on a Sunday afternoon from the parking lot behind the Marble Arch Hotel on Richards Street, shows some of the variations in the Vancouver downtown skyline: on the left, the railing and edge of the innovative Cathedral Square, an underground electric substation surmounted by an urban park, across the street from Holy Rosary Cathedral; in the middle, at 522-24 Richards, a bay-windowed, clapboard rooming house; on the right, the Marble Arch hotel, completed in 1913 to the design of Emil Guenther for the owner, A. Hyndman.[1] Visible in the background is the Seymour Building, the best example of the Skyscraper Gothic style in the city.

1 City of Vancouver heritage inventory.

BEHIND THE MARBLE ARCH HOTEL

M·KLUCKNER '89

DOWNTOWN IN THE 1950S

Built in 1891 by the Canadian Pacific Railway Company, the Vancouver Opera House adjoined the company's Hotel Vancouver (to the right of the hotel in the postcard); the brick building on the left is the Granville Mansions. During its sales campaign in the late 1880s for West End residential lots, the CPR promised to construct an Opera House for the city, but only commenced work when some of the disgruntled home-owners threatened litigation. Twenty years after it opened, the CPR sold the Opera House to private interests; it subsequently operated as a vaudeville theatre and movie palace, spending its final years as the Lyric Theatre before being demolished in 1969 to make way for the new Eaton's store.

↑ MAP ADJOINS ON PAGES 40-4

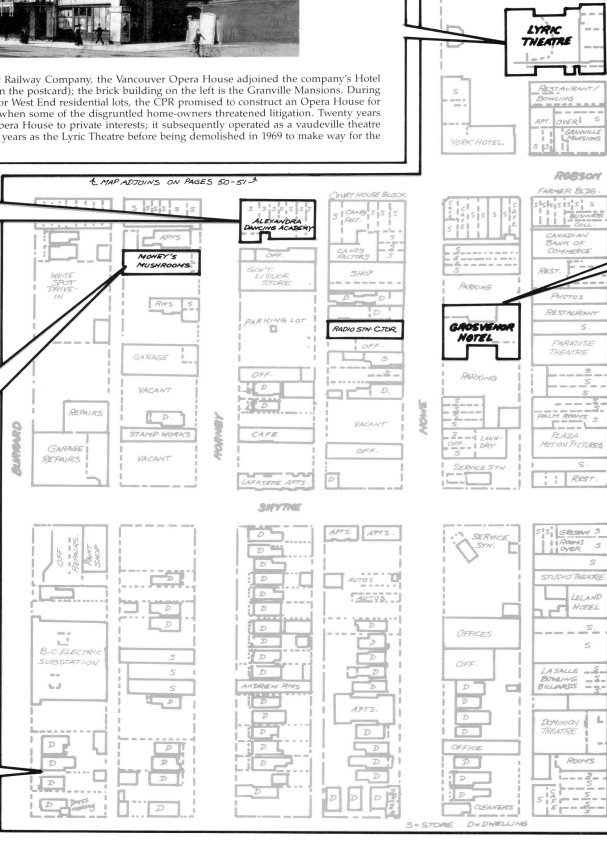

EATON'S PARKING LOT (SEE PAGE 42)

Beloved of a generation of party-goers, the second-floor Alexandra Dancing Academy, nicknamed "the Gonorrhea Track," was conveniently located around the corner from the downtown all-night liquor store at 826 Hornby. Radio station CJOR, with studios a half-block away, broadcast live from the Alexandra beginning in 1932.

A little brick building at 823 Hornby Street was the headquarters of Money's Mushrooms, the brainchild of William Taylor Money. Born in Virginia in 1895, Money emigrated to Canada and worked for the Bank of Montreal, served in the Canadian Garrison Artillery during the First World War, then worked in the bakery business until 1928. That October, he bought a small farm in Burnaby and started to grow mushrooms. He had obtained the exclusive agency for Chester County Sterilized Spawn from Pennsylvania, and with the help of that company's technical expert, Jimmy Gahm, he was able within three years to become successful both at growing them and at convincing other farmers to grow them, and had set himself up as a wholesaler and distributor.

On the site of a handful of frame houses, the B.C. Electric Railway Company built the most significant office tower of the postwar period. Completed early in 1957, the lozenge-shaped glass and porcelain skyscraper by architect Ron Thom set a design standard which the postwar city was often unable to live up to, and single-handedly pulled the city's growth away from the waterfront to what had been a crumbling residential area south and west of downtown.

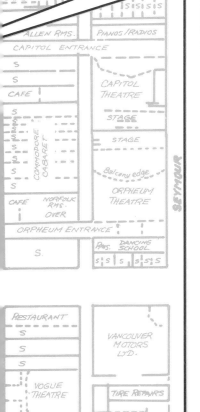

Following an unsuccessful attempt by heritage advocates to save the Birks Building (page 43), the construction of Vancouver Centre and the Scotia Tower proceeded between 1974 and 1977. Birks, the Montreal-based jeweller, entered the Vancouver market by purchasing Trorey's Jewellers at Granville and Hastings, and in 1913 moved uptown to its newly completed, terracotta, curved-fronted office tower, taking the old Trorey's clock with it. A later generation of eastern investment, including Eaton's and Cadillac-Fairview with land-assembly help from the city, began the redevelopment of the Georgia and Granville corner in the late 1960s with the Pacific Centre superblock. The Vancouver Centre development connected a new Birks Building via a mall with the rest of the underground labyrinth. Less lamented than the Birks Building, but a landmark in its own right, was the Strand Theatre, now the site of the 34-storey Scotia Tower. The austere street façades of these new buildings, especially that of Eaton's, and the strong winds channelled earthward by the forest of towers, encourage customers to avoid the outdoors and to seek instead a passage through the underground malls. The old Trorey's clock, known for generations as the Birks Clock, is still on the corner.

Another downtown landmark was the Grosvenor Hotel, built in 1913 by Edgar Baynes (page 23). The hotel's long-time manager was the 1930s-era bandleader Bob Lyon (1910-87), whose connections with the entertainment industry, including a wartime stint as entertainment liaison officer for General Douglas MacArthur in Australia, dovetailed with the operations of radio station CJOR, with offices for owner and founder George Clarke Chandler in the hotel and studios across the street. Eventually, the studios moved into the hotel basement. The Grosvenor was demolished in the early 1980s, by which time CJOR had moved to Fairview; even the radio station was taken suddenly off the air, in 1988, sixty-two years after its founding, and replaced by the "classic rock" station CHRX.

VPL 13255

The postcard shows "Theatre Row" in the 1940s, looking towards the mountains from a point just north of Nelson Street. Granville Street was always *the* downtown street for strollers and cruisers in cars, brightly lit and exciting, a version for earlier generations of what Robson Street is today. The unfortunate decision in the early 1970s to convert it into a pedestrian mall prompted the movement northwards of the street people who had always been a feature of Granville between Nelson Street and the bridge. Granville Mall still has all the theatres visible in the postcard, and maintains a tenuous hold on respectability, anchored by the city-owned Orpheum Theatre, visible in the middle distance. The campaign to "Save The Orpheum" in the mid-1970s saved its magnificent interior from division into several small cinemas; the resulting restored theatre is home to the Vancouver Symphony Orchestra.

Post Office and Winch Building, Vancouver, B.C.

One of the great victories for heritage preservation in the city was the federal government-sponsored restoration and conversion of the old Post Office, customs warehouse, and Winch Building into a complex of shops and offices called the Sinclair Centre, in honour of the long-time Liberal cabinet minister who is better remembered by the public as Pierre Trudeau's father-in-law. The postcard shows the view looking northeast from the corner of Howe and Hastings about 1910.

Granville Street, Vancouver, B. C.

Granville Street downtown was an exciting, automobile- and tram-choked street, the sidewalks busy with pedestrians protected from the rain by an almost continuous series of awnings. This postcard view from the 1920s looks northward to the mountains, with the clock tower of the old Post Office — now the Sinclair Centre — visible in the distance. The crossing just past the Colonial Theatre sign is Dunsmuir Street. The sign "Don't Argue" is part of the slogan of a local tobacconist: "Don't Argue, Con Jones Makes The Best Tobacco!" Midway down the block, past the "Don't Argue" sign, on the left-hand side of the street, is the red-tinted façade of the James Inglis Reid shop (page 45). The tall grey building in the right middle-distance is the Rogers Building (next page). In the decades since this postcard was published, changing shopping habits have diminished the economic viability of many of the types of stores which used to attract the crowds and create such a lively street scene; individual ownership, and the resulting individual style of each of these little buildings, has been lost in a wave of mass advertising and corporate concentration. Such a level of capital creates malls like the Pacific Centre, and architects have responded eagerly to the task of turning buildings in upon themselves, leaving imposing but austere façades on the streets. The block to the immediate left of the photographer, between Georgia and Dunsmuir, was demolished in the early 1970s for the second phase of Pacific Centre, including the IBM and Stock Exchange towers. The latest addition to the Pacific Centre complex, extending north from Dunsmuir almost to Pender, presents a somewhat more lively face to the street than the inhospitable blank façades of the earlier sections.

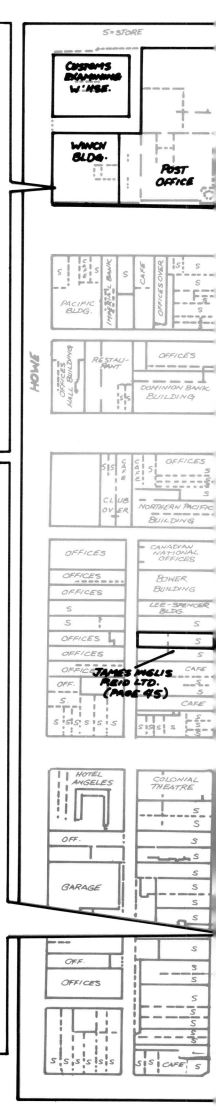

CORDOVA

HASTINGS

PENDER

DUNSMUIR

GEORGIA

The photograph looks west from Seymour Street to Granville along Pender, with the 1912 Rogers Building visible in the middle distance. It shows the cheerful clutter once so typical of Vancouver's downtown, a result of the many booms and busts in the local economy. The 1887 building on the right, originally called the Delmonico Hotel, and the buildings adjoining it to the west, have been replaced by a stark, multi-storey concrete parking garage. The fine buildings in the immediate area of the Rogers Building, including the temple-like 1908 Bank of Commerce at the southeast corner of Hastings and Granville (a designated heritage building), the 1905-10 assemblage now called the Sinclair Centre (also designated), the 1925 Bank of Montreal at Granville and Pender (a conservative design quite out-of-date when completed), the 1912 Seymour Building (page 37), and the 1912 London Building on Pender, are excellent examples of the kind of stone and marble-faced, reinforced concrete buildings which probably would have filled the downtown area had it not been for the 1913-14 depression. The last three buildings have no heritage designation, and thus can be demolished more or less at will; the London Building and the Bank of Montreal are part of an entire block which has recently been "assembled" for redevelopment. The Rogers Building is the legacy of Jonathan Rogers, a builder, developer, parks board chairman, and philanthropist who had a profound effect on Vancouver's growth. A building such as this raises the question: should it become a designated heritage structure, for which it qualifies either on architectural merit or as a monument to the work of a great citizen, or should its fate be left to the vagaries of the market?

The owner of the Rogers Building in the late 1920s was a flamboyant soldier of fortune by the name of Major-General Francis Arthur Sutton. Born in Essex in 1884, he was educated at Eton and went to Argentina at twenty to engage in railway work. Five years later, he travelled to Mexico and worked for Lord Cowdray, who had cornered Mexico's oil output through his business and political machinations. Sutton returned to England at the outbreak of the war, lost his right arm at Gallipoli, became consulting engineer to the United States government on the manufacture of trench mortars, and after the war went to Siberia, where he engaged in gold dredging until put out of business by the Bolsheviks. Moving on to Shanghai in 1921, he established factories to manufacture trench mortars for one of the warlords fighting over territory in the aftermath of the demise of the Chinese emperor; in 1922, he joined Marshal Chang-Tso-Lin, reorganized the marshal's artillery and became director-general of his arsenal, thus aiding the defeat of General Wu-Pei-Fu in the 1924 battle for Beijing. By now known as "One Arm" Sutton, he moved to Vancouver in 1927 with his wife of seventeen years, two daughters, and evidently a considerable fortune from his adventures. One of his purchases was the Rogers Building; another was Portland Island in the Gulf of Georgia, where he established a racehorse training and breeding farm and a summer home. He had his autobiography published in New York, and became something of a public figure: "many a city man remembers his fierce, oath-sprinkled addresses before service clubs," said one account.[1] But the Depression destroyed the value of his investments, and in 1933 legal action was taken to foreclose on his Portland Island property. Roy Manzer, the counsel for the island's mortgagor, "alleged the general had resumed his Chinese name and lived and carried on like an Asiatic warlord at the head of a great army."[2] He lost his local investments, including the Rogers Building, which Jonathan Rogers had to take back, and left the city to return to the Far East. In 1938, he was arrested by the Japanese in Seoul and thrown into jail.[3] After his release, he drifted south to China, and was in Hong Kong at Christmas, 1941, during the Japanese invasion. Sent to a Japanese prison camp, he was "reported to have been savagely tortured," and died in 1944.[4]

1 *Sun*, November 21, 1938.

2 *Province*, October 10, 1933.

3 *Sun*, November 21, 1938.

4 *Province*, November 23, 1944. Other biographical information from *Who's Who in Canada*, 1930-31 edition, page 669.

Hotel Vancouver, Vancouver, B.C. Love Photo.

103,903. J.V.

C.P.R. Hotel Vancouver, Vancouver, B.C. Canada.

1 It was a building of exceptional quality, designed for the CPR's first-class world travellers. Photographs of its interior, such as the 1889 one by William Notman, N.P.A. 2146, published in *Eyes of a City*, CVA, show an extraordinary four-storey interior galleria above the lobby.

The fate of the first two Hotels Vancouver at the southwest corner of Georgia and Granville is a reminder that real-estate speculation and the demolition of local landmarks is nothing new to the city. The top postcard, published about 1910, shows the original, gabled 1886 Hotel Vancouver and its additions to the west and south, built as demand increased.[1] Also visible in the gap between the building in the left foreground — demolished in 1912 to make way for the Birks Building (demolished 1974) — is the Vancouver Opera House (page 38), demolished in 1969. Responding to the increased demand for first-class hotel space, the Canadian Pacific

Railway Company commissioned Francis Swales to design a second Hotel Vancouver — the lower postcard — which was completed in 1914. That building, with its exceptional ballrooms, meeting rooms and roof garden, was probably the finest ever built in the city. It remained open for the pitifully short span of twenty-five years — in 1939, in a sweetheart deal with the Canadian National Railway, which had been required as a condition of entry into the city to build a downtown hotel, the CPR agreed to close its hotel, and to allow the CNR's new edifice at Georgia and Burrard to assume the name Hotel Vancouver.

The CPR's former hotel thereafter saw use as a militia headquarters during the Second World War, then became a returned servicemen's hostel for about 1,200 people, operated by the Citizens Rehabilitation Council. The press speculated in May, 1947, that the hotel property was to be purchased by Eaton's, which had only served B.C. through its catalogue operation until it established a heavy-goods showroom and warehouse at 526 Granville Street early in 1940. Eaton's intended to open a fully fledged department store in the city, and got into the market in 1948 with the purchase of Spencer's department store on Hastings Street (now the bones of the Harbour Centre). The company confirmed its purchase of the old Hotel Vancouver, and the Hotel York property at the northeast corner of Robson and Howe, in March, 1948. John David Eaton announced that all the buildings on the site would be demolished in the near future to make way for a new, fully modern department store.[2] Two days later, the newspapers announced that Eaton's had also bought all but one twenty-five-foot lot (due to one home-owner's recalcitrance) on the block bounded by Smythe, Howe, Hornby and Nelson, for a parking lot and mail-order warehouse.

Objections to the planned demolition came from the Architectural Institute of B.C. and the Vancouver Tourist Association, who joined forces to urge the hotel's rehabilitation.[3] Several days later, the board of trade added its voice to the call, but J.D. Eaton said that no one was interested in it as a hotel, and keeping it was uneconomical.[4] The hotel was demolished in the spring and summer of 1949. The result was the scene in the postcard above, which looks eastward in the 1950s from the lawn in front of the Courthouse (now the Art Gallery), across the Eaton's parking lot. The buildings in the distance are the Hudson's Bay Company, Birks (demolished 1974), and the 1912 Vancouver Block. The old Hotel Vancouver site remained as a parking lot for almost twenty years, until Eaton's participated in the development of the first phase of the Pacific Centre.

The architect of the second, and finest, Hotel Vancouver was Francis Swales, born in Oshawa, Ontario, in 1878. He received his professional training at the Atelier Masqueray in New York, Washington University, and the École des Beaux Arts in Paris. Before coming to Vancouver, he collaborated on the design of buildings at the Louisiana Purchase Exposition, the St. Louis railway terminal, the San Francisco customs house, the Cairo opera house, and a number of hotels and major stores, including The Ritz and Selfridge's in London, England. He returned to Canada in 1911, and in addition to this hotel, he designed a hotel for the CPR at Glacier and coordinated extensions to the Chateau Frontenac in Quebec. In Vancouver, he lived at 1743 Pendrell Street.[5]

2 *Province*, March 18, 1948.

3 *Sun*, December 23, 1948.

4 *Sun*, December 28, 1948.

5 *Who's Who & Why*, 1921 edition, page 1517.

THE ORILLIA

VPL 11371

The photograph above looks west along Robson Street from the corner of Richards, in 1952; it shows the four houses that once stood on the northwest corner there, but have since been demolished for a parking lot. Visible past the newly constructed Farrell Building that dominates the centre of the photograph is The Orillia, built in 1903, which survived until 1985.

A many-dormered rooming house built above a row of ground-floor shops by the architects Parr & Fee, The Orillia was the last of its kind in the city. For many Vancouver residents, it was a site of great nostalgia because of its billiard parlour and "Sid Beech's," a Mexican restaurant that for decades was a popular late-night hangout. The architects, Hamilton Doyle & Associates, who were given the commission by the Hong Kong-based owner of The Orillia to design a replacement for the site, rejected proposals by the city's heritage advisory committee to build a new tower with The Orillia restored inside it; the owner rejected a last-minute appeal by the mayor, which followed months of demonstrations and lobbying by city heritage supporters. On the first Sunday morning in May, 1985, The Orillia was demolished.[1] The new tower, called Vancouver House, has had prominent "for lease" signs attached to it since its completion, and has yet to attract a main-floor tenant.

1 "Landmark Bites Dust," *Province*, May 6, 1985.

JAMES INGLIS REID

A genuine piece of old Vancouver ceased business at the end of 1986. James Inglis Reid Limited, the Scottish butcher with the tiled, sawdust-covered floors and the window showcases filled with cured hams and bacon, had been a fixture at 559 Granville Street since 1916. In this case, it was the business itself which formed part of the city's heritage, rather than the building which housed it. Changing shopping habits in the downtown area, the store's aging staff, and the owners' unwillingness to open Sundays made it impractical for the firm to join the northward march of Pacific Centre. The owners — the daughter and son-in-law of James Inglis Reid — sold the building and its property and retired.

Reid arrived in Vancouver from Scotland in 1906, feeling that the expansion of chain stores there made his future as an independent shopkeeper tenuous. Following several years in business on East Georgia Street near Main, Reid leased the main floor of 559 Granville; the next year, 1917, he hired "Horatio" Nelson Menzies, and together they developed the Scottish treats, including sausages, haggis, oatcakes, and black and white puddings, which remained features of the store for nearly seventy years. During the Robbie Burns season each year, the store made as much as four tons of haggis, which was shipped all over the continent. Reid's slogan, "We Hae Meat That Ye Can Eat," was an adaptation of Robert Burns's "The Selkirk Grace."

As the years passed and the store's reputation grew, Reid was able to take over the other floors in the building, and eventually to buy it; during the Depression, he sold shares in the business to his regular employees. He had decided to retire in 1945, at the age of seventy, and was going to sell the business, but instead passed it on to his son-in-law, Gordon Wyness, to manage it. Mr. Wyness, an engineer by profession, managed the store for its last forty-one years.

As indicated in the drawing below, the store was much more than the unique, sawdust-floored trading area that customers saw: it was a four-storey manufacturing plant, with curing and smoke rooms and a bakery.[1]

The little brick building which stood at 559 Granville and housed the James Inglis Reid butcher shop was built in 1902. Its architect was George William Grant (above). Born in Pictou, Nova Scotia, in 1852, Grant arrived in British Columbia in 1885, and practiced in New Westminster before moving to Vancouver in 1887.[2]

1 Information from visits to the store and conversations with Gordon and Alison Wyness.

2 *Who's Who & Why*, 1913 edition, page 290.

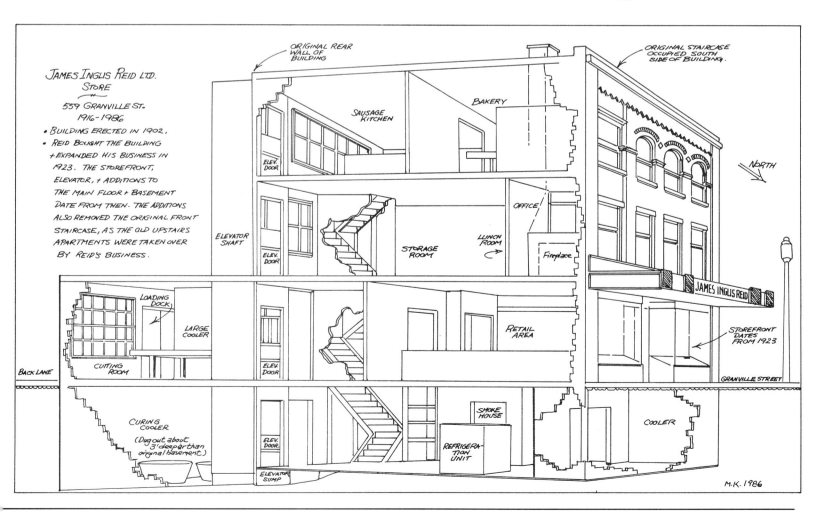

JAMES INGLIS REID LTD.
STORE
559 GRANVILLE ST.
1916-1986

• BUILDING ERECTED IN 1902.
• REID BOUGHT THE BUILDING + EXPANDED HIS BUSINESS IN 1923. THE STOREFRONT, ELEVATOR, + ADDITIONS TO THE MAIN FLOOR + BASEMENT DATE FROM THEN. THE ADDITIONS ALSO REMOVED THE ORIGINAL FRONT STAIRCASE, AS THE OLD UPSTAIRS APARTMENTS WERE TAKEN OVER BY REID'S BUSINESS.

ORIGINAL REAR WALL OF BUILDING
ORIGINAL STAIRCASE OCCUPIED SOUTH SIDE OF BUILDING.
SAUSAGE KITCHEN
BAKERY
ELEV. DOOR
NORTH
ELEVATOR SHAFT
ELEV. DOOR
OFFICE
STORAGE ROOM
LUNCH ROOM
Fireplace
JAMES INGLIS REID
LOADING DOCK
LARGE COOLER
RETAIL AREA
STOREFRONT DATES FROM 1923
BACK LANE
CUTTING ROOM
ELEV. DOOR
GRANVILLE STREET
CURING COOLER
(Dug out about 3' deeper than original basement.)
ELEV. DOOR
SMOKE HOUSE
REFRIGERA-TION UNIT
COOLER
ELEVATOR SUMP
M.K. 1986

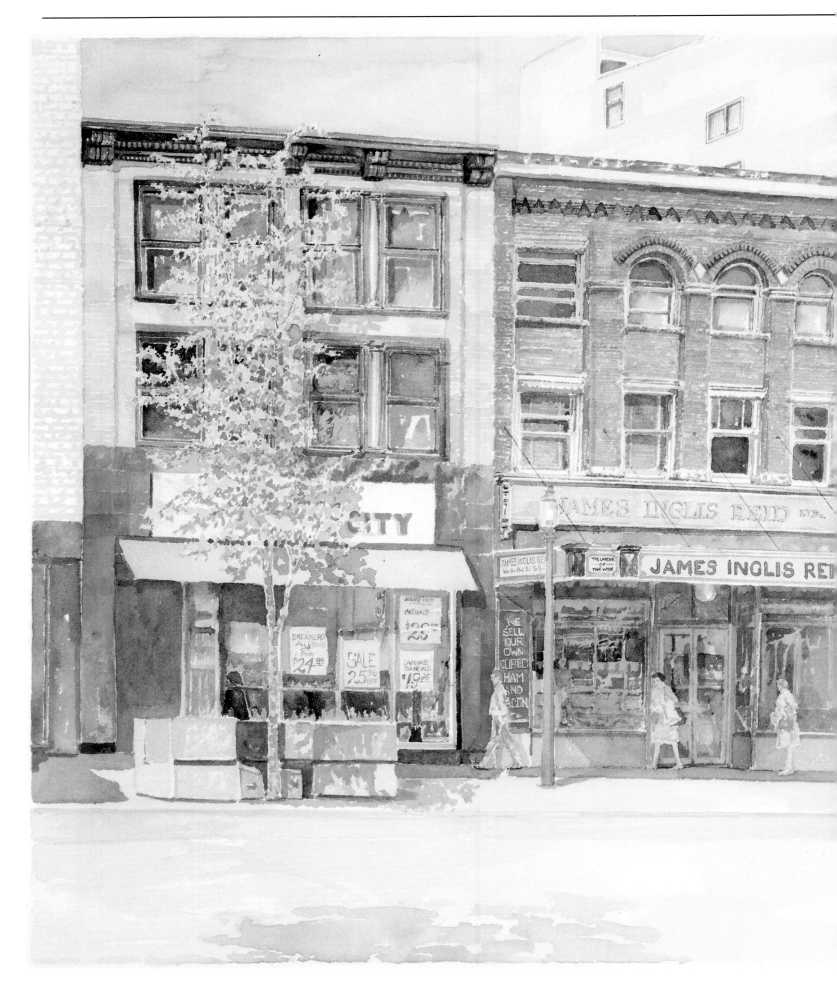

Reid's butcher shop at 559 Granville, as it appeared in the summer of 1986.

THE GEORGIA MEDICAL-DENTAL BUILDING

The heritage *cause célèbre* of the late 1980s was the Georgia Medical-Dental Building. It represented everything that a building should have needed to be preserved in mature, sophisticated, rich, post-Expo Vancouver: a large, solid, well-built, brick and terra cotta, fifteen-storey skyscraper only sixty years old; a good example of art deco architecture and one of the better buildings constructed in the city in the 1920s; a local landmark, for years the prestigious address for physicians and dentists, highlighted by the three nurses, nicknamed the "Rea sisters" (Pya, Dya, and Gonna), gazing down on passersby from the parapet nine storeys above the sidewalk. The emotional response of the citizens of Vancouver to this building and to its demolition make it difficult to objectively assess whether, in fact, it was as good as its proponents claimed; whether the developer's facts and figures, allegedly substantiating their claim that the building was economically unsaveable, presented the entire picture; or whether it was another example of Vancouver's penchant for newness taking precedence over long-term concerns for the fabric of the city.

The announcement that the Shon Group, which had owned the GMD since the early 1970s, planned to demolish it and replace it with a postmodern skyscraper mimicking the shape of the Hotel Vancouver across the street, stimulated an unprecedented amount of discussion during 1988 and the early months of 1989 on the merits of heritage preservation. The argument against preservation was firstly one of numbers — the GMD renovated would still be only a "class C" office building and command per-square-foot rentals of only $15 to $20, while the new "class A" tower would command $40[1] — and secondly of aesthetics and the broad question of the public's conception of the worth of the building.[2] The mayor and the majority of city council, who were in favour of development and against heritage designation per se, could not be rallied to the building's cause. Some said it was ugly, others homely; the public, at least according to letters to the editor of the leading Vancouver newspaper,[3] had no definite opinion on the value of the building, other than that it was something of a landmark which evoked nostalgia. Council's refusal to designate it as a heritage building and compensate the Shon Group for the loss of its profit was the ultimate thumbs down. Preparations for the building's demolition took longer than anticipated, as it was so strongly constructed, but in the presence of a large crowd and national television cameras, one morning in May, 1989, it was imploded, landing in a monstrous, three-storey-tall heap of bricks and plaster and bits of twisted metal. The nurses, and some of the art deco cladding, had been grudgingly removed by the developer weeks before and deposited safely in the architectural graveyard of the Vancouver Museum.

The watercolour shows the Georgia Medical-Dental Building from the west, across Burrard Street, with the 1889 Christ Church Cathedral — the oldest surviving church in Vancouver — almost beneath it. It was designed in the late 1920s by the celebrated local firm of McCarter and Nairne, whose Marine Building, designed at almost the same time and erected at the corner of Burrard and Hastings, is one of the art deco masterpieces of North America.[4] The architects must have assumed that Christ Church was an insignificant parish church that would soon be removed and replaced by an office tower, for they designed the GMD as a two-sided building — its two good sides facing Georgia and Hornby streets — on a three-sided lot. The fire escape and the bare-brick, boxy sides of the GMD showed the "unneighbourly" back side to what was, in the late 1920s, the residential West End to the west (see map, pages 50-51). From that aspect, the GMD always looked like a prime example of "façadism" — the tacking of a decorative façade onto a box. Perhaps there was simply not enough money to finish its west wall. It was like the old story of the building with the Queen Anne front and the Mary Anne back.

Christ Church Cathedral, the "establishment" Anglican church built on the edge of what was, in the 1890s, Vancouver's fashionable residential district, narrowly missed demolition in 1974, when a proposal to replace it with an office tower and underground sanctuary was submitted to city council. There followed Vancouver's first great debate on the merits of heritage and the public value of a church building. On December 17, council declared Christ Church to be an historic site, and the owner of the neighbouring property agreed to pay Christ Church $300,000 a year for 106 years, in return for a density transfer,[5] which eventually resulted in the extra height of the Park Place Development. The proposed office tower on the Christ Church site, by Arthur Erickson, was to have been set away from the street, and would not have solved the aesthetic problem of the GMD's fire escape.

1 *Vancouver Sun*, "Lament for a Landmark," by Elizabeth Godley, March 18, 1989, page D3.

2 Perhaps there is little "worth" in an old building in Vancouver, or perhaps the problem was more specifically that there was little perceived worth in the Georgia Medical-Dental. The developer's per-square-foot rental calculations were certainly accurate, and the economic argument for demolishing the building was sound, but only if the building were removed from its context and treated purely as a commodity, and if no dollar value were placed on its landmark status and stylistic richness.

3 *Sun*, ibid.

4 The Marine Building is a designated heritage building and one of the classic arguments for heritage preservation: it is historically very significant, a triumph of design and construction, a splendid local landmark, and has always commanded high rents from good, long-term tenants. This pedigree has not kept it intact, however, for a heritage designation protects only the exterior, and so the floor of its lobby and its windows have been needlessly modified in the name of "improvements."

5 *Province*, December 18, 1974.

GEORGIA ST. AT BURRARD, VANCOUVER.

M. KLUCKNER 1989

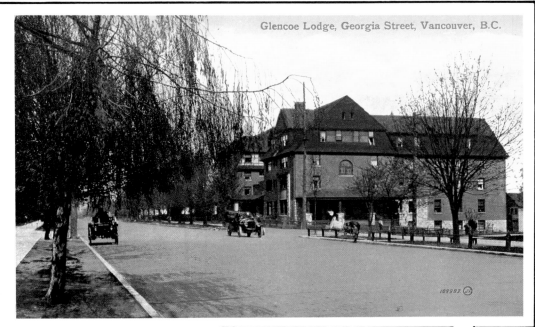

Glencoe Lodge, Georgia Street, Vancouver, B.C.

The lease of the former Glencoe Lodge property to the Standard Oil Company — two lots at $225 a month — in May, 1935, put a gas station and its accompanying parking lots on the strategic northwest corner of Georgia and Burrard, kitty-corner from the Hotel Vancouver. Glencoe Lodge, as it appears in the World War One-era postcard above (photographed from directly in front of the future site of the Hotel Vancouver), was a much-expanded, converted 1886 house, operated as a residential hotel after 1906, when B.T. Rogers of B.C. Sugar bought it as an investment. Rogers hired a tall, angular Scotswoman, always known as *Miss* Jean Mollison, the former operator of the CPR's Chateau Lake Louise, to manage it. With her bony face framed by a beribboned straw hat, Miss Mollison soon became a familiar sight striding, never just walking, through downtown Vancouver; she created a very respectable, recherché, little hotel, which offered musical evenings, a drama group headed by the playwright and educator L. Bullock-Webster, and a quiet dining room. Glencoe Lodge became known far and wide as a good address for people awaiting the completion of their new houses, as well as a permanent address for respectable couples, such as Balfour, Guthrie & Company assistant manager Harold Stephen Cove and Mrs. Cove, and the stockbroker C.M. Oliver and Mrs. Oliver.

B.T. Rogers died in the summer of 1918; his will stipulated that his four sons and widow were to receive the stock in the B.C. Sugar Refinery, while his three daughters were to get only the income from Glencoe Lodge and a couple of other pieces of Vancouver property, the inference being that they would marry men of means. Mrs. Rogers had agreed in March, 1931, to let Miss Mollison continue at half rent during the Depression, but when one of her two elder daughters, who had married musicians, was having difficulty making ends meet, Mrs. Rogers felt forced to change her decision about the hotel's future. That November, she terminated Miss Mollison's tenancy and signed the lease over to a man named F.W.M. Rowe; his underfinanced attempts to run Glencoe as the Belfred Hotel brought him to grief and landed Mrs. Rogers in court as a defendant in an unsuccessful legal action by two unpaid renovation contractors. Having failed to find a profitable lessee for the hotel, Mrs. Rogers had the building demolished in 1933, and two years later signed the lease with the Standard Oil company. The property remained until 1970 as a gas station — a highly visible example of the city's half-finished, automobile-oriented downtown — at which point it was redeveloped as part of the Royal Centre complex.[1]

One of the long-term residents of Glencoe Lodge was the stockbroker Charles Mason Oliver. Born in Teeswater, Ontario, in 1870, Oliver joined the Canadian Pacific Railway at the age of fifteen and worked in Winnipeg for several years, then spent the following five years in the United States before arriving in Vancouver, still in the employ of the CPR, in 1898. He was sent to Rossland for seven years, in charge of the railway office there, and started a brokerage business in 1905. Returning to Vancouver in 1907, he founded C.M. Oliver & Company, still a prominent part of the local brokerage scene.[2]

1 Information from *M.I. Rogers*, pages 61, 140 and 141.
2 *Who's Who in Canada*, 1930-31 edition, page 1325.

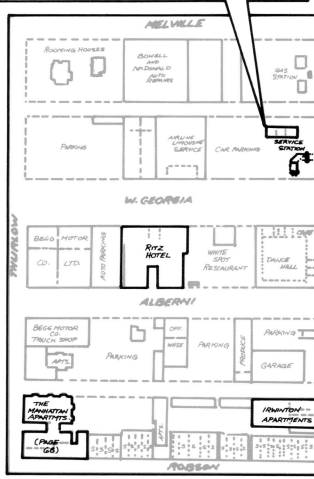

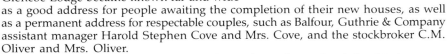

The map shows the state of the Georgia-Burrard area of downtown in 1955, demonstrating conclusively how much of it was still parking lot — a result largely of the economic doldrums of the previous twenty-five years. The Manhattan Apartments (page 68) and the Irwinton Apartments, the only two substantial buildings on the block west of Burrard between Alberni and Robson, have been restored. The almost-vacant lot across Burrard from the Irwinton became, in 1956, the site of the city's main library, superseding the Carnegie Library at Hastings and Main; in the three decades since, the system has outgrown its headquarters, and is constructing a new main library building elsewhere. The dance hall at the southwest corner of Burrard and Georgia was built on the formerly hallowed ground of the impressive wooden Wesley (Methodist) church, demolished following the completion in 1933 of R.P.S. Twizell's St. Andrew's-Wesley United church at Burrard and Nelson; the year after the original of this map was drawn, the dance hall became the site of C.B.K. Van Norman's 19-storey Burrard Building, the first office tower to be built in Vancouver after the Depression. Just west of this spot was the Ritz Apartment Hotel, started during the First World War as a YMCA building. It remained unfinished for several years due to the failure of the fund-raising campaign. When completed, it was used as an apartment building, and after 1929 as the Ritz. It was demolished in 1983, lamented by many locals, as was the Devonshire, for the demise of its beer parlour.

Lieut.-Col. Edward John Ryan's contracting company built the "new" Hotel Vancouver at Georgia and Burrard, as well as parts of the University of B.C. campus; beginning in 1926, he organized and planned the hydroelectric plant, spa, and resort at Harrison Hot Springs, and built the hotel there. Born in Quebec in 1884, Ryan came to Vancouver in 1909, operated a contracting business until 1914, then joined the Irish Fusiliers of Canada, with whom he served in France and won the D.S.O.[3]

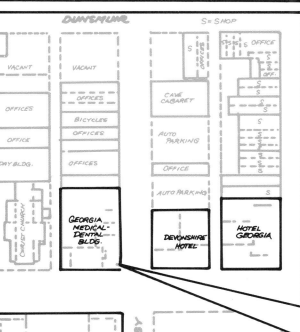

Two postcard views of the corner of Georgia and Howe, looking northwest. Both cards show the three 1920s-vintage buildings which lined the north side of Georgia Street. Nearest, and the only one still standing, is the Georgia Hotel, opened in 1927 by the Prince of Wales. In the middle is the Devonshire Hotel, beloved for its comfortable ambience and more recently for its beer parlour; it was imploded in the summer of 1981, and its site is now occupied by the Bank of Hong Kong. Farthest along, and imploded in the spring of 1989, is the 1929 Georgia Medical-Dental Building, seen here from where its architects intended it to be viewed (see the discussion on the previous pages). The top view is from the early 1930s, taken from a front window of the "old" Hotel Vancouver. Visible are the hoarding around the construction of the "new" Hotel Vancouver, on the extreme left; boulevard trees and the residential West End beyond; old houses on Howe Street just north of the Hotel Georgia; and in the distance on the waterfront at the foot of Thurlow, the buff-coloured Immigration Building, with its segregated (white and Oriental) dining room and washrooms, demolished in 1976 to provide truck and trailer parking for the CPR docks. The bottom view, taken in the 1950s from one of the back windows of the Lyric Theatre (page 38), shows the changes of twenty-odd years: on the left, the completed new Hotel Vancouver, and, in the foreground, the parking lot which had been the site of the old Hotel Vancouver. Note also the Marine Building in the right distance, and the B.C. Electric's Brill trolley-coaches, with their buff-yellow paintwork and red "Thunderbird" insignia.

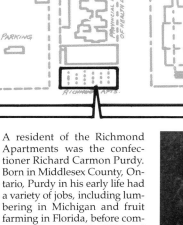

A resident of the Richmond Apartments was the confectioner Richard Carmon Purdy. Born in Middlesex County, Ontario, Purdy in his early life had a variety of jobs, including lumbering in Michigan and fruit farming in Florida, before coming to Vancouver in 1907 and organizing the chocolate manufactory which still bears his name. He claimed that his stores were the first in Vancouver to introduce ordering by telephone.[4]

3 *Who's Who in Canada*, 1930-31 edition, page 969.

4 *Who's Who and Why*, 1921 edition, page 164.

The watercolour shows the view, across yet another parking lot, of the backs of the 1898 Victoria House facing Homer Street (on the left), and the interconnected 1908 Victoria Block facing West Pender Street (in the middle). It is a part of downtown that progress has left alone, where, for pedestrians, the views from the lanes are as interesting as the views from the streets, and where it is possible in one glimpse to see the historical layers of the city's development.

The recently renovated Victoria House dates from the time of grassy boulevards and vacant lots on Pender Street, as seen in the old colour postcard on page 57. The Victoria Block was built only ten years later, but by that time the Courthouse, and much of the business growth in the city, had moved westward to the Granville Street area; its tenants now include a used bookstore and a small cafe, much like the tenants of the other buildings in the 300-block West Pender, where low rents and comfortable old buildings combine to make it an appealing and affordable address for small, lively enterprises. A contrast to these modest brick buildings is the fine office building on the extreme left — at the southwest corner of Pender and Homer — which represented a major development in office building planning: there is no internal light-well, and all of the offices face to the outside;[1] although its main floor has been modernized and now lacks the original high ceiling and mezzanine, the rest of the building retains the marble, fine tilework, and woodwork of an earlier era. Built in 1912, only four years after the Victoria Block, it is a product of the resurgent economy of the years just before the First World War. Its builder and major tenant was the Dominion Trust Company, a promoter of the speculative

1 Kalman, *Exploring Vancouver 2*, page 97.

real-estate boom through its involvement with characters such as Alvo von Alvensleben. Dominion Trust's bankruptcy in October, 1914, and subsequent liquidation for about thirty cents on the dollar rocked the B.C. economy, which had already been driven to its knees by the collapse of real-estate prices and the pending bankruptcies of the Grand Trunk Pacific and Canadian Northern railways, and drove hundreds of small investors and savers into penury. The public enquiry into Dominion Trust's affairs and the Conservative provincial government's lax regulatory practices was a major factor in that government's downfall in 1916.

Towering over all these buildings is the revolving observation deck and restaurant of the Harbour Centre on Hastings Street. Built in the mid-1970s on the site of the old Molson's Bank and Eaton's department store, Harbour Centre housed a Sears department store that soon after opening became a financial failure. Eaton's had bought its way onto Hastings Street with the 1948 takeover of the Spencer's department store chain, but had plans, finally realized in 1970, to move uptown to Georgia and Granville (see page 42); the abandoned Spencer's/Eaton's buildings were extensively renovated, and tied together with an office tower and shopping mall, but West Hastings Street, even with the venerable Woodward's department store a few blocks to the east, was no longer the place where shoppers wished to be. The former Sears portion of Harbour Centre now houses the downtown campus for Simon Fraser University.

The parking-lot area in the foreground and the balance of the block south to Dunsmuir Street were cleared in the spring of 1990 for new B.C. Hydro office buildings.

THE INNES-THOMPSON BUILDING

The south side of Hastings Street between Seymour and Richards, to date intact, is one of the best office-building streetscapes in the city, being comprised of three buildings, each solidly built, in good condition, and representative of three types of architecture from distinct periods of the city's growth. The watercolour shows a partial view of the three, centring on the Innes-Thompson Building in the middle, as they appear from just across Hastings Street in front of the Harbour Centre.

The oldest of the three is the Innes-Thompson Building, built in 1889, and one of the few buildings outside of Gastown to have survived one hundred years. Its construction dates from a period when the Canadian Pacific Railway had its own office next door (to the left), and was actively promoting the sale of commercial property in the area.[1] Frederick Colleton Innes was the first established realtor in Granville, having opened his office as F.C. Innes & Company in 1885. Early in 1887 he was advertising land for sale and for lease on Cordova, Hastings, and Granville streets.[2] The architect of the Innes-Thompson Building was Charles Osborne Wickenden, whose other significant surviving work in the city is Christ Church Cathedral at Georgia and Burrard streets (see page 48).[3]

A contrast to the Innes-Thompson Building's homely Romanesque arches is provided by the office tower on the left, at the corner of Seymour and Richards, which was completed in 1913 and was for a time the second-tallest building in the city (after the World Building/Sun Tower at Beatty and Pender).

Called the Weart Building after J.W. Weart, a lawyer and the general manager of the Investors' Guarantee Corporation, it was to have been completed as in the architect's drawing on these pages, with Skyscraper Gothic cresting which was then becoming the fashion in New York, and showed up in Vancouver in the Seymour Building (page 37) and later in the Stock Exchange Building at Pender and Howe. The onset of a depression in 1913 is the probable explanation for the lack of the planned detailing on the Weart Building.

Weart (1861-1941) moved west from Ontario and took up residence in Burnaby in 1896 — he was reeve of Burnaby in 1910-11. At the turn of the century, he was a member of the Liberal party and a supporter of "Fighting Joe" Martin; he ran unsuccessfully against Francis Carter-Cotton in the 1907 provincial elections, and finally won office in the 1916 elections, after which he was chosen Speaker of the legislature.

Besides owning the Weart Building — in whose penthouse he lived for a time — he was one of the founders of the Terminal City Club and developer of the Metropolitan Building.[5] The

Architect's drawing of the Weart Building.[4] It is ironic to note that, even in 1912, the architect replaced the Innes-Thompson Building (on the right) with a more modern, imposing structure.

1 Its next-door neighbour to the right (west), was at that time the Bank of British Columbia, built in 1887 and the first masonry building erected west of Gastown. See Kalman, *Exploring Vancouver 2*, page 90.

2 The "Thompson" partner of Innes-Thompson is untraceable. Innes's real-estate advertisements include one in the *News* supplement of January 1, 1887, Pho. 33, CVA. His house in the early 1890s was at the northeast corner of Hastings and Burrard streets.

3 Kalman, *Exploring Vancouver 2*, page 292.

4 Drawing reproduced from the 1912 anonymous publication *Vancouver Today*, CVA.

INNES-THOMPSON BUILDING, HASTINGS STREET

Weart Building was renamed the Standard Bank Building, after its main floor tenant between 1915 and 1946.

The most recent member of the trio is the Union Bank of Canada Building on the extreme right, built in 1919-20, a bunkerlike example of the Second Renaissance style from the period when banks felt that ultraconservative architecture was appropriate to their mission. It was designed by the architects Somervell and Putnam, whose other efforts in the city include the Bank of Montreal at Pender and Granville and the London Building around the corner on Pender (page 41), the decorative Merchants' Bank on Pigeon Park at Hastings and Carrall, the B.C. Electric building across Hastings Street from the Merchants' Bank, the Seymour Building, the Birks Building at Georgia and Granville (page 43), and "Shannon" (pages 137-139).[6] The Union Bank of Canada Building became the local headquarters of the Bank of Toronto (renamed the Toronto-Dominion Bank in an amalgamation), and was reduced to the status of a branch only when the Toronto-Dominion moved to Pacific Centre in the early 1970s.

The fate of the Innes-Thompson and Toronto-Dominion buildings became an issue in the summer of 1987, when a proposal surfaced from an ownership group to demolish them and build a hotel-office complex on the block between Hastings and Pender. An alternative was proposed, coordinated by architects working with the Heritage Committee of the Vancouver Community Arts Council, which sought to achieve a compromise between the density and economic demands of the demolition/redevelopment scheme, yet save the façades of both buildings. The developer's architects then produced revised plans that would retain only the façades of the Toronto-Dominion bank, as they felt that the Innes-Thompson façade was insignificant architecturally. The fate of the Innes-Thompson Building, at this writing, remains uncertain.

5 Obituaries published in local newspapers on February 12, 1941.

6 Kalman, *Exploring Vancouver 2*, page 291.

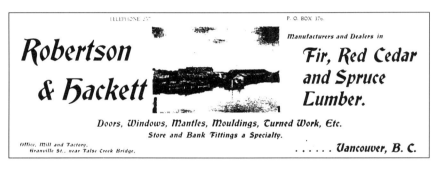

David Robertson (left), with his partner George William Hackett, owned one of the largest integrated lumber companies in the province, Robertson & Hackett Sawmills, with headquarters in an 1888 mill underneath the north side of the Granville bridge. Robertson & Hackett were also well established as contractors; they built many of the substantial office and institutional buildings in the old city, including the turreted stone Bank of Montreal built in 1891 on Granville Street (demolished); the Bank of British North America, later called the Spencer's Building, at the northwest corner of Hastings and Richards; the first unit of the B.C. Sugar Refinery warehouses along Powell Street; the B.C. Electric building at Carrall and Hastings; the first unit of the 1914 (second) Hotel Vancouver at Georgia and Granville; and the Kensington Apartments (which the firm owned until 1949). Robertson was born in Fifeshire, Scotland, in 1850, and apprenticed with contractors in Edinburgh and Manchester; striking out on his own, he built an addition to the Liverpool Safe Works, then immigrated to Canada, settling first in Toronto, before moving to British Columbia in May, 1888. As well as contracting and sawmilling, Robertson & Hackett had a sash and door factory, and the Canadian Wood & Coal Company. Following the elder Hackett's death in 1919, his twenty-eight-year-old son George Robertson Hackett (right) became vice-president and managing director of the sawmill and affiliated operations, including Dominion Mills Limited on the north arm of the Fraser River. Hackett's 1931 biography noted that the operations had ''an annual capacity of one hundred million feet of lumber, and employs upwards of five hundred men.'' The company had retail yards in Vancouver, Kamloops, Penticton and Oliver, and shipped lumber and wood products to ''all parts of the world by rail and cargo.''[1] Fire destroyed the old False Creek mill on December 16, 1953; it had been closed for a year and was in the process of being dismantled in preparation for the construction of a new Granville Bridge.

1 Information from *Who's Who in Canada*, 1930-31 edition, pages 1061 and 1463; advertisement from *Vancouver of Today Architecturally*, c. 1900, CVA.

A postcard view from about 1905 looking northeastward from the roof of the Labour Hall at 585 Homer Street. The only recognizable survivors of this scene are: in the dead-centre of the card, the buff-coloured, three-storey, bay-windowed Victoria House (page 52); and, to its right in the distance — just to the left of the domed building — the white Flack Block at 163 West Hastings Street, built with the proceeds of a Klondike gold fortune. The domed building is the Courthouse, built in 1888 and demolished at the beginning of the First World War, after the provincial government had erected a new building — now the Vancouver Art Gallery — uptown in the "CPR precinct." The sailing ships in the distance are loading lumber at the Hastings Sawmill, the enterprise founded in 1865 which provided the raison d'être for Gastown; at the time of this photograph, the sawmill was part of the B.C. Mills, Timber & Trading Company. The photographer was overlooking the backyards of a carpenter, a machinist, an engineer, and a boarding house.

Although in recent years the most visible part of Vancouver's skid row, the unit-block East Hastings — the near block of the postcard below — was for the first half of this century a respectable, thriving shopping district. An indication of this was the presence of Brown Bros. Florists, Nurserymen and Seedsmen at 48 East Hastings Street. Proprietor Joseph Brown (above) left Kent, England, for the United States and, after nearly twenty years of slowly working his way west, arrived in Vancouver in 1898. His nursery at Hammond, twenty-four miles east of the city on the CPR line, was said to be the largest in western Canada.[1] The rejuvenation of this part of Hastings Street has recently commenced with the renovation for residential use of the Holden Building (now called the Tellier Tower) at 16 East Hastings by the Downtown Eastside Residents' Association. Built in 1911 (and thus not appearing in the postcard below), the Holden Building's major claim to recognition is its service from 1929 to 1936 as Vancouver's City Hall.

A postcard view looking east from the corner of Carrall and Hastings, about 1908. The photographer was on the roof of the building that was the predecessor of the B.C. Electric Railway Company building — the famed head office building and interurban depot built in 1912, surviving today as a bank. The bay-windowed, turreted building on the right is the Pennsylvania Hotel, to which time has not been kind; it survives today without its turret, in the middle of what has become Vancouver's skid row. The 1906 Pantages Theatre in the distance, at 142 East Hastings, was Alex Pantages's first in Vancouver (his second one, built in 1917 and later known as the Beacon, would be directly behind where the photographer stood on Hastings Street). Sold to Charles Royal (page 91) the year the second theatre opened, this first Pantages Theatre went through an astonishing number of guises as cinema, theatre, and meeting hall. It was bombed in 1933 when rented to the Workers Unity League, and in 1953 was the venue for a production of Tobacco Road *that resulted in the arrest and conviction of cast and crew for staging an immoral performance. After a period as the counterculture's City Nights theatre, the building survives today as a Chinese cinema. The second Pantages Theatre was demolished in the early 1970s for a parking lot. Also visible in the postcard, just above the "Pantages" sign, are the rounded domes of the Carnegie Library, now a community centre, at the corner of Hastings and Main. This area of the city remains almost intact, with most of the buildings seen in this card still extant, because of the local economic slump, already well in progress when the B.C. Electric Railway Company moved to its new office tower at Burrard and Nelson (page 38).*

1 *Who's Who & Why*, 1921 edition, page 578.

THE ARCO HOTEL

The Arco Hotel on Pender Street east of Abbott was recently removed from the city's heritage inventory due to a combination of factors, including its deteriorated condition, the difficulty of improving its earthquake resistance, and the fact that it is not part of a unified period streetscape. Regardless, the old commercial hotel remains something of a landmark, standing as it does on the edge of the neglected but historic Hastings Street area. Built in 1912 by the contractor W.H. Braunton for John Walker, it was one of the first buildings erected on what had been a swampy inlet of False Creek.

Before 1912, when that spur of False Creek was filled, Pender Street was not connected with what was then called Dupont Street, and is now East Pender; the little swamp was the unofficial dividing line south of Hastings Street between white Vancouver and Chinese Vancouver. When the city extended Pender Street eastward across the filled swamp, it expropriated all but six feet of the corner property of the Chinese business consortium known as Sam Kee; the following year, out of spite, the group erected the Sam Kee building at East Pender and Carrall, now publicized by *The Guinness Book of World Records* as the narrowest commercial building in the world.[1]

The Arco Hotel was first known as Patricia Lodge, and later called The Ritz Hotel for a time before the new Ritz, now demolished, opened on West Georgia Street. The name "Arco" dates from the 1930s. The land directly south of the hotel — at the point-of-view of the painter — is slated to become part of the International Village, the first phase of the development of the Expo lands.

The Woodward's revolving "W" has been a fixture on the Vancouver skyline since the late 1950s. The "W" replaced a two-million-candlepower, four-foot-diameter searchlight installed in 1927 atop the eighty-foot "Eiffel Tower" visible in the watercolour. The tower and its illuminated letter surmount a five-storey extension to the Woodward's main store that contains elevators and two 25,000-gallon water tanks.[2]

Although the revolving "W" is still clearly visible above the Gastown skyline, little remains of the Woodward family association with British Columbia's oldest chain store, founded in 1892. In November, 1989, following years of reports in the press about the scale of its financial losses and months of rumours, the last two Woodward members on the company's board of directors — the one-time heir apparent, executive vice-president and chief operating officer John Woodward, and his younger brother Kip — left the company's board of directors. Both were great-grandsons of founder Charles Woodward. Control of the company will likely pass to out-of-province groups, including Toronto-based Cambridge Shopping Centres.[3]

1 The Sam Kee building has been restored by its current owner and occupant, the Jack Chow Insurance Agency.

2 John Atkin and Roger Neate, "Interesting Objects," a pamphlet published in association with the World Artifex Society, 1989.

3 *Vancouver Sun*, November 17, 1989.

THE ARCO, PENDER STREET

M.KLUCKNER 1989

DOWNTOWN SOUTH

Between the downtown end of the Granville Bridge and Robson Street, where the modern central business district begins, is an unfinished, semi-established area of Vancouver, dotted with small warehouses, offices, autobody shops, nightclubs, a few apartment buildings and even the occasional wooden house, all stitched together with parking lots and billboards. For most Vancouverites, it is an area to be driven through. To its west is the residential West End, and the spur of modern development around the Courthouse and Robson Square; to its east is the historic and rejuvenated Yaletown warehouse district; to its south, along the shores of False Creek, are the high-density residential and office developments between the bridges and on the former Expo lands. Now known as Downtown South, this previously neglected piece of Vancouver is an area ripe for some kind of massive redevelopment.

Granville Street between Drake and Nelson has been an area of high crime for decades. The 1922 murder of Constable Richard McBeath in front of the Austin Hotel was only an extreme example of the activities in what had already become an unsavoury part of town. The reputation has persisted until the present, the area being associated with violence and drug dealing in the hotels along Granville, and sordid prostitution in the darkened side streets. The scale of the social disintegration in Downtown South has been heightened by the failure of the early-1970s Granville Mall experiment,[1] which had two unfortunate consequences: it blocked automobile traffic on Granville north of Nelson and led to an influx of street people onto the wide sidewalks and benches there; and it diminished Granville's importance as a traffic artery in the blocks close to the bridge, making respectable commercial activity even more difficult. A few blocks away, Richards Street near Helmcken has become the haunt of street prostitutes since a provincial government edict cleared them from the West End.

In June, 1987, city council agreed in principle to the rezoning of Downtown South to create a new high-density residential neighbourhood, and thus also restore commercial vitality to Granville Street. Council accepted boundaries for the rezoning as Pacific Street on the south, Homer and Beatty streets on the east (wrapping around the Yaletown district), Robson Street on the north, and a zigzag of Howe, Nelson, Hornby, Helmcken, and Burrard streets on the west; within these boundaries, density was to be increased to a level at least double that in the West End, enticing private developers and creating a very urban environment for residents, who would live near their jobs and not put added strain on the city's overtaxed transportation systems.[2] The densities proposed allowed for a forest of towers of more than twenty storeys and threatened all of the old buildings in the area, some of which have significant historical value and are listed on the city's heritage inventory, but none of which have heritage designation (protection from demolition). As well, the towers would in all likelihood limit the view of the mountains from Granville Bridge and the south shore of False Creek. Although the rezoning proposal appeared to have a juggernaut's momentum, it suddenly stalled in October, 1989, due to nagging concerns about the quality of life in such a super-high-density area, unresolved questions about the fate of heritage buildings along Granville Street,[3] and the city's inability — without an enabling amendment by the provincial government to the City of Vancouver charter — to collect a fee from developers to pay for public amenities within the new area. But these are temporary setbacks, and as certain as the rains of November, a rezoning and redevelopment of Downtown South will occur.

1 A noble experiment, like Prohibition, by the city in the early 1970s, to make Granville Street between Nelson and Hastings a pedestrian and transit mall. It is in the process of being rethought.

2 City council minutes of May 30, 1989; minutes of Standing Committee of Council on Neighbourhood Issues and Services, April 13, 1989 and April 27, 1989; manager's report on rezoning of downtown south to high density residential, April 5, 1989.

3 James Lowe, "Vancouver Downtown South," Arts Vancouver, October, 1989.

4 Barry Broadfoot, "Trouble with Harry," Sun, May 3, 1968.

5 Photograph and information from Who's Who in Canada, 1930-31 edition, page 1100. Obituaries published in Vancouver newspapers on March 17, 1982.

Free-standing billboards are not a new blight on the Vancouver landscape. The "king of the billboards" in early Vancouver was Harry John Duker, born in St. Louis in 1889, who with his $100 in savings started an outdoor advertising company in Vancouver before he was twenty years old, and sold it for $300,000 in 1930. Nicknamed "Totem" for his size, Duker had come to Vancouver to try out as first baseman for the Vancouver Beavers; he did not get the position, but was asked instead to become the club's secretary.[4] He became the "number one clubman in Vancouver," involved with golf (he was a four handicap), the Vancouver Aquarium, the B.C. Automobile Association, the Queen Elizabeth Theatre, Kerrisdale Community Centre, and the Miss Vancouver pageants. His wife, nicknamed "Aunt Margaret," was a co-founder of the Crippled Children's Hospital and a tireless worker for the Children's Aid Society — she was named "Vancouver's Good Citizen" in 1947. Duker himself received the same award twenty-one years later. He died at age 96 in 1982.[5]

The Homer, under a milky city sky in the summer of 1989.

Other than the Granville Street heritage buildings, mainly well-built hotels and banks which could be integrated into the redevelopment of the street, there are a few important historical buildings scattered through the area, none of which under current city heritage policy is likely to survive a major zoning change. The most important of these, for the simple reason that it is the oldest house in Vancouver, is the quaint little yellow house at 1380 Hornby Street, built in 1888 and now occupied by Umberto's restaurant (see the photograph on page 63). At the opposite corner of Downtown South, at 863 Hamilton Street, is one of the best, and last surviving, Queen Anne-style houses in the city: built in 1895, it is typical of the type of house built when Downtown South was suburban.[6] And, for aesthetic reasons — and the fact that it provides affordable housing — there is The Homer, a classic rooming house.

Situated at the northeast corner of Homer and Smithe streets, The Homer is a non-family residence, with (in the watercolour) a family-oriented billboard across the street, erected on the edge of yet another Vancouver parking lot. Although The Homer is quite dilapidated, and the alterations to the coffee shop on the main floor (in the watercolour hidden from view by the cars) are not in character with the upper storeys, it is a unique building in the San Francisco "bay window style," a U-shaped structure with continuous corner bays and a plaster swag relief on the upper storey. It was built in 1914, after the demise of Recreation Park.

Recreation Park was a five-acre playing field southeast of Smithe and Homer. A large timber grandstand provided seating for the crowds that came to watch Bob Brown's Aberdeen Baseball Club, and events such as the memorial service for Edward VII in May, 1910. So popular was it that in March, 1906, the B.C. Electric Railway Company built a four-block-long streetcar line to provide access to it from Robson and Granville. The line ran east along Robson to Homer Street and south to Smithe Street, where a long siding was installed opposite the entrance to the park.[7] The baseball team stayed there until Athletic Park opened in 1913 at the south end of the Granville Bridge. By 1914, Recreation Park had disappeared.

6 A proposal under discussion in the spring of 1990 would retain this house and restore its few Victorian neighbours, creating a little heritage enclave on the plaza of a large redevelopment planned for that block.

7 Ewert, *The Story of the B.C. Electric Railway Company,* page 64.

THE KITSILANO TRESTLE

The two western quarters of a four-part Vancouver panorama, photographed by Truman & Caple from 7th Avenue between Oak and Spruce in Fairview in 1893. On the extreme left is the forest of the Kitsilano Indian Reserve. The closer of the two trestles is the original Granville Street Traffic Bridge, opened on January 4, 1889 — its swing span is clearly visible just to the left of the join in the two photographs. The further bridge is the original Kitsilano Trestle, with its fixed span clearly visible, connecting the developing Yaletown area of downtown with Kitsilano Point. Note the exceptional width of False Creek, which was filled repeatedly over the years to create more industrial land, and in the centre the sandbar encircled by pilings — an unsuccessful private pre-emption attempt — that, during the First World War, was filled with dredge spoil and became Granville Island. The clearing fires in the West End are at about Nicola Street. The big boarding house at the north end of the Granville Bridge stood at the northwest corner of Beach and Granville; the enterprise on the waterfront there was Wallace's Marine Ways. The two white houses directly behind it belonged to George Magee, and stood at Burrard and Pacific. The houses on the ridge are on

One of the most historically significant structures in the city was the Kitsilano Trestle, which by the time of its demolition in 1983 had become a hazard to navigation on False Creek, a superfluous part of the B.C Hydro Railway system, and something of an antiquated eyesore compared with the sleek new developments and yacht basins in that part of town. The trestle connected the Vancouver & Lulu Island Railway line, better known in modern Vancouver as the Arbutus Corridor, with the Canadian Pacific Railway Company's yards and roundhouse on the north shore of False Creek, and the B.C. Electric Railway Company's downtown streetcar system. Early in the 1980s, when the CPR traded that land to the provincial government, it triggered an ongoing series of changes to one of Vancouver's few remaining inner-city industrial areas, including the redevelopment of the north shore of False Creek between Burrard and Granville bridges, Expo 86, and subsequently the Concord Pacific redevelopment of the Expo lands. The industrial timbre of False Creek had begun to change a decade earlier, when the city cleared away the wasteland of mills and foundries on the south shore and redeveloped it with housing and parks; concurrently, private investment and the federal government restored the cluster of warehouses on Granville Island, changing it into a colourful, tin-roofed collection of public markets, shops, studios, restaurants, and theatres.

The Canadian Pacific Railway built the original Kitsilano Trestle in 1886, replacing it with an almost identical one with an added swing span in 1902; although a homely, utilitarian structure, the earlier one was intended as part of the railway's mainline to its proposed Kitsilano Point ocean docks and terminal.[1] The first surveys of the future site of Vancouver in the 1870s, to determine its suitability as a railway terminus, had suggested that English Bay was the ideal site for an ocean port, a conclusion confirmed by CPR general manager W.C. Van Horne, who in 1885 stated that: "owing to the extreme force of the tide at the First Narrows, the entrance to Burrard Inlet will be almost impractical, except at low tide . . . ."[2] Late in 1886, the year the CPR mainline reached the coast, and also the year of Vancouver's incorporation and the Great Fire, the railway extended its line from Burrard Inlet to the north shore of False Creek, built

CVA DIST.P.31-2

the trestle across the narrows near the Indian village of Snauq, and extended the line westward to the foot of Trafalgar Street — the western limit of DL 526 — where it erected a small cairn. The sidecutting in the cliff face above the beach, now the pathway between Trafalgar and Balsam streets leading to the Kitsilano Yacht Club, is the original right-of-way.[3]

In defiance of opposition from civic politicians and business leaders, who resisted the installation of a fixed bridge and the consequent blocking of navigation on the creek, the railway company continued to talk of building its roundhouse, railyards, and the aforementioned ocean docks on Kitsilano Point, on the modern site of the Planetarium and museums. It took some generous tax incentives from the city to motivate the railway instead to build its yards and roundhouse on the north shore of False Creek, where the latter remains today, and to develop the port on Burrard Inlet.

In 1902, when the CPR laid the tracks of its subsidiary, the Vancouver & Lulu Island Railway, from Kitsilano to Steveston, it demolished the old trestle, replacing it with the "modern" one that survived until recently. That V&LI line, leased by the CPR to the B.C. Electric Railway Company in 1905, became the latter's interurban railway line, operating from a terminus on the downtown side of False Creek, across the trestle, through Kitsilano, Kerrisdale, and Marpole to Richmond and Steveston.

The BCER also used the Kitsilano trestle for its streetcar system connecting Kitsilano beach with the city. The BCER abandoned its Richmond-Vancouver interurban system in 1958, and used the line subsequently, as did its corporate successor B.C. Hydro, as a freight route. The CPR in 1986 declined to renew the old BCER lease, and resumed use of the line, connected with its mainline in the absence of the Kitsilano Trestle by a route along the south shore of False Creek. Now potentially strategic to Vancouver's growing rapid transit system, the V&LI line is one of two probable routes for the SkyTrain to take to Richmond (the other, which would cause more technical and financial problems but would link more commercial and high-density residential areas to the downtown, is Cambie Street).

Davie Street near Thurlow. The arrow indicates the 1888 George Leslie house at Pacific and Hornby streets, now occupied by Umberto's Restaurant. The only other survivor from this scene is the Yale Hotel, built in 1890 and originally called the Colonial Hotel, visible behind the four two-storey white houses on Pacific Street between Seymour and Richards. The CPR's railway track is visible running along False Creek.

1 Both sides of False Creek — the downtown District Lot 541 and the south shore District Lot 526 — were part of the CPR's 1885 railway grant.

2 Patricia E. Roy, "Railways, Politicians and the Development of Vancouver as a Metropolitan Centre," unpublished M.A. thesis, University of Toronto, 1963 (available at UBC Special Collections), pp.7-12, cited in Burkinshaw, *False Creek*, page 14.

3 J.S. Matthews, CPR notes, CVA.

With the exception of the Ocean Construction cement plant on Granville Island and a few mills and storage yards east of the Cambie Street Bridge, there is no evidence left of the old False Creek — once the smokiest, most polluted, most densely concentrated area of heavy industry in the city. In the years before the catastrophic False Creek fire of July, 1960, the south shore was a solid line of heavy industry: at the foot of Birch Street was Sigurdson Millwork and the Darnell Lumber Company; between Alder and Spruce streets the looming, Dickensian Vancouver Machinery Depot; at the foot of Oak Street the B.C. Forest Products mill; west of the foot of Laurel the B.C. Fir & Cedar Lumber Company; and from Laurel to Willow the Alberta Lumber Company. The Alberta Lumber Company sales office illustrated above, built in 1912, stood at 790 West 6th until 1983, and outlasted by a decade the mills and wharves and beehive burners on the creekshore. Further east, between Ash and Cambie, was the Vancouver Engineering Works, a business controlled by George Walkem; the Walkem Machinery buildings illustrated on the next page, a landmark of sorts just to the west of the Cambie Bridge, survived until 1986. Next to the Vancouver Engineering Works and nestled along the west side of the old Cambie Bridge (more properly called the Connaught Bridge, and dismantled in 1984) was Johnston Terminals.[1]

One of the great curiosities of False Creek, which survived until July, 1981, was the Sweeney Cooperage, tucked almost underneath the downtown end of the Connaught Bridge, with a street address of 49 Smythe. The firm was founded in 1889 by Michael Sweeney of Carbonnear, Newfoundland, and expanded greatly during the life of his son Michael Leo Sweeney (1886-1977). It had merged with a number of other barrel-making operations and carried on business as the Canadian Western Cooperage during the period 1921-1939, but Sweeney was

able to buy out the other investors and, in 1940, changed the name back to Sweeney Cooperage Limited. In addition to the False Creek plant, Sweeney owned barrel plants in Victoria and Montreal and was president of the Canadian Cooperage Association. A noted athlete and a prominent Roman Catholic, Sweeney also found time to be president of the B.C. Automobile Association during the mid-1940s.[2] He was also president of the tourist association, and wore as his trademark a straw boater, even in the rain, to prove that it was liquid sunshine.[3] The public got to see the workings of the old cooperage during the occasional time when it sold off its old iron-banded, oak-staved whiskey barrels, which found many new uses, including as backyard strawberry planters.

(Left) One of the sawmill owners on the south shore of False Creek was Thomas Andrew Lamb, whose Lamb Lumber Company and False Creek Lumber Company had offices at 953 West 6th Avenue, just east of Oak Street. Born in New Brunswick, Lamb spent his early working life in cheese factories before venturing to the Yukon in 1903, where he mined for several years. At the age of thirty, he decided to come to British Columbia with his brother; in 1912, they founded the Lamb Lumber Company. In addition to these operations, he was a director of the Western Canada Magic Silver Black Fox Company. He lived in Shaughnessy Heights at 1937 Hosmer Avenue.[4]

(Right) Frank Wilkinson founded Wilkinson & Company Steel and Wire Merchants in 1910 at 846 Beach Avenue, near the north end of the Kitsilano Trestle, on a site now completely redeveloped with highrise condominiums and yacht marinas. His business manufactured wire, nails, bale ties, and barrel hoops, and advertised itself as ''one of the biggest distributors in British Columbia of galvanized sheet, steel plates, shapes and bars, wire rope, Canada plates, tin plates and triangle mesh concrete reinforcement.''[5]

1 See page 91 for a biographical note on the founder, Elmer Johnston.

2 *Who's Who in British Columbia,* 1944-46 edition, page 249.

3 Obituaries published in Vancouver newspapers on September 19, 1977. See also J.S. Matthews news clippings in CVA for articles on the cooperage itself.

4 *Who's Who in Canada,* 1930-31 edition, page 539.

5 *Who's Who & Why,* 1921 edition, page 83.

ARMSTRONG, MORRISON & COMPANY

The growth of the Lower Mainland and the stupendous changes to its transportation system have all but erased the legacy of Armstrong, Morrison & Company. In the Vancouver area, only their greatest construction feat, the 1904 railway bridge across the Fraser River at New Westminster, survives, but at the time of the First World War there were five Armstrong & Morrison bridges across False Creek. The earliest was the Great Northern Railway trestle, connecting the GNR's terminus — the building that later became the Marco Polo restaurant at Pender and Columbia — with the railway mainline extending through the Grandview Cut and across the above-mentioned Fraser River railway bridge. Next was the 1908 bascule span on Main Street, replacing an old trestle dating from the early 1870s. A moveable span at Main Street became necessary because of the city's plan to dredge the False Creek mudflats east of Main Street to create a port, to be connected with Burrard Inlet by a canal along the old high-tide "canoe route" at Campbell Avenue.[1] Because the city made a deal with the GNR in 1910 whereby the latter filled the mudflats east of Main Street for a railway terminus, the bascule span was never needed, and eventually found its way to Victoria, where it became the Johnston Street Bridge across the Upper Harbour. The third Armstrong & Morrison span was the 1909 Granville Bridge, under which Granville Island was created. It survived until the current Granville Bridge opened in the mid-1950s. The fourth span across the Creek was the 1912 Connaught Bridge, the venerable traffic-jam creator that survived until 1983. The fifth, crossing a spur of False Creek, was the old Georgia Viaduct.

Alexander Morrison and William Henry Armstrong formed their partnership in 1892, and were associated in the early years with a contractor named Dan McGillivray. Their first efforts included the New Westminster waterworks and the Heatley Avenue engineering and ironworks, which they sold in 1901 to Vancouver Engineering Works. Subsequently, the firm devoted its energies to contracting and specialized in bridge construction; in addition to the Vancouver-area bridges above, it built seven bridges on the Canadian Northern (now CNR) line from Lytton to Kamloops, the bridge across the Columbia River at Trail, the Kettle Valley Railway bridge across the Fraser River at Hope, and the first highway bridge across the Pitt River near Coquitlam.[2] The firm became associated with Stuart, Cameron & Company during the 1930s on projects such as the construction of the foundations for the Lions Gate Bridge.

(Left) Born in Motherwell, Scotland, in 1852, Alexander Morrison served an apprenticeship as a builder and millwright and worked in the shipbuilding yards on the Clyde before immigrating to Quebec in 1871. After two decades of contracting work there, he came to British Columbia in 1891. In addition to his construction work and interests in the city's Scottish societies, he owned a ranch near Keremeos, where he grew "thirty acres all apples and small fruits." In Vancouver, Morrison lived at 1185 Harwood in the West End. (Centre) The corpulent William Henry Armstrong (1857-1946) left his home in Stratford, Ontario, to join the bridge construction department of the Grand Trunk Railway, worked subsequently for the Canadian Pacific Railway, and was trainmaster and general roadmaster for the CPR in Vancouver from the time of the railway's arrival on the west coast in the mid-1880s. He formed the partnership with Morrison in 1892. Other than the Ancient Landmark order of the Masons, his major interest was motoring, and he claimed to have "brought to and operated the first automobile in Vancouver, 1899." Morrison lived in a large stone house at the corner of Comox and Jervis. (Right) The successor to the founders of Armstrong, Morrison & Company was William Carey Ditmars (1865-1960), born in St. Catherines, Ontario. Following several years in Vancouver as a representative of the John Doty Engine Company of Toronto, Ditmars joined Armstrong & Morrison in 1897, became a partner in 1903, and took over the entire firm in 1924. Like Morrison, Ditmars maintained a ranch at Keremeos. He built the notable Georgian Revival brick house at 3637 Pine Crescent in Shaughnessy Heights. As well as his construction interests, he was involved in gold-mining companies, the Vancouver Granite Company, and spent some of his spare time as an active member of the Vancouver Pioneers Association.[3]

1 The 1905 City Engineering plans appear in Burkinshaw, *False Creek*, page 30.

2 Information from *Who's Who and Why*, 1921 edition, pages 230 and 255; *Who's Who in Canada*, 1930-31 edition, page 1311; and Matthews news clippings in CVA.

3 Obituaries published in Vancouver newspapers on December 9, 1960.

CVA BU. P. 788

For the twenty years before Tudor Manor was built in 1927, the West End had been undergoing a slow transition from family-occupied houses to rooming houses and apartment buildings. The best of the surviving apartment buildings from these early years are the 1909 Banff at the corner of Bute and Georgia (now isolated by the westward expansion of the city's central business district); the 1909 Beaconsfield at 884 Bute Street; the 1910 Holly Lodge at 1210 Jervis Street; the 1912 Sylvia Court Apartments, now the Sylvia Hotel at Beach Avenue and Gilford; and the 1912 Kensington Place at Beach Avenue and Nicola Street.

Although it had outlived its economic usefulness according to 1980s West End standards, Tudor Manor's Beach Avenue façade was saved in a complicated 1988 redevelopment. The suites behind it were removed and completely replaced, and a concrete tower was built up through the back of it, at the eastern end (the near end of the photograph) of the original building. With its little "hats" which are supposed to echo the Tudor roofline of the original, the tower bears the post-modernist stamp of the prolific architect Paul Merrick; according to Merrick, there is no other apartment building like it in the world.[1]

Tudor Manor, at 1311 Beach Avenue, as it appeared in the spring of 1928, just before completion.

Two of the residents of the Sunset Beach area, before it became the apartment and rooming house neighbourhood of the 1930s, were Major Alexander Henderson, K.C. (top) and Miles Penner Cotton (bottom). The barrister Henderson (1861-1940) was born in Oshawa and educated at Osgoode Hall in Toronto. Immediately after completing his legal education he came west to British Columbia, and was called to the B.C. bar in 1892. He soon embroiled himself in Liberal politics and was elected to the provincial legislature from the New Westminster riding in 1898. It was a period in B.C. politics without formalized political parties,[2] and Henderson gravitated to the faction led by Cariboo rancher Charles Augustus Semlin, who formed a government on August 12, 1898. Semlin invited into his government the Conservative Vancouver newspaperman Francis Carter-Cotton as minister of finance, and the Liberal Vancouver lawyer Joseph "Fighting Joe" Martin as attorney general; although representing the same government, the two men fought viciously both inside and outside the legislature, until finally, following a row in Rossland on June 20, 1899, Semlin demanded Martin's resignation. Alexander Henderson was asked to be the replacement attorney general and served until the end of the following February, when Semlin's government was suddenly dismissed by Lieutenant-Governor Thomas McInnes. In an unprecedented move that resulted in his dismissal by Prime Minister Laurier, McInnes asked Martin to form a government — "Fighting Joe" thus became B.C.'s shortest-serving premier, from March 1 to June 14, 1900, when he went down to electoral defeat. Henderson also was defeated in that election, and quit politics.[3] The Conservative coalition government led by James Dunsmuir, which had won the election, appointed Henderson to a county court judgeship; he resigned that post in 1907 to take an appointment as commissioner of the Yukon, and left that in 1911 to form the legal partnership of Henderson, Tulk and Bray.[4] He continued "in harness" until a sudden illness three weeks before his death.[5] Miles Penner Cotton was born in Kingston, Ontario in 1878, and studied engineering at Queen's University. He spent ten years with the engineering department of the CPR, and made contacts which helped him to secure the contract for curbs, sidewalks and streets in Shaughnessy Heights.[6]

1 Quoted in "Towering Tudor," *Vancouver Sun*, March 25, 1989, page C1.

2 A person might be known as a member of a federal party, but if he (there being no women in politics before 1917) ran for provincial office, it was as an independent. This continued until 1903, when Richard McBride appealed to the voters to elect him and his Conservative caucus.

3 Information on the governments of the period is in Howay and Scholefield, *British Columbia From the Earliest Times to the Present*, and in *Victoria The Way It Was*, pages 86-9.

4 The partner Tulk was Albert Edward Tulk, the liquor dealer who built the splendid house known as "Rosemary" at 3689 Selkirk in Shaughnessy Heights.

5 Information from *Who's Who in Canada*, 1930-31 edition, page 992. Obituaries published in Vancouver newspapers on December 14, 1940.

6 Information from *Who's Who & Why*, 1921 edition, page 915. Obituaries published in Vancouver newspapers on March 17, 1941.

ROBSON STREET

The restoration of the Manhattan Apartments at the corner of Thurlow and Robson streets is one of a handful of successful heritage preservation projects in the West End. Robson Street has changed so drastically in the past twenty-five years, from a folksy European "Robsonstrasse" to the sleek fashion and restaurant street of today, that there seemed to be little room left for a heritage building. The postcard above is from the period 1910-1915.

Designed and built in 1908 by the prolific firm of Parr & Fee (page 74), the Manhattan was a speculative venture by the lumbermill owner William Lamont Tait, who actually moved there from his grand folly "Glenbrae" (page 108) in 1920. It was the earliest apartment building in the city that did not have a house-like gable; instead, it had a flat roof, and used a deep courtyard, visible on the left side of the postcard, to bring light into the interior of the building. According to the architectural historian Harold Kalman, it "formed the model for countless later apartment buildings,"[1] most of which, including the Trafalgar Mansions on Nelson and the Simpson Apartments at Denman and Davie, have since been razed.

As the city changed around it, the Manhattan became just another rather rundown West End apartment building; by the 1960s, when tenants were seeking the flashy new highrises that had sprouted all over the West End, and were able to choose among them with the help of generous "first month's rent free" bonuses from anxious landlords, the Manhattan was dilapidated, pigeon-spattered, and thoroughly grimy. In 1975, its owner, Sunco Developments, applied for a demolition permit. However, both the city and the tenants wished to explore methods of restoring the building and involved the Canada Mortgage and Housing Corporation in a search for financing. In 1979, the owner made a second demolition application, but was again persuaded to reconsider, although there had been little progress on the restoration plans. Eventually, the tenants formed the Manhattan Cooperative Housing Association, intending to purchase and renovate the building themselves, but the owner then decided not to sell. Following further discussions, the tenants' cooperative took a thirty-five-year lease on the residential portion of the building, and with government financing were able to hire an architect and a contractor to renovate it. The owner restored the commercial portion. In 1983, the Manhattan received the Credit Foncier Award for Restoration Projects.[2]

No matter how much reconstruction Robson Street undergoes and how much it changes, it remains one of the most vibrant shopping and promenading streets in the city. Named for the unlucky B.C. premier John Robson,[3] the street became a commercial one after streetcar tracks were laid along it in 1895; the Denman Street end was considered so remote that the Vancouver Street Railway Company, which was also in the land development business, offered free passes as an inducement to new settlers.[4] After the Second World War, it became the European shopping street in the city, and earned the nickname "Robsonstrasse" for its large number of German businesses. Fortunately for its long-term viability, none of the plans from the 1960s and 1970s to rebuild it as a pedestrian shopping mall ever came to fruition.

1 Kalman, *Exploring Vancouver 2*, page 123.

2 *Heritage West*, Winter, 1983, page 26.

3 Robson assumed the office on August 3, 1889, upon the death of A.E.B. Davie, and himself died in office in July, 1892, from blood poisoning which developed after he jammed his finger in the door of a cab in London, England.

4 Conversation between Fred Salsbury and J.S. Matthews, October 23, 1943, quoted in Matthews "Streets and Place Names," CVA.

The last two houses on Robson Street await the certainty of demolition, most likely in 1991, when the lease on La Côte d'Azur expires. Both are examples of the Edwardian Builder style — the gabled Vancouver Box — and were built in 1903-4 by a carpenter-contractor named Thomas Hunter, who lived at 1106 Melville Street. Between 1927 and 1937, 1216 Robson Street — the house on the left — was the home and gallery of the noted "abstract" photographer John Vanderpant (1872-1937).[1]

For most of the past twenty or so years, the two houses have formed a little French enclave amid the German atmosphere of "Robsonstrasse." Opened in 1968, La Côte d'Azur at 1216 Robson was Maurice Richez's first foray into the Vancouver restaurant business. Its comfortable atmosphere is reminiscent of inns of the French countryside, and it was one of the early harbingers of the sophisticated restaurants that have become quite common in Vancouver in the eighties and nineties. The green house next door, at 1222 Robson Street, was for a long time Le Bouquinier, a French-language bookstore. Most of the 1200-block Robson has been assembled for redevelopment by Gammon International, the Hong Kong-based Quan family's investment company.[2]

1 Obituary in *Sun*, July 25, 1937. For further information, see Hill, Charles C., *John Vanderpant*, National Gallery of Canada, 1976, available at the Vancouver Public Library.

2 Sean Rossiter, *Vancouver* magazine, June, 1989.

"GABRIOLA"

Looking in a northwesterly direction from the corner of Davie and Nicola at "Gabriola," and the newly completed Angus Apartments, in the winter of 1925-26. English Bay is down the hill to the left. Visible behind the nearest telephone pole is a sign advertising the apartments for rent. The brick apartment buildings were demolished in the 1970s, and "Gabriola" was restored for use as a restaurant.

1 The information herein, unless otherwise noted, is from Mrs. B.T. Rogers's diaries, excerpted in *M.I. Rogers*, pages 27, 54, 55, 129 and 130.

2 B.T. Rogers was an accomplished gardener, and maintained elaborate greenhouses and conservatories at both his houses. Both his business and pleasure trips often seemed to revolve around the purchase of or the discovery and digging up of ferns; he traded palms with Lord Mount Stephen; and the Duke of Westminster's gardener dropped by one day in 1896 to inspect his roses, including an especially fine Gloire de Dijon.

The grand residence "Gabriola" at 1531 Davie Street, now The Mansion restaurant, was B.T. Rogers's second house in Vancouver. The first, called "The Bungalow" and designed by R. Mackay Fripp in 1890, stood just west of the corner of Georgia and Nicola. Aided by the economic activity stimulated by the Klondike gold rush, Rogers's B.C. Sugar Refinery prospered in the booming Vancouver of the late 1890s, and with the birth of his third child, Ernest, in 1898, Rogers felt that it was time to begin planning for a bigger house. Mr. and Mrs. Rogers had decided by August, 1899, that either six lots somewhere on Haro Street, or the vacant block of Davie Street west of the corner of Nicola, would be a suitable site for the new house. Mrs. Rogers noted in her diary that her husband gave her the four lots immediately west of Nicola as a Christmas present that year, and that on the last day of the year he decided to buy the fifth and last lot on the block.[1]

Rogers commissioned the Victoria-based architect Samuel Maclure to design the house, and the latter visited Vancouver in mid-January, 1900, to discuss plans with the couple. Progress was swift thereafter: on February 2, Maclure brought over the elevations; early in May they decided upon a stone veneer to be quarried on Gabriola Island, and by the end of June all the studding was erected; on July 12, one of the Bloomfields, probably James, brought over the stained-glass designs. Mrs. Rogers first referred to the house as "Gabriola" in her diary the following April. They moved in on July 11, 1901.

The family, including the four children born between 1900 and 1912, lived in "Gabriola" for the next twenty-four years, but only ten years after building it, following a lengthy trip to England, B.T. Rogers began to plan for an even bigger house with extensive gardens and room for livestock. Construction commenced on the new "Shannon" estate (page 137), but thanks to wartime labour shortages it was still incomplete when Rogers died suddenly in the summer of 1918. His widow, who found "Shannon" grandiose and too reminiscent of her late husband, had little desire to finish it, so the new house stood as an incomplete shell, but with finished outbuildings, established gardens, staff, and livestock, through the early 1920s.[2]

Then, on January 2, 1925, she wrote in her diary: "signed the agreement with Bentall re apartment building on Davie Street." "Bentall" was Charles Bentall, owner of Dominion Construction, which had been building "Shannon." Bentall evidently had convinced her to finish "Shannon," convert "Gabriola" into an apartment building, and finance the latter project herself. In March, she formed the Angus Apartments, Ltd. (Angus was her maiden name); that month, workmen started demolishing "Gabriola's" greenhouses, and by the end of September, 1925, she wrote: "saw the apartments that are ready for occupation and the demolished parts of the old house."

PETER CHERNIAVSKY

The hallway and main staircase of "Gabriola," probably about 1910. On the staircase landing, visible today to patrons of the restaurant that now occupies the house, is a stained-glass window by the Bloomfield family, installed there on May 28, 1901.

PETER CHERNIAVSKY

The two elder Rogers daughters, Mary on the left and Elspeth on the right, in front of the Stanley Park "hollow tree" about 1907. The girls kept their horses in the coach house and stables that stood facing Nicola Street behind "Gabriola," and rode through the West End, as did B.T. Rogers himself, to reach Stanley Park. The house and its greenhouses and outbuildings originally occupied all five lots on the block of Davie Street west of Nicola and most of the adjoining lots facing Pendrell Street. Mary and Elspeth Rogers married respectively Mischel and Jan Cherniavsky, the cellist and pianist of the world-travelling Cherniavsky Trio; Jan Cherniavsky (1892-1989) was a familiar figure for decades on the Vancouver music scene and was one of the organizers of the Vancouver Opera Association. The old coach house and stables became the Angus Garage after Mrs. B.T. Rogers converted "Gabriola" into an apartment building, and were demolished in the late 1970s, after Dominion Construction restored the house and converted it into a restaurant.

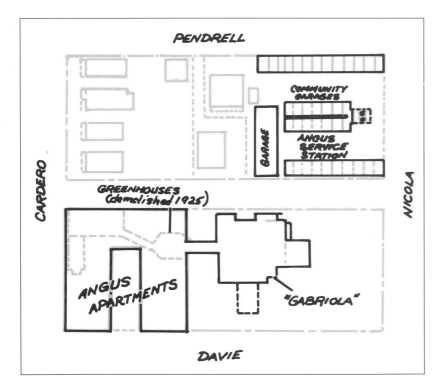

The "Gabriola" block on Davie Street, adapted from Goad's Atlas, 1912 *and the* Insurance Plan of Vancouver, January, 1955.

The West End around the time of the First World War was a respectable and comparatively diverse (for the time) neighbourhood, containing lavish houses for some of Vancouver's long-established wealthy residents, frame builders' houses (such as the Comox Street ones in the postcard on the next page), new apartment buildings, and even quaint little cottages such as that of lifeguard Joe Fortes, the B.C. Mills prefab (page 19), and the Gilford Street houses (page 83). Below are photographs of two of the finer West End houses, reproduced from the promotional booklet *Beautiful Homes*.[1]

"Argoed," the home of Jonathan and Elisabeth Rogers, stood at 2050 Nelson Street, a half block from Stanley Park. Jonathan Rogers died in 1945, but his widow, Elisabeth, one of the major supporters of artistic and community activities in the city, lived on in the house until her death at age 83 in 1960.[2] As her husband had done, she left in her will unprecedentedly large bequests to charity, including this house "to the governing council of the Salvation Army to be used as a home for aged women and women convalescents and to be named the Elisabeth Rogers Home for Women."[3] An auction at the house, on June 28, of all the items not specifically listed in the will drew throngs of people; a newspaper article, describing the 1942 Packard, full-sized billiard table, silver, jewellery, and oil paintings, was headlined "Era Ends Under Gavel."[4] But the fine old house never became the memorial to Mrs. Rogers that she had wished; later that year, the Salvation Army announced that it was selling the house for $200,000. "We can accommodate a much larger number of women if we sell the home and construct a building specifically suited for that purpose," said Brigadier John Steele.[5] The house was sold, and demolished in 1962 to make way for the construction of an eleven-storey apartment block. There is no Elisabeth Rogers home for women in Vancouver.

The home of the lumberman Edwin C. Mahony, who invented the B.C. Mills, Timber & Trading Company's prefabricated modular wall system, which stood at the northwest corner of Comox and Chilco.

1 Undated pamphlet, published circa 1915, in CVA, Und-831.

2 Obituaries published in Vancouver newspapers on January 23, 1960.

3 *Province*, June 10, 1960.

4 *Province*, June 29, 1960.

5 *Sun*, December 12, 1960.

The West End, looking down Comox Street, Vancouver, B.C.

A John Valentine & Sons postcard from about 1915, looking west along Comox Street toward Stanley Park from the roof of the Gainsborough Apartments. The first street crossing Comox is Nicola Street; the house on the northeast corner, and most of the houses on the north side of Comox west of there still exist. The white apartment building at the corner of Comox and Cardero is the Grace Court; beyond it, on the left of Comox Street, is Lord Roberts school.

Three residents of the St. Paul's Church area of the West End in the early 1920s were Nina de Pencier (far left), E.L. Cave-Brown-Cave (left), and A.C. Cohen (right). Nina Frederica de Pencier was the wife of Adam Urias de Pencier, the rector of St. Paul's Anglican church from 1908-10 and later Bishop of New Westminster;[1] she was the daughter of Lt.-Col. Frederick Wells of Toronto, one of the old landowners of that city, whose family sold Henry Pellatt the land for his famous castle "Casa Loma." The de Penciers were pillars of the Anglican establishment of the West End, who congregated at the splendid wooden St. Paul's at Jervis and Pendrell, built in 1905. Very little remains in the West End reminiscent of this era, other than the church itself, the Fee house (page 74), and "Gabriola" (page 70).

Another Anglican with excellent social credentials, who lived at 1221 Cardero Street, was Edward Lambert Cave-Brown-Cave, the grandson of Sir John Robert Cave-Brown-Cave, BART. The Cave-Brown-Cave moniker came to the former through his mother — he was the sixth son of a man named Ambrose Sneyd, but evidently adopted his mother's surname to assure the title's lineage to his son. Coming to Canada in 1886, Edward Cave-Brown-Cave spent two years as the private secretary to Sir John Lister-Kaye, BART., who was interested in farming in the "Canadian Northwest"; he then worked for the general manager of a Manitoba railway, before coming to Vancouver in 1901, and joining the British Columbia Assay and Chemical Supply Company. His recreation included cricket, lawn tennis, and golf, and he was president from 1910 to 1919 of the Vancouver Lawn Tennis Club.[2] His son Clement Charles ascended to the 300-year-old baronetcy following the death of his uncle Sir Rowland in 1943; the news took several days to reach Vancouver, as the baronet had been known in his London hospital only as Rowland Cave, and was identified eventually by a daughter, who was a missionary in Africa.[3] The new baronet was able to enjoy his title for a little more than a year, as he died suddenly in April, 1945; the title then passed to his fifteen-year-old son Robert, who lived on with his mother in Vancouver in a house at 1290 Matthews, which they called "Stanford House" after the family seat.

A man of rather different background was Abraham Charles Cohen, resident in the early 1920s at 1253 Pendrell Street. Born into a Jewish family in Riga, Russia, in 1881, he immigrated to New York City, where he worked as a knitter before volunteering for the United States army during the Spanish-American War of 1898. Subsequently, he moved to Vancouver, and worked in the knitting business with Mackay, Smith & Blair. In 1914 he founded the Universal Knitting Company, "Manufacturers of Sweaters, Sweater Coats, Bathing Suits, Athletic Jerseys, Knit Goods and Novelties for Women and Children, 303 Pender Street West." The company flourished, developing a large export business to Japan, New Zealand, Java, and South Africa; by 1921 it employed over a hundred people.[4]

As the years passed, the old families moved away, and the old houses were converted into suites and housekeeping rooms. A new type of resident moved into the West End, occupying the gracious apartments in buildings such as the Queen Charlotte at 1101 Nicola Street. The noted barrister Adam Smith Johnston (far right) was one such; he sold his old house on Laurier Avenue in Shaughnessy Heights, and moved to the Queen Charlotte. Johnston (1888-1948) was "Vancouver's most colourful lawyer of the old school." A sartorial sight-to-see with his flowing locks, cigar, erect bearing, and exquisitely groomed clothes, he was generally considered "the best-dressed man in Vancouver."[5]

1 *Who's Who & Why*, 1921 edition, page 474.

2 *Who's Who & Why*, 1921 edition, page 48.

3 *News-Herald*, December 24, 1943.

4 *Who's Who & Why*, 1921 edition, page 1040.

5 Information from *Who's Who & Why*, 1921 edition, page 582, and from obituaries published in local newspapers on October 14, 1948.

THE FEE HOUSE

Thomas Fee (1860-1929)[5]

Thomas Arthur Fee and his partner John Edmeston Parr left a more extensive and varied legacy of buildings to the City of Vancouver than any other architectural firm. Born in eastern Canada about 1860, Fee trained briefly as an architect in Minneapolis,[1] and arrived in Vancouver in the 1890s, living first in a house at 747 Hamilton Street. He was enamoured of the United States, and probably influenced by the architect-developers who operated in a free-wheeling manner in southern California during the 1880s;[2] his pro-American, pro-annexation beliefs got him expelled from the Vancouver Board of Trade on September 30, 1914. Fee had also made a statement in support of the German-Canadian speculator Alvo von Alvensleben, who had been unable to return to Canada following the outbreak of the First World War; that, probably as much as his pro-American beliefs, contributed to his ejection.[3]

Parr & Fee operated its very successful business from the Fee Block at 570 Granville Street (now razed), and contributed a tremendous number of buildings to the Vancouver skyline. The firm's earliest surviving edifices are probably the Ralph Block at 126 West Hastings Street and the Carleton Hotel at the southeast corner of Cambie and Cordova, both dating from 1899. Their work in the early years of the new century included The Orillia (page 44), the two houses at Broughton and Pendrell (the watercolour on the next page), and the two Edwardian Builder houses that survive as part of the Comox-Pendrell streetscape (page 77). During the booming economic years between 1908 and 1913, the firm designed a number of commercial buildings, including several hotels on Granville Street, the 1907-12 Malkin warehouse at 57 Water Street (now The Old Spaghetti Factory and other businesses), the 1908-9 flat-iron Europe Hotel on Maple Tree Square, the 1908 Manhattan Apartments on Robson Street (page 68), the 1909 Filion Block at 204 Carrall Street and the 1910-12 Vancouver Block skyscraper at 736 Granville Street. During that period, Parr and Fee also designed the turreted Mount Pleasant Presbyterian Church at 10th and Quebec, and are credited with the erection of "Glenbrae" in Shaughnessy Heights (page 108).[4]

1 Kalman, *Exploring Vancouver 2*, page 137.

2 "The great land boom of the 1880s threw the Southern California architect directly into large speculative enterprises," notably the partnership of Samuel and Joseph Cather Newsom, who "devoted a considerable amount of their professional energies to designing new towns, housing developments, hotels, and office buildings, and sometimes even invested their own monies in these speculative ventures." Gebhard and Winter, *Architecture in Los Angeles*, page 14. Vancouverites spent much of the time from about 1898 until 1914 in the thrall of a similar land boom.

3 Castell Hopkins, *Canadian Annual Review of Public Affairs*, 1914 edition, page 704.

4 Kalman, *Exploring Vancouver 2*, architect index, page 290, and City of Vancouver Heritage Inventory, page 25.

5 Photograph from *Vancouver of Today Architecturally*, pamphlet circa 1900, CVA Und-506.

The only surviving house that Thomas Fee built for himself is the one at the northwest corner of Broughton and Pendrell, erected in 1903. Fee lived there only briefly, before moving in 1907 to his new, much larger house at the corner of Gilford and Comox (now demolished). Subsequently, the house at 1119 Broughton Street was divided up into housekeeping rooms, disfigured with fire escapes, and for years called "Holly Manor." The watercolour was painted in March, 1989, and shows how later development, especially the brick Pendrell Apartment House on the left, took over parts of the house's grounds, leaving the distinctive turret practically on the property line. Adjoining "Holly Manor" on the north side, at 1111 Broughton (visible in the middle ground of the watercolour), is another house built at the same time by Fee; now stucco-covered, it has, if anything, a more interesting floor plan — a cross like a Byzantine church, with a turret at its south end and a bay, like the apse of a church, at its north end. The brick apartment building in the background, at 1091 Broughton Street, is The Gainsborough.

A redevelopment of "Holly Manor," which will move the house forward on the lot and erect an eight-unit, four-storey structure behind, was approved by city council in October, 1989.

THE COMOX-PENDRELL HOUSES

The watercolour on the facing page shows some of the houses on the south side of Comox Street, looking west from near the corner of Thurlow. These houses, with those adjoining them to the west (the right of the painting) and the block of houses facing Pendrell Street with which they share the back lane, form the so-called Comox-Pendrell Character Area — the last major intact grouping of houses in the West End. Built during the period from 1893 to 1905, each house is an example of the variations in the Queen Anne and Vancouver Box styles. More importantly, they form the kind of varied streetscape typical of old Vancouver. The houses on the block are owned by the parks board, which, in its quest for open space, cleared the block immediately to the north to create Nelson Park; it had similar intentions with this block, but now appears willing to undertake some sort of heritage restoration. Meanwhile, several of the houses are continuing to deteriorate.

The block-long streetscapes of Craftsman houses in Kitsilano, illustrated on pages 26-29, are unusual in that few builders were sufficiently organized or had enough financial backing to erect more than a few houses at a time. Most building firms at the turn of the century were composed of a few men, a few hand tools, and a horse that could pull an excavation bucket. Thus, styles changed down the lengths of almost any block; as well, the real-estate market was always so volatile, and there was so much subdivided land thrown on the market during the period from 1886 to 1940, that blocks were developed with a few scattered houses, then a vacant lot filled in later with something completely different, and so on. Most of the intact groupings in any one style are Craftsman houses, dating from about 1912-14 — the frantic end of the Vancouver boom, when the city's economy was strongest and population growth greatest.[1]

Two other groups of houses in the West End have recently been restored. The most visible and least successful restoration is the group of Vancouver Boxes on Pacific Street just west of the Burrard Bridge. In order to finance the preservation of eight of the ten, they were moved forward on their lots and reestablished in pairs behind a low red-brick wall and atop an underground garage, so that an apartment building could be inserted behind them along the lane. The result has made the houses stand out glaringly, aggravated by the lack of any significant period landscaping, and their arrangement in pairs bears more resemblance to late 1970s Kitsilano townhouse construction than to Edwardian Vancouver subdivisions. They have lost the look of old Vancouver.

The other West End restoration is in the unusual block bounded by Barclay, Nicola, Haro, and Broughton, and is an innovative project to create a heritage park in the midst of the

1 Other groups of matching houses in this book are the elaborate Craftsman houses at Nelson and Cardero (page 80), the little cottages on Gilford Street (page 82), and the Vancouver Boxes on Alberta Street (page 97), barely visible on Cypress Street (page 107), and on Lakewood Drive (page 162). There are streets scattered throughout the city with groupings of later styles of houses, such as the Spanish Colonial Revival ones of the twenties and thirties, the Art Deco and "art stucco" bungalows from the thirties, and the ubiquitous "VLA houses" — the little stucco and siding boxes for returned servicemen and families built under the Veterans' Land Act in the late 1940s and early 1950s. Burkeville (page 186) is an example of Second World War workers' housing — not too different from the VLA houses of Fraserview.

The unusual apartment building at 934 Nicola Street, removed during the 1980s as part of the development process of Barclay Heritage Square.

OLD HOUSES ON COMOX STREET, WINTER DAY   MICHAEL KLUCKNER 1990

high-density, highrise West End. Before its restoration in the mid-1980s, the block contained a very odd assemblage of houses, most significant of which were the rambling 1890 house known as Barclay Manor and the unusual 1892 Queen Anne house of the Roedde family. These two houses, the old builder's house between, and the mixture of frame houses and small apartment buildings around the rest of the block, presented a discontinuous but typically "Vancouver" streetscape, such as the one on Comox in the watercolour above. Convinced by citizen action not to demolish the houses and clear the block, the city and parks board have collaborated on what is now called Barclay Heritage Square, and the restoration of Barclay Manor, the Roedde house, and several other houses around the periphery. Roedde House is in use as a heritage attraction and venue for meetings, Barclay Manor is a senior citizens' centre, and the other houses are divided and rented as apartments. However, the buildings which were not as significant *architecturally* were removed. With no back lanes and no linear, fence-delineated Vancouver back gardens, and a lacy Victorian gazebo inserted next to Roedde House, the result is stagey, with the splendidly restored houses standing out of natural context like an architectural petting zoo.[2]

This raises another question regarding the fate of the Comox-Pendrell streetscape (especially the houses on Pendrell Street): if it is "restored," to bring out all the original architectural detailing and separate the houses from their fenced, overgrown, but very typical Vancouver landscape, will it still look like Vancouver? Is there a pure style of house that, when restored and stripped of all its additions and fire escapes, is representative of the old city? Or is it the soft-edged evolution of houses such as these, and the landscaping surrounding them, that makes them worth saving as Vancouver heritage?

A few of the houses on Comox Street just west of Thurlow, painted in the winter of 1990. All are quite dilapidated, but only the two on the left, at 1110 and 1114 Comox, show the effects of being "roominghoused." These two houses on the left are examples of the Queen Anne style. The two almost identical houses to the right of them, both built in 1904, are examples of the Vancouver Box. The furthest one along, at 1122 Comox, was designed for S.J. Steeves by the productive firm Parr and Fee; using their plans, Steeves then erected the house immediately to the east at 1120 Comox.[3]

2 The term "architectural petting zoo" was coined by the head of the National Trust for Historic Preservation in the United States, referring to Los Angeles and its Heritage Square assemblage of old Bunker Hill houses, which were moved onto the site from elsewhere; cited in Gebhard and Winter, *Architecture in Los Angeles*, page 27.

3 Allen Parker and Associates, *Vancouver Heritage Inventory Summary Report*, page 25.

Beach Avenue along English Bay was lined with fine wooden houses. The photographs on this page were taken by the amateur photographer A.L. Yates in the late 1950s and show, from top to bottom, the 1000, 1100 and 1200 blocks. The photographs were taken in response to the city's decision in 1956 to rezone the West End to allow highrise apartments. Within fifteen years, all of these houses had disappeared.

ANDRA PARK IN NOVEMBER   M·KLUCKNER 1989

The last two houses along English Bay are the little cottages visible above, built in 1899 at the corner of Bidwell and Harwood. At that time, Bidwell Street did not run through to Georgia Street, and the only construction on it was a group of houses between Burnaby Street and the beach, including these two little survivors. They were probably built by a bricklayer named James Jeffery or Jeffey of 133 Keefer Street, although it is also possible[1] that they are the work of a man named John Jeffers, who was listed in the 1900 directory as a carpenter, but is listed in the 1899 and post-1900 directories as a conductor for the B.C. Electric Railway Company. The houses were connected to the water mains along Beach Avenue on June 7, 1899.[2]

1 The handwriting on the water permit application is almost illegible.

2 City of Vancouver water records, CVA. For both of these houses, the water was initially supplied just "for domestic use" — meaning a tap — but not for a bathtub or a water closet.

NELSON + CARDERO, VANCOUVER

APARTMENT
ZONED SITE

RON SMITH

736-3831

M·KLUCKNER

One of the best remaining groups of Craftsman houses in the West End stands at Nelson and Cardero, painted in the spring of 1989. The watercolour looks north on Cardero Street from the corner of Nelson, and the houses — 1609 Nelson only partially visible on the left, 1605 Nelson at the corner, and 985-7 Cardero on the right — were all completed late in 1908 for a man by the name of James G. Birkeston. The scene realizes the intentions of the early residents of the West End, most notably in the fully grown boulevard trees on Cardero and the mixed shrubberies around the houses, a sharp contrast to recent restoration efforts, such as Barclay Heritage Square and the Pacific Street houses, that have separated the buildings from the landscape. The few remaining houses in the West End, such as these, are like little postage-stamp parks amid the straight lines and concrete of later generations.

The photograph looks in a southwesterly direction to the corner of Gilford and Georgia, at the Horse Show Building, erected in 1898 and reportedly second only in size, for a building of its type, to Madison Square Garden in New York City.[1] From the time it opened until it was converted into an armoury in 1914 for the Irish Fusiliers, it was the scene of well-attended, gossipy equestrian events, and rallies and public meetings. Many local residents still had their own stables, and men like B.T. Rogers and A.D. McRae rode their own favorite mounts, while families entered their broughams and victorias and teams for judging. Following the outbreak of the First World War, the building became the Stanley Park Armouries, and burned to the ground in an enormous conflagration on the night of March 18, 1960. The land has been vacant ever since, with the armoury's old concrete foundations still visible on the south side of the lot.

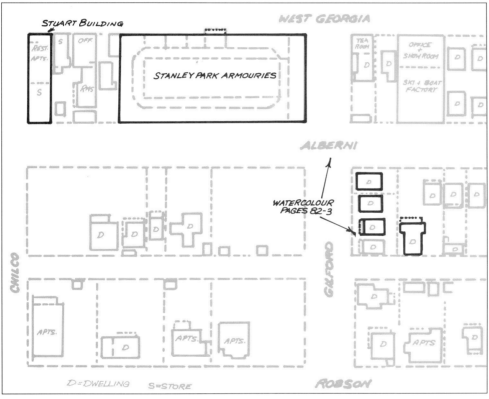

COURTESY OF VANCOUVER SUN

The razing of the Stuart Building, in July, 1982, was the inevitable culmination of years of real-estate speculation, and the consequent reluctance of its absentee owners to maintain it. A classic example of demolition by neglect, the Stuart had been a solid, well-built, bay-windowed apartment building, surmounted by a distinctive tower — a quaint landmark that complemented picturesque Lost Lagoon. In 1909, when the Stanley Park causeway was still a trestle bridge and Lost Lagoon was a tidal inlet, the mill owner W.W. Stuart, who lived on the site, demolished his own house and built the apartments, as he felt that a spot so near the terminus of the Stanley Park streetcar line was ''too strategic to be 'wasted' by a private house.''[2] The modern owners also exercised their right to demolish in 1982, leaving the lot ugly and vacant, except for a bicycle rental company's temporary structure, ever since.

In the house at 1952 Alberni, across the street from the Stanley Park Armouries — headquarters of the First Battalion of the Irish Fusiliers of Canada — lived its major and paymaster, Mathew Joseph Crehan. In civilian life, he was a senior member of the firm of Crehan, Mouat & Company; in 1905, he helped to organize the Institute of Chartered Accountants of British Columbia. He had been an active militia member before the War, first with the B.C. Horse regiment, then with the Irish Fusiliers. In the 1920s, he became involved with the plethora of veterans' organizations, including the Army and Navy Veterans Association, the Great War Veterans Association, the Council of United Battalion Auxiliaries, and the Comrades of the Great War, which coalesced into the Royal Canadian Legion. He also managed to attain the honorary presidency of the South Vancouver Mothers' and Wives' Association of Soldiers and Sailors! Born and educated in Galway, Crehan was president for three years of the Irish Association of B.C. In his Who's Who biography, he listed his religious affiliation as ''free thinker.''[3]

1 Photograph from *Vancouver Today*, pamphlet published about 1912, CVA 1912-19. Statement about size by J.S. Matthews, Bu.P.554.
2 Kalman, *Exploring Vancouver 2*, page 254.
3 *Who's Who & Why*, 1921 edition, page 212.

Although they comprise potentially one of the most desirable sites in Vancouver, the blocks of Georgia Street and Alberni near Stanley Park have deteriorated sadly over the past thirty years, leaving garbage-strewn vacant lots at the point where the Stanley Park causeway emerges into Vancouver. There were once a few large buildings in the area: the Denman Arena and the Georgia Auditorium, and the Horse Show Building, later known as the Stanley Park Armouries. Other landmarks, such as the Stuart Building at Georgia and Chilco, fell victim to long-term land speculation. Although little more than cottages, the Gilford Street bungalows (above), a mere block from the park, survived until 1989 — again due to long-term land speculation. Ironically, while these little houses survived, a comparatively substantial building — the reinforced concrete Chatsworth Apartments at 1950 Robson Street, built in 1940 — was demolished at the age of forty-five, again due to market forces.

Coal Harbour is still crowded with boats and boathouses, but most of the boat-building businesses that used to line Georgia Street, with sheds and wharves extending down to the water, have gone. The oldest yard still extant is W.R. Menchions & Company on Cardero, incongruously adjoining the luxurious Bayshore Inn. William Rod Menchions came to British Columbia in 1897, when he was twenty-six years old, and went to work with Wallace's Shipyards, then on False Creek. He went into business for himself in 1909 at the current site. Another

Looking down Gilford Street towards Alberni, with Georgia Street and Coal Harbour in the background, in early January, 1989. Built in 1904, the little row of bungalows on Gilford Street was the last vestige of the modest housing dating from the years when Coal Harbour was an industrial and sawmilling backwater.[2] The vacant land in the left middle-distance is the site of the old Stanley Park Armouries, which burned down in 1960. There was originally a fourth house in the row, demolished about 1985, that occupied the vacant lot in the foreground. The oldest house visible in the watercolour is the unpainted grey one on the extreme right. Built probably in the early 1890s, before there was a lane between Robson and Alberni, it sat at the extreme rear of its lot and had a street address of 1890 Alberni. Following years of little maintenance on the houses, and skyrocketing land values in the area, the tenants were evicted and the houses boarded up, but the plywood over doors and windows did little to deter transients, and a neighbourhood rumour alleged that they had become "crack houses." They were razed in April, 1989, but redevelopment did not commence until a year later.

long-time Coal Harbour boatbuilder was Albert Charles Benson, an Australian who came to Vancouver in his teens and worked for Turner's Boat Works before starting business for himself on False Creek in 1922. He moved to Coal Harbour in 1937; A.C. Benson Shipyards had its office at 1705 West Georgia Street.

No trace remains of the old auditorium that stood at the northwest corner of Denman and Georgia, or the arena that adjoined it to the north. The arena was one of the first artificial ice surfaces in the country, built in 1911 by the Patrick brothers, who owned Vancouver's Stanley Cup-winning hockey team, the Millionaires. It burned in the summer of 1936, nine years after the Patricks had completed the Georgia (also known as the Denman) Auditorium. Over its three decades of existence, the auditorium was the venue for everyone from world-famous classical musicians to politicians, evangelists, boxers, and wrestlers; between 1942 and the early months of 1945, it was used as an aircraft plant by Boeing.

It became a casualty of the opening of the Queen Elizabeth Theatre, and was sold by its owners — Lieutenant-Governor Frank Ross and Colonel Victor Spencer — to Johnston Terminals for $15,000, its value as scrap.[1] The auditorium site is now parkland; rumours in the early 1970s that the site was to be developed with highrises led to its occupation as a "people's park" by protesters.

1 "Old Auditorium Beaten to Death by Wreckers," *Sun*, September 4, 1959.

2 The nearest bungalow, at 746 Gilford, was built by a carpenter named George Johnson; its next-door neighbour, at 744 Gilford, was built by carpenter D. Strathie. They were first occupied by an accountant and an electrician.

STRATHCONA

The fate of Strathcona — the residential neighbourhood to the east of Chinatown — is an ongoing concern for people who support the preservation of the city's heritage. It is one of the most intact "character areas" in the city, containing a mixture of Gothic Revival, Queen Anne, and Edwardian Builder houses, some interesting apartment buildings and row housing, a few cottages little more than shacks, and the occasional landmark left from the generations of immigrants who have passed through since the 1890s — Lutheran and Ukrainian churches, Italian stores, and a Jewish synagogue. It was the most multiracial and is the most urban of Vancouver's old neighbourhoods, but, because it is Vancouver, this diversity takes place within the context of detached wooden houses on narrow lots, with tiny, nondescript front yards, and intensely private, individualistic back yards and lanes.

Strathcona is one of the few parts of the city that has a garden landscape that, although not the original one, has been around for so long that it is looked upon as traditional.[1] The area became Chinese in the early 1950s, when its Italian and other European working-class residents moved to East End suburbs such as Grandview, and changes in Canadian immigration law superseded the Oriental Exclusion Act of 1923. The 1923 Act had itself superseded decades of increasingly punitive head taxes; largely because of this, the Chinese population of Vancouver was composed largely of men. Most had come alone to Canada seeking their fortunes and, because of exploitation by labour contractors and pitifully low wages, had been unable to save enough money to return. Those who were not household servants often lived in somewhat squalid tenements in Chinatown. During that time, Strathcona was a multiethnic, but generally white, neighbourhood. Following the repeal of the Chinese Exclusion Act in 1947, and the enfranchisement of Orientals, Chinese families began to arrive and moved eastward into the old wooden houses, just as they were being vacated by the Italians.

By the time of the First World War, the Strathcona streets had been pretty much filled with houses and other buildings. Its residents during the decades since, including the newly arrived Chinese in the 1950s and 1960s, had little financial ability to maintain and update the houses; the ubiquitous absentee landlords, like those elsewhere in the city, had their hearts set on long-term speculation and eventual demolition and redevelopment, and thus had little desire to put money into maintenance. So, with almost no redevelopment pressure from outside, the neighbourhood slowly crumbled. As was the case in practically every city in North America during those years, paternalistic planners, politicians, and interested citizens considered the area a slum and made plans to raze and "renew" it. In the 1960s, two pieces of the Strathcona jigsaw puzzle were bulldozed and replaced with public housing — McLean Park, on the edge of the Chinatown commercial district, and Raymur Park several blocks to the east.

Concurrently, traffic planners were looking at the area as the likely route for a freeway link through Chinatown and downtown, connecting with highways on the north shore via "the Third Crossing." Citizens' groups organized to save the neighbourhood and fight the freeway, as part of their larger agenda of unseating the entrenched, development-oriented, Non-Partisan-Association-dominated city council. Success came in stages: first, in 1969, council made a cautious philosophical move away from wholesale urban renewal; second, in 1971, the senior levels of government agreed to fund five million dollars worth of repair and renovation to the older houses, as part of an experimental project to seek an alternative to urban renewal; and third, in 1972, the city finally scuttled its plans for the Third Crossing and freeway system, after managing to complete only the new Georgia Viaduct. In the civic elections of November, 1972, citizens voted away the Non-Partisan Association's majority, replacing it with a reform slate headed by Arthur Phillips.

The five-million-dollar renovation fund became the model for the federal government's two "community-sensitive" restoration programs — the Neighbourhood Improvement Program and the Residential Rehabilitation Assistance Program — which eventually supported community efforts across the country and in Vancouver districts such as Kitsilano. RRAP gave grants and loans directly to home-owners and landlords to fix up their houses. The result was the preservation, in a manner of speaking, of the old wooden houses, although the money in many cases financed the destruction of some houses' original features, the graceless conversion of others into suites, the replacement of original wooden siding and shingles with asbestos tiles, stucco, and even hideous brick-printed papers, the defacement of façades with poorly designed fire escapes, and some eccentric paint jobs. There was little concern with the consistency of the streetscapes, and even less for historical authenticity. At the same time, some owners and speculators were building "Vancouver Special"-type infill. In the long run, the most positive aspect of these 1970s initiatives was to buy the houses some time, which allowed public sentiment

1 The gardens seen mainly in the East End around "Vancouver Specials" and typically involving red-brick walls, wrought-iron gates, statuary, and very carefully considered, formal garden layouts of roses, lilies, and brightly coloured bedding plants are another example of a garden landscape that has been around for so long it seems to be the original one.

2 There is a parallel with the shift in values that contributed to the closure of James Inglis Reid Limited (page 45).

3 One of the best examples of this is the gutting and rebuilding as condominiums of the decrepit old synagogue/Gibbs' Boys Club at the corner of Pender and Heatley.

4 As well, there is the inevitable increase in property values and rents, the conversion of affordable rental housing to more expensive types, and the dislocation of long-established, poor residents from the neighbourhood.

THCONA GARDENS, VANCOUVER

Strathcona backyards in the summertime — a view from behind the south side of the 700-block East Pender, looking east, in the summer of 1989. The cottage partly visible on the left is 732 East Pender, built in 1892 for a butcher, which is in the process of being restored. Its backyard is untended, not the case with the two houses to the north, which have their long, narrow, fence-delineated lots completely planted with vegetables. Beans climb up the characteristic crossed sticks to a height of about eight feet; bok choy is picked and hung on the line to dry, sometimes sharing the line with salted fish and laundry. The green house at 738 and the red-trimmed one at 742 have interconnected fire-escape/porch structures like a catwalk. Both of these houses were built as an investment in 1907 by the rancher William Latimer, who lived next door in the brown house, at 746 East Pender.

and private money to see in them some value as *restored* — not just renovated — Vancouver houses in a restored Vancouver neighbourhood.

As well as buying time, the Strathcona rehabilitation project kept the community's social fabric more or less intact, preserving the unique back-garden landscape recorded in the watercolour on these pages. Nowhere else in the city is there anything like these sheltered pools of golden green light, with the first crop of vegetables harvested in May and old Chinese women moving slowly between the planted rows, sometimes carrying a chamber pot for fertilizing the garden, other times gathering the crop or hanging vegetables to dry on the clotheslines. As well, the area is one of a decreasing minority in the city where people still hang laundry outside, rather than drying it in machines indoors. It seems likely that this type of backyard landscape is doomed, if only because the thrifty extended families that created it are dying off, and their descendants are becoming integrated into the North American system of values.[2]

This old-new Strathcona is also threatened by the "new-old" — the penchant for inner-city living that has made the Strathcona neighbourhood fashionable[3] and the corresponding move to restore the old houses. Strathcona is being gentrified, but it is a mixed blessing: on one hand, the dilapidated old houses are being preserved; on the other, it spells the demise of the unique, ethnic neighbourhood and its garden landscape.[4] The air is alive with the sounds of gentrification — of handsawing and sanding, and backyard brick-paving for car parking — a contrast with the power hammers and staplers, tilesaws and big diggers of the construction boom elsewhere in the city. Gentrification of a neighbourhood is a social issue as well as a heritage one. It is possible to see it, in an era of little government largesse for "soft" projects, as the only likelihood of some sort of preservation of an area such as Strathcona. But the social versus heritage issue, expressed so clearly in this neighbourhood, is one of the conundrums facing those who wish to preserve it.

Japanese Church, Vancouver, B.C.

One of the curious old landmarks of Japantown was the Vancouver Buddhist Church, built in 1906 at the corner of Jackson and Powell adjacent to Oppenheimer Park. Recently demolished, it has been replaced by a new church, serving the Japanese community that has reestablished itself — at least commercially — in the area, forty years after it was forcibly relocated at the onset of the Pacific half of the Second World War. The "hanging arch" window in the church's main gable was a feature of many houses during that period;[1] it is interesting to see that style of window return, often with a sunburst pattern of plastic rails laminated between the panes of a double-glazed window, in the thousands of "Developer Georgians" built in the recent Vancouver housing construction boom.

1 Kalman, *Exploring Vancouver 2*, page 67.

2 C.D. Rand was one of the directors of the Vancouver Electric Railway & Light Company — *Vancouver Daily News-Advertiser*, June 26, 1890 (reporting on the first day of trials for the street railway).

3 Land and taxes were cheap in South Vancouver, and there were few building restrictions, allowing the more independent of the new settlers to "tame the West" at their own speed. (See page 166.) Deviations from Vancouver's rigid grid system are much more common in the East End, where many little surveys of small holdings took place.

4 Records of the Vancouver Water Works Company indicate permit applications in a sequence, all for different owner-occupants, on this block of "Princess Street," implying that the houses were already standing, and had been drawing their water from wells. Permit number one using "city water" is the building at 300 Alexander Street, connected to the new Capilano water mains in October, 1888.

5 Vancouver water permit number 547, CVA.

Two of the oldest houses in the city stood on Pender Street near Dunlevy, just east of the Chinatown commercial district. The one on the right, at 451 East Pender, is probably the second-oldest house in the city still standing on its original lot — it was built in 1889, the year after the little Yaletown house on Hornby Street now occupied by Umberto's Restaurant. Both 451 East Pender and the Hornby Street house are examples of the Queen Anne style, featuring an asymmetrical façade, bay windows, and a plethora of decorative woodwork. Similar to 451 East Pender is the 1895 house at 863 Hamilton Street. The house on the left in the watercolour, with a street address of 449 East Pender, is slightly different. Built two years after its neighbour, its square, projecting bays, hipped roof, and steep façade are more typical of the type of house built by the thousands in San Francisco during the 1880s. Like the 1894 Shaw house in Fairview, illustrated on page 98, 449 East Pender Street mixes elements of the Eastlake style and the Queen Anne style.

By the late 1880s, although Vancouver was only a few years old, land was already being subdivided into narrow lots for this sort of suburban house, to be sold to the thousands of migrants streaming into the railway-created "instant town." In the East End, the Vancouver Improvement Company, created by a group of capitalists including David Oppenheimer, Israel Powell and C.D. Rand, subdivided land to sell to builders and helped to finance the street railway extensions into their bailiwick;[2] On the west side, the Canadian Pacific Railway subdivided its land and developed what in the long run became the centre of the city, around the corner of Georgia and Granville. By comparison, elsewhere in the city, and especially in the Municipality of South Vancouver,[3] purchasers of land were in many cases virtual homesteaders, and contractors bought land carved from small, crown-grant district lots, rather than from the subdivided and planned holdings of a big syndicate.

These houses are the last two survivors of a solid row of houses built on what was then called Princess Street. Several houses, including number 451, were standing and occupied before the summer of 1889.[4] Number 451 was built for Joseph Cameron, an engineer in a planing mill. The much-altered house still standing to its east (to the right of the watercolour), was occupied by the Palmer family, including two brothers who were coal merchants and probably a sister named Emily who was a photographer; behind their property was a public stable for four horses.[5] In the summer of 1891, the house at 449 East Pender was connected to the water system for a man named William J. Barker, listed in city directories as a nurse.

There is no record of who built these two surviving houses, although it was likely a carpenter, such as George Walker, who built the house that used to stand at 429 East Pender; he boarded at the southeast corner of Hastings and Main Street, according to the 1889 city directory. Although they usually built interior finishings and kitchen cupboards from scratch, carpenter-contractors like Walker were able to buy the windows, doors, and decorative woodwork, such as porch brackets and roof cresting, for houses such as these from the numerous sash and door factories operating in the Vancouver area, one of which was Fairview Sash & Door, whose advertisement appears on page 64. The quality of woodwork these factories turned out was astonishing, but not cheap. One surviving catalogue of "sash doors, mouldings, and other interior and exterior finish" of the period was put out by the British Columbia Lumber

and Shingle Manufacturers' Association[6] in 1906 — it offers the "ship's wheel" gable ornament visible on 451 East Pender for $6.00, a tidy sum for that time, representing almost two days' wages for a carpenter.

The watercolour shows the houses as they appeared early in the summer of 1989. The house on the left at 449 East Pender had been empty for some time, while the owner of both houses developed plans for their restoration with the architect Allan Diamond. To try to keep transients out, the owner and the city had nailed plywood over doors and windows, which the transients regularly removed. On August 27, 1989, 449 was severely damaged in a fire, which spread to the roof of 451 and burned the attic; the former had to be demolished. Regardless of this setback, restoration is proceeding, and 449 will be rebuilt to its original specifications.

The houses at 449 and 451 East Pender, just east of the Chinatown commercial district.

6 CVA brochure 1906-23.

Fishing in the early days was a relatively simple affair. Stories from "the good old days" are invariably the reverse of "the one that got away" tales: one scoop of the gill net caught more fish than could be sold to the cannery; a man could go out in a canoe and catch salmon by hitting them with his paddle, especially around the mouth of the Capilano River; on certain days, you could run across the Fraser River (in some versions, Coal Harbour) on the fish's backs; and most tellingly, there was no point going fishing when you could have your pick of a boat's catch for fifteen cents.

Although there are still operating canneries along the Steveston waterfront on the Fraser River, with trollers and trawlers and seiners moored in many of the sloughs nearby, there is little evidence remaining of the salmon fishing fleet on the Vancouver waterfront. The original purpose of the Nine O'Clock Gun in Stanley Park — as a start-stop signal in the 1890s for commercial fishermen, who started fishing at six in the evening and stopped when it fired again, usually a half-hour later — has been almost lost in time.[1] And the Campbell Avenue fishermen's wharf is gone.

Dating from the late 1920s, the Campbell Avenue wharf was established in the middle of a very industrial part of Vancouver just to the west of the B.C. Sugar Refinery, hemmed in against the shoreline by the multiple tracks of the Canadian Pacific Railway. It quickly became

Five of the men with businesses on the Vancouver and Steveston waterfronts in the early part of this century. (Far left) Captain Richard Edward Gosse, born in Spaniards Bay, Newfoundland, in 1852, came to British Columbia in 1887 after years of fishing and sealing experience off the Labrador coast. Over the next twenty years, he built fourteen canneries along the B.C. coast, including ones on the Fraser River, Rivers Inlet, Skeena River, Barclay Sound, and at Anacortes in Washington State. A half-dozen of these he continued to own as president of the Gosse-Millerd Packing Company, with offices at 597 West Hastings Street — the old Molson's Bank Building.[2]

(Left) W.J. Blake Wilson was vice-president of Burns & Company, the Calgary-based meat-packing concern, which maintained an abattoir at the foot of Woodland Drive. Born in rural Ontario, he left the family farm to move west in 1890, and went into partnership with Pat Burns in 1903. His influence was felt throughout the community, as he was also the president of Home Oil Distributors, vice-president of the Pacific Great Eastern Railway and B.C. Pulp and Paper Company, and director of a bewildering array of companies, most significant of which were the Royal Bank of Canada, the Canadian Pacific Railway, the Great Northern Railway, the Vancouver, Victoria & Eastern Railway, the Montreal Mutual Life Assurance Company, and Dominion Bridge Company. He lived at 1238 Tecumseh in Shaughnessy Heights.[3]

(Centre) Innes Hopkins was the managing director of B.C. Marine Limited, a shipbuilding and repairing "marine railway" at the foot of Victoria Drive, founded in 1897. He could trace his ancestry to a seventeenth-century Knight of Coventry, and was the son of the noted Conservative and historical chronicler[4] John Castell Hopkins and Trianda Phelia Boyd Heu de Bourck, a clergyman's daughter. He lived at 3738 Selkirk in Shaughnessy Heights.[5]

(Right) The president of B.C. Marine Limited was Edward James Coyle, who also was president of the tugboat and towing firm Pacific Coyle Navigation Company and of Coast Stevedoring Company. Born in Stayner, Ontario, in 1870, he joined the Canadian Pacific Railway while in his teens and was transferred first to Winnipeg, then Vancouver, then Portland, and finally back to Vancouver in 1898, where he rose to the position of assistant general passenger agent. In 1908, he formed a partnership in the towing industry as Greer Coyle Company, and over the next twenty years he expanded his interests around the waterfront. He lived at 1190 Matthews in Shaughnessy Heights.[6] Coyle was also a notorious impaired driver. In one incident in 1933 he had been drinking and ploughed into a turning car at 10th and Granville, killing a woman passenger; he was acquitted of manslaughter, but had his license suspended for five years.[7] Ten years later, he drove through the wooden guardrail at the north end of Granville Bridge and plunged eighteen feet into the yard of the Robertson & Hackett sawmill. Although the front of his car was completely crushed, he suffered only minor abrasions. In that case, he pleaded guilty to a charge of dangerous driving and had his license suspended for two years.[8]

(Far right) James Edward Hall was president of the Vancouver Milling and Grain Company, and president of the Vancouver Grain Exchange. His company dealt in grains, cattle feed, and chicken supplies and was the manufacturer of flour brands, including "Royal Standard" and "Wild Rose"; it had a flour mill and grain elevator on the Vancouver waterfront, branches in New Westminster, Victoria, Nanaimo, and Mission, and an interest in a grain distribution company with offices throughout the Far East. At the age of twenty-eight, he made an advantageous marriage to Ethelwyn Ceperley, the daughter of H.T. Ceperley (page 168). His "who's who" biography noted that "Mr. Hall is a frequent visitor to the Orient, and is a great believer in the future development of trade with the Far East." Probably because of the amount of travelling he did, he preferred apartment living, although for a brief period in the early 1920s he lived in the fine Craftsman house at 1963 Comox Street, one of the few designated heritage buildings in the West End.[9]

1 According to J.S. Matthews, the gun was "originally placed there as a time signal to salmon fishermen to start or stop fishing. At first fired at 6 p.m., but its usefulness for such purpose having ceased, it was continued as a nine o'clock signal — before 1898" (notes to St.Pk.121, CVA). Another version came from Brockton Point lighthouse keeper William Jones, who claimed in a 1922 interview that it had been his duty to set off a stick of dynamite each night at 9 p.m. to aid ships' masters in setting their chronometers. The gun superseded the dynamite in 1894 (cited in Steele, *The Stanley Park Explorer*, page 48).

2 *Who's Who & Why*, 1921 edition, pages 522 and 1527.

3 *Who's Who in Canada*, 1930-31 edition, page 1083.

4 Most notably of the *Canadian Annual Review of Public Affairs*, published annually from 1900 until his death in 1922.

5 *Who's Who & Why*, 1921 edition, page 586.

6 *Who's Who in Canada*, 1930-31 edition, page 1057; obituaries published in Vancouver newspapers on November 19, 1949.

7 *Province*, March 14, 1934.

8 *Province*, April 6, 1944.

9 *Who's Who & Why*, 1921 edition, page 555.

THE MARINEVIEW CAFÉ

M.KLUCKNER '89

a splendid, ramshackle collection of fish company sheds, an icehouse, fish boats, the smells of the briny deep, and the constant racket and detritus of huge flocks of gulls. All could be observed from the front windows of the Marineview Cafe, which for about fifty years was operated by three generations of the Gurney family. The Marineview was one of the classic cafes of Vancouver — crowded at lunchtime by all sorts of people drawn to its fresh seafood and downscale ambience, it was frequented the rest of the day by fishermen, shore workers, and railwaymen, enjoying lengthy coffee breaks and yarning. Although there are many vantage points along the waterfront where one can see the "tourist harbour," or the recreational harbour, the Marineview was one of the few public places in the harbour's industrial area whose windows looked out on the "working" harbour.

Changing times, and the declining west-coast fishery, evidently caused the National Harbours Board to rethink the use of its land at the foot of Campbell Avenue. The Marineview Cafe closed at the end of October, 1989; the building that housed it and the icehouse were demolished soon after. The fish companies and the wharves were removed in the spring of 1990.

The view from the Marineview Cafe, looking north towards the mountains, on the morning of October 5, 1989. On the extreme left of the watercolour is the grey-metal gooseneck spout down which the ice cascaded into the holds of the old, unrefrigerated trollers.

1033 KEEFER STREET

The watercolour shows a very fine little Vancouver Box that stood at 1033 Keefer, in the enclave of Strathcona cut off by the Raymur Park housing project. Built in 1900 for Augustus Dixon, a millhand for Robertson & Hackett, it was very similar to the Dustman house plan on page 21, and slightly smaller than the Kerrisdale version of the same style illustrated on those pages. Like the cottage at 3556 Victoria Drive (page 165), it fell stylistically between the highly decorated but asymmetrical Queen Anne, and the purposeful, symmetrical Edwardian Builder. The landscaping and beautification in the foreground is a result of the area's Neighbourhood Improvement Program in the 1970s. This watercolour is from sketches done in 1982; for the current scene, and a good example of unsympathetic infill, see the photograph on page 199.

MOUNT PLEASANT

Main Street divides the historic Mount Pleasant neighbourhood into two neat halves. The eastern one, stretching east to Clark Drive and occupying the slope above the Canadian National/Burlington Northern railyards, south to about Kingsway, has been one of the social failures of Vancouver, a high-crime district with a street prostitution problem concentrated around the Kingsgate Mall just east of the Broadway-Kingsway intersection. Until the 1960s, east Mount Pleasant was a stable residential area made up of fine, turn-of-the-century houses, but it began to show signs of abandonment, as resident owners moved away and sold out to absentee landlords. When the slope north of Broadway was rezoned for lowrise apartments, developers jumped at the opportunity, erecting numerous bland, boxy buildings, like strips of toothpaste along the streets. Some owners stayed and restored their houses, but they were soon a minority. The construction in the early 1980s of the King Edward Campus of Vancouver Community College on the site of the China Creek cycle track was expected to stabilize the area, but its real impact has been to provide a steady supply of poor immigrants, attending its English Language Training programs and with little mobility and knowledge of the city, to rent the deteriorating apartment buildings and houses on the surrounding streets. The neighbourhood to the south of Broadway has fared little better, especially since prostitutes and their retinue, pushed out of the West End by citizen pressure and government edict, have settled there, too. An active community group, and sympathetic planning and development permit decisions from City Hall, may save the remaining intact "character" streets and restore some stability to its populace.

The western part of Mount Pleasant is quite a different story. The residential area south of Broadway and west of Ontario Street contains a wide cross-section of very old homes, which were awaiting the inevitable demolition to make way for three-storey apartment buildings until the arrival, in the mid-1970s, of the Davis family (page 94). Responding to the possibility of preserving some of the historic character of the area without having to spend any tax money, the city rezoned part of West Mount Pleasant to allow for conversions and renovations that retain the old houses, paid for by a bonusing arrangement that allows a developer to build infill housing on some sites.[1] The result has reinforced the settled, historic ambience of some neighbourhood blocks, unlike most others in the city, attracting to adjoining blocks new buyers with a desire to preserve and conserve. West Mount Pleasant is one of the few heritage success stories in the city.

(Left) In the house that stood at 3023 Quebec Street lived the actor and theatre proprietor Charles Elliott Royal, the owner and manager of the Empress Theatre at the southwest corner of Hastings and Gore.[2] Born in Independence, Oregon, in 1880, Royal started his career in vaudeville in New York and over the years played everything from comic opera to drama, as well as touring with his own stock company through the United States, Canada, Hawaii, and Alaska and writing a number of plays, novels, and songs, including "In a Hammock That Just Holds Two."[3] (Middle) The Rev. Roderick George MacBeth, pastor of St. Paul's Presbyterian Church at 18th and Glen Drive, lived in the house at 355 West 11th Avenue. He initially trained to be a lawyer; while still a student, he served as a lieutenant in the Winnipeg Light Infantry during the 1885 Riel Rebellion. After being admitted to the bar in Manitoba, he practiced law for only a year before enrolling in a seminary in Princeton, New Jersey. He subsequently held pastorates all over the country before settling in Vancouver in 1915. He was the author of several books, including The Making of the Canadian West, The Romance of Western Canada, The Romance of the Canadian Pacific Railway, Our Task in Canada, *and* The Burning Bush and Canada.[4] *(Right) The founder of the huge Johnston Terminals firm was Elmer Johnston, who lived at 3090 Alberta Street. Born in Bradford, Ontario, in 1883, he moved with his family to Portage La Prairie and worked on their farm until the age of twenty-one. His first job in Vancouver was with Mainland Transfer Company, which he left to start his own firm in March, 1913.[5]*

1 The RT-6 zoning by-law for that area is written to ensure that redevelopment decisions are negotiated between builders and the planning department, in order to encourage the retention of the large old houses. A developer who is willing to fit his plans in with the character of Mount Pleasant is rewarded by being allowed to build to a higher density, but anyone who wants to go his own way — as is the case in other zones where builders erect unsympathetic monster houses in defiance of the neighbourhood's established character — cannot build anything large enough to justify the effort.

2 The theatre was demolished in 1940 — the last performance there was *Abe Lincoln of Illinois*, starring Raymond Massey — cited in John Atkin and Robin Fitzgerald, "Theatres," a pamphlet published by the Heritage Committee of the Community Arts Council of Vancouver, 1989.

3 *Who's Who & Why*, 1921 edition, page 1259.

4 *Who's Who in Canada*, 1930-31 edition, page 818.

5 *Who's Who in Canada*, 1930-31 edition, page 2022; obituaries published in Vancouver newspapers on October 22, 1949.

St GEORGE St. MOUNT PLEASANT

Looking down the hill along St. George Street towards 6th Avenue in Mount Pleasant. The two "double houses," as they were called when they were built in 1911, separated by the little cottage on the lane, are unique designs in the city. On a winter's day, as one looks down the hill towards the blue-grey mountains, they constitute a uniquely Vancouver streetscape — regrettably, not least because the buildings are so dilapidated, and the old, almost unpainted boards on the cottage and grey duplex are bleached in the winter light.

These two duplexes, the green one at 2236-40 St. George and the grey one at 2216-18 St. George, were erected in 1911 by John McKenzie and John Ross respectively; it does not appear that either man lived there after the buildings were finished, so it is reasonable to assume that

they were developers. In the directories of the period, there are several John Rosses and John McKenzies listed as carpenters or builders.

Time has not been kind either to these buildings or to the surrounding area. Over the past twenty years, the adjoining blocks have been largely redeveloped with three-storey apartments and, although this block of St. George Street is directly across from Mount Pleasant elementary school, prostitutes regularly work the street. A local time signal of sorts is the activity each morning just before the eleven o'clock liquor store opening.

The property on which the grey duplex stands is up for redevelopment, with the duplex's demolition as the probable result.

THE DAVIS FAMILY

HORSE CHESTNUTS IN EARLY NOVEMBER, MOUNT PLEASANT

There are a few ways by which the old houses in a neighbourhood can be restored. The least likely is for government to do it: costs can be immense,[1] and the conventional (or at least majority) political logic in a city like Vancouver is that spending significant sums on heritage attracts few short-term votes. A slightly more likely possibility is for some type of heritage foundation, blending government support and money with private funds, to finance approved and supervised restorations, but such an organization has not yet received enough political support in Vancouver. Another way to maintain the character of old neighbourhoods is to make heritage renovations attractive to private developers by offering bonuses (for greater density than allowed by the zoning, or allowing construction of infill buildings) that help to finance the extra work involved with a proper renovation. It is important here to make the distinction between *real* heritage, in which old buildings are restored within their historical context, and ersatz heritage, in which new buildings are designed to look old, or old buildings are moved to new locations and restored. The two may look the same, but there is no intellectual or emotional significance to the latter. Quite simply, it is the difference between the main street of an old town, such as Victoria or Nelson in British Columbia, and "Main Street, U.S.A." in the heart of Disneyland.[2]

The only truly successful restorations occur when individuals make the "leap of faith," and decide that, in spite of the costs and headaches, a historic building or streetscape is simply too valuable to lose. In West Mount Pleasant, the Davis family made just such a commitment, when they decided in the 1970s and 1980s that the surviving houses in the 100-block West 10th Avenue should be saved and restored.

1 The budget for the city's restoration of Barclay Manor at 1447 Barclay Street in the West End was more than half a million dollars, according to the sign posted in front of it during the restoration.

2 One is credible, like a history book, while the other is suspect, like a historical novel. See footnote number 3 on page 173.

3 The Fairview line started operating on October 22, 1891. The $150,000 spent on it — five times the original estimate — greatly overextended the resources of the Vancouver Electric Railway & Light Company, which had undertaken the project in anticipation of a land boom on the south shore of False Creek, especially on the Fairview Slopes which the Canadian Pacific Railway had just

Horse chestnuts, and an old, immobilized bicycle, its basket planted with geraniums, on West 10th Avenue in Mount Pleasant at the beginning of November, 1989. The little half-gable visible on the extreme left is the cottage at 144 West 10th; the red and green houses are respectively 148 and 150 West 10th, and the beige house partly visible in the background is 166 West 10th, the oldest house in Mount Pleasant, which the Davis family restored first in the mid-1970s.

John R. Davis was an engineer for Imperial Oil; with his wife Pat, and university-student sons John and Geoff, they lived on the west side of the city, in Point Grey. In the mid-1970s, they renovated and resold a few Point Grey houses. They then heard about a dilapidated and very old house for sale at 166 West 10th Avenue, in the middle of a block that was duplex-zoned, but was to all intents and purposes awaiting an upzoning and the eager arrival of apartment developers. Having barely looked through the door to confirm that it was in its original condition, the Davises bought number 166 to restore. Research determined that the house had been built at the corner of 11th and Columbia, a couple of lots to the southwest, and was moved to its present site in 1891 for a teamster named Robert Moore. The year 1891 saw the inauguration of the ill-fated Fairview streetcar line[3] between the south shore of False Creek and downtown; it was only five years after the incorporation of the city, a time when Mount Pleasant was mainly stumps interspersed with a few shacks, dairy farms, and the Doering & Marstrand brewery — all long-since demolished, although one brewery building remains at 7th and Scotia. Thus, the Davis restoration project was certainly the oldest house left in Mount Pleasant, and one of the oldest houses in the city (in the watercolour above, it is the beige-coloured house partly visible in the background).

The house was unquestionably a dump. Its sills sat almost at ground level, with the earth heaped up along the wooden sides — presumably to insulate the unheated, dirt-floored basement. Thus, the wood was rotten all the way around the perimeter, and termites had infested not merely the floor joists, but even the dining room wall from floor to ceiling. All four members of the family worked together full time for two years, removing and cataloguing all the old

put onto the market, and in which the VER&L Company had received 68 lots in return for providing the service. The line crossed False Creek from downtown on the original Granville trestle (photograph, page 62), and climbed what was then called Centre Street to 9th Avenue (now Broadway). The 9th Avenue track between Granville and Main was a nightmare to install, as it had to cross seven streams on seven wooden bridges of as much as 150 feet in length. At Main Street, then called Westminster Avenue, the line returned to downtown, crossing yet another trestle over False Creek. The Fairview Slopes project, along with many early Vancouver businesses including the VER&L Company, succumbed to Vancouver's economic doldrums in 1892 and 1893 — the woodwork, rebuilding the studding and replacing rotten framing, rewiring and replumbing, until they were able to reassemble the house into its original condition. In 1976 the restored house was designated a heritage building, and received the city's first heritage plaque.

Then, the four houses numbered 140, 144, 148, and 150 West 10th came on the market, for sale only as a unit, in anticipation of the city-supported change to apartment zoning. In the watercolour, the red house is number 148, and the green house 150; to the right of the latter, between it and the beige-coloured 166 West 10th, is a little 1890s "granny cottage" at 156 West 10th, set back on its lot, not visible from that angle, and not for sale at that point; the yellow gable partially visible on the left is part of the 1899 Queen Anne cottage built at 144 West 10th for the grocer Fred Walsh. The houses at 148 and 150 West 10th are of a later generation — they are examples of the Edwardian Builder style, and were built in 1907. All were in terrible condition, but as demolition was the inevitable result of doing nothing, the Davis family decided to buy them. Together they formed Mount Pleasant Developments, sold their Point Grey house, moved into 166 West 10th Avenue, and, with $75,000 as a down payment, went shopping for financing. Only the Royal Bank's commercial loans division, and its manager Claude Prutton, could see the social significance of their plans and agreed to lend them the money.

John Davis took early retirement from Imperial Oil, and his two sons decided to forego conventional careers and threw in their lot with the family renovation business. A carpenter named Gary Fink joined the group, and together they restored the four houses; they managed to keep afloat financially by renovating houses elsewhere in the city and because the Royal Bank stood behind them, even when interest rates exceeded 20 percent in the early 1980s. John Davis died in 1983, but his widow and sons continued the project.

In 1984, the little turn-of-the-century "granny cottage" at 156 West 10th, with a dirt kitchen floor, termites, no studs in the back wall, and a stream in the half-basement, came on the market; to protect it from potential townhouse-builders and preserve the continuity of the streetscape, the Davises bought it, too, restored it, and moved in after selling 166 West 10th to friends. They kept the four houses in the row to the east and rented them out. In addition, they have restored the houses across the street, at 115 and 117 West 10th, and the house to the west of 166 at 170 West 10th. Their efforts won a City of Vancouver Heritage award in 1980 and a Heritage Canada award in 1981 for the preservation of an historic streetscape.

Using a standard balance sheet or "bottom line" approach, it is difficult to justify this sort of restoration. Pat Davis maintains that "you cannot do a proper job and make money." Any one of their houses can illustrate this: perhaps the most skewed is the case of the tiny orange cottage at 117 West 10th, bought for $75,000 in 1980, on which they spent $325,000, including their time costed out at far below what they could have earned elsewhere for house renovations. The city, which at that time was uninterested in the restoration of anything anywhere, let alone in Mount Pleasant, would not allow the Davises even to put an addition onto the back.[4]

The restoration of two other houses within a stone's throw of the Davis group demonstrates the possibilities. Of the two, the true restoration is the magnificent 1908 Colonial Revival house at 2631-2633 Columbia Street. It was restored immaculately, but at great expense, in the early 1980s by Mary "Twigg" White, who sold it at a loss; however, the two subsequent owners have each sold at a profit, and the current value of the restored house has now exceeded its cost in the early 1980s plus the cost of the restorations. The other example is the stone house at 124 West 10th, renovated under the city's bonusing scheme, which allowed owner/builder Richard Fearn to erect the infill "Isis Cottage" at the back of the lot. Throughout West Mount Pleasant, especially in the streets around City Hall where there remain some massive and splendid houses from the boom before the First World War, this sort of bonus infill and renovation-cum-restoration has worked quite well. It is preserving and stabilizing the historic streets in a part of the city which would otherwise — because of its proximity to megadevelopments such as City Square at 12th and Cambie and the possibility that Cambie Street may become the rapid transit route to Richmond — be razed and rebuilt with very high-density housing.

local results of a worldwide depression — and the Fairview line ceased to operate on May 14, 1893. It was revived the following year under the banner of the Consolidated Railway and Light Company, the predecessor in Vancouver of the B.C. Electric Railway Company, and became profitable after Fairview and Mount Pleasant began to be settled around the turn of the century. See Ewert, *The Story of the B.C. Electric Railway*, pages 22 and 30.

4 Interview with Pat Davis, November, 1989.

RIA STREET - CLEARING SKY   M. KLUCKNER 1990

Over the past forty years, the industrial and warehousing area around False Creek has expanded southward, replacing much of the Mount Pleasant residential area east of Cambie Street and north of Broadway. Most of the blocks of simple wooden houses there, dating from the 1890s and 1900s, are gone; the few remaining scattered houses are, in most cases, showing the effects of prolonged neglect.

Other than the few dozen surviving houses in the area and apartment buidings like the 1912 Quebec Manor at 7th and Quebec, the only legacy of the area's residential past is Jonathan Rogers Park, occupying the block bounded by Columbia, Manitoba, 7th, and 8th. Rogers (page 72), a long-time parks commissioner, felt that the residents of Mount Pleasant deserved a new park once Strathcona Park became the site, in the mid-1930s, of Vancouver's City Hall. As the city had made no effort to create a new park, Rogers bequeathed $100,000 in 1945, stipulating that the money be used to buy parkland in the West Mount Pleasant area north of Broadway.[1]

The postwar housing crisis and the city's inability to make a decision on a location delayed the process until, in 1950, park commissioners stated that the area stipulated in Rogers's will had become too industrialized and land prices had become too steep to make a park worthwhile.[2] Nevertheless, the properties committee of council decided on the block at 7th and Columbia, and made plans to acquire the few dozen houses there. A year-and-a-half later nothing had been done, and Rogers's widow publicly criticized city council for not spending her husband's bequest.[3] The newspapers took up the call, but it was 1956 before the houses were purchased and clearing was well underway; by that time, Rogers's bequest, with interest, was only half the money required to develop the park. Regardless, the park opened, but the industrial and commercial trend in the area was so far advanced that, by the late 1950s, it served a much smaller community than that envisioned by its benefactor.

These five houses are all examples of the Vancouver Box, and were built in 1907. The four farthest along were built by the carpenters Little and Brown, and connected to the city water supply in September. The nearest one, at 2128 Alberta Street, and two houses to the south of it (one of which has been demolished), were erected by the carpenters Whiting and Rogers that spring.

1 *Province*, December 29, 1945.
2 *Sun*, April 12, 1950.
3 *Sun*, November 4, 1952.

97

FAIRVIEW

570 W. 7TH AVENUE, VANCOUVER.

1 The 1891 "Steamboat House" at 1151 West 8th Avenue was built for Sir John Watt Reid, but is remembered usually for a later occupant — the lieutenant-governor and *Province* newspaper publisher Walter Nichol. It is the oldest in the area on its original foundations, but has been modified and modernized with glass walls around its porch that disguise its late-Victorian features. The other notable very old house on the Slopes is Hodson Manor, erected in 1894 on 8th Avenue just west of Hemlock and moved in 1974 to its present location at 1254 West 7th Avenue, where it serves as offices and performing space for Early Music Vancouver and other cultural groups.

2 Teamster Robert Moore was one such Mount Pleasant resident (see page 95).

The house at 570 West 7th Avenue, nearly a block west of Cambie, is one of a handful of old houses remaining on the Fairview Slopes. It has the added distinction in the neighbourhood of being the oldest stylistically intact house still on its original foundations.[1] Built in the early part of 1894 for James Shaw, it was connected to the new city water system in Fairview that June; the owner paid only for a bath connection, not for a water closet, the latter being presumably outdoors at the rear of the lot. The house has the asymmetry of the Queen Anne style, and uses elements of the Eastlake style, notably the square bay windows with brackets, the division of surfaces into panels surrounded by board moulding, and the elaborate gingerbread detailing in the gables.

Three years before this house was built, the Canadian Pacific Railway Company had subdivided and placed on the market "The Fairview Slopes," its first south-of-False-Creek subdivision, at a time when Fairview and Mount Pleasant were little more than stumps and gullies and mud, interspersed with the houses of a few adventurous owners.[2] For Shaw, however, access to downtown was a relatively simple matter across the nearby Cambie Bridge, built for $12,000 and opened in July, 1891, by Leamy's sawmill.

Shaw died not long after the house was completed, but his widow, Emma, lived on there for a number of years. In the subsequent decades, it survived almost in a time warp, hidden away at the industrial end of Fairview Slopes; its most recent coat of paint probably dates from around the end of the Second World War. It is a classic example of the truism that the houses in the worst shape are the best ones to restore, as they are the most intact. Unfortunately, the house sits on land which is zoned for commercial use, rather than for residential or office use, either of which might allow the house to fit into a new development.

General Hospital, Vancouver, B.C.

A postcard of the original Vancouver General Hospital, probably from 1905, the year the building was completed, but before any landscaping was undertaken. The city's public hospital moved to Fairview following a plebiscite in January, 1902, on whether to replace the aging and overcrowded 1888 City Hospital located on Pender Street between Cambie and Beatty downtown. Grant and Henderson were the architects, and an example of their work here survives today as the old portion of the Heather Pavilion.

The technological complexity and institutionalized organization of modern medicine dwarfs these heroic individual beginnings, and has in addition rendered old hospital buildings obsolete and allegedly dangerous:[1] the last remnants of Grant and Henderson's Fairview Building are scheduled to be razed as part of the ongoing development of VGH, as is the oldest surviving section of St. Paul's Hospital, built in 1916. Neither will make way for new, modern hospital buildings — the city intends to leave the cleared land as park.

Known as Fairview, the neighbourhood between Broadway and the old city boundary at 16th Avenue, bounded on the west by Burrard Street and the east by Cambie, was well established with solid and substantial houses by the First World War. It was an area midway in prestige between lower-middle-class Kitsilano and upper-middle-class Shaughnessy Heights, deserving perhaps the appellation "Lower Shaughnessy" with which modern real-estate agents have labelled the area north of 16th Avenue. Very few of the fine old houses remain; in their place are a mixture of apartment buildings, including the city's best collection of 1920s and 1930s Tudor Revival and Mission Revival lowrises that, although in impeccable condition, are not "valuable" enough for the land on which they sit and are being picked off one by one by developers looking to build highrise luxury condominiums. The two houses illustrated here were built just before the First World War; the photographs were published about 1915 in the booklet Beautiful Homes.[2] *The top photograph is the home of realtor Montgomery Smith at the northwest corner of 14th and Hemlock (now demolished). The bottom photograph is the very fine Tudor Revival home of lawyer A. Lawrence P. Hunter, which still stands, surrounded by period landscaping including a stone fence, clipped hedges, and a fully grown monkey-puzzle tree (not yet planted when this photograph was taken), at 1306 West 12th Avenue.*

1 Especially to earthquakes, as old St. Paul's and the Heather Pavilion are made of brick and stone.

2 An undated pamphlet, Und-831, in CVA.

One of the finest Craftsman houses in Fairview, which so far has eluded the southward march of apartment redevelopment, is the old Shelly home at 1104 West 15th Avenue. "Will" Shelly had a distinguished business career and a rather mixed political one, but in a number of significant ways he left his mark on the city. This house and its former owner raises the question: how does a city like Vancouver commemorate a life such as his? A plaque could be erected in front of this house, or the house itself could be protected from demolition. But perhaps the importance of the owner does not justify retention of the house, and if the city chooses to designate a building, it should do so purely on architectural grounds. In any event, Shelly surely deserves some sort of civic commemoration either in Stanley Park or on Grouse Mountain for his part in their history.

Like so many other Vancouverites, William Curtis Shelly came from eastern Canada. Born in Jordon, Ontario, in 1878, he and his brother Frederick spent a dozen years in the bakery business in St. Catharines before selling out and moving west in 1910. They started Shelly Brothers, which rapidly grew to be the largest bakery in British Columbia. Shelly's Vancouver headquarters and bakery was at 601 West 10th Avenue, on the edge of today's Vancouver General Hospital precinct, but the firm had bakeries in Victoria, Nanaimo, and New Westminster. Shelly bought his own grain and had it milled to his specifications, this branch of the business becoming Four X Mills. He organized Canadian Bakeries in 1926,[1] and also built the Shelly Building at 117 West Pender Street. But his greatest legacy was the promotion and development of Grouse Mountain Highway and Scenic Resort in the 1920s, which put the first tramway, lodge, and modern ski area onto the north shore.[2]

Shelly entered city politics in 1919 and won an aldermanic seat, but chose to contest the next set of elections for a parks board position; he was soon elected chairman and remained in that position from 1922-27. During that period, the legal status of the squatters in Stanley Park, mainly living along the shore near Brockton Point, became an issue, resolved in the so-called Squatter Eviction Trials of the 1920s.[3] Only one squatter, an old native woman known as Aunt Sally, was able to prove her right to the title of one acre of the park by virtue of having lived there for more than sixty years. Her case proven, she received a number of offers to purchase her land, all of which she refused, but late in 1925 Shelly heard that she was about to accept an offer from a private firm that was hoping to erect an apartment building there. Shelly approached city council for $18,000 — the asking price for the acre — but was turned down, so he and his lawyer Leon Ladner (page 112) went to the park to negotiate with Aunt Sally. In short order, they had struck a deal, by which Shelly bought it himself with $17,500 of his own money! City council eventually reimbursed him, but refused to pay him interest.[4]

After nearly a decade in civic politics, Shelly entered the provincial arena as a Conservative in the July, 1928, elections. He was elected, and was promptly invited by Premier Tolmie to enter his cabinet as minister of finance. Tolmie's new government was notable for its number of rookies: of the eleven members of cabinet, only four had any legislative experience. It was their misfortune, after two years in office, to see the province sink into the depths of the Great Depression, upon which they demonstrated conclusively over the next few years their inability either to do anything about it, or to convince the electorate that they had any idea of what to do. Shelly was one of the neophytes with whom political life did not agree. A newspaper account describes his time in the legislature: "(Shelly) was the financial heart of the government, and the financial critic of the opposition was Mr. A.M. Manson, now a member of the Supreme Court bench. Mr. Manson was a caustic and unsparing critic. He held back no punches and he pummelled the government's policies unmercifully. It was all in the game with him, of course, but to Will Shelly it was no game at all, but in dead earnest. 'I have never been talked to like that in my life and I don't like it at all,' he told me in the corridor, after Manson had put him to the wall."[5] Shelly did not seek reelection, which was fortunate for him, as the Tolmie government was annihilated in the 1933 elections.

Although he lacked political magic, Shelly was for twenty years considered to be the most skilled amateur magician on the west coast. He was one of the founders of the Vancouver Magic Circle and during the Second World War gave numerous free magic performances to servicemen and families. By that time he had moved to the house at 1563 Matthews Avenue in Shaughnessy Heights, where he was visited by the newspaper reporter Jack Scott. "Mr. Shelly is the only member of a large family who is a magic addict, and he explains this by saying 'one nut is enough,' " wrote Scott. "We first went on a tour of the sections of the Shelly home devoted to magic. In the basement there is an amazing workshop where Mr. Shelly personally

William Curtis Shelly

1 In 1961, Canadian Bakeries merged with McGavins — whose plant at Broadway and Arbutus had on its roof a huge sculpted hand holding a loaf of bread. See *Province*, February 14, 1961.

2 Biographies in *Who's Who & Why*, 1921 edition, page 1476, and *Who's Who in Canada*, 1930-31 edition, page 1282.

3 For details on the squatters' community there, and the trials, see Steele, *The Stanley Park Explorer*, pp. 39-46.

4 Speech by Shelly at the Stanley Park 50th Anniversary dinner in 1939; city archivist J.S. Matthews confirmed the story and noted that "we might by this time have had a privately owned institution, operating for profit, in the middle of our great park." See Matthews news clippings under W.C. Shelly, CVA. Richard M. Steele, in *The Stanley Park Explorer*, gives the purchase price as $15,500, page 18.

5 D.A. McGregor, "From an Angle on the Square," a newspaper column in the *Province*, August 16, 1951.

6 Jack Scott, "Our Town," column in the *Vancouver News-Herald*, August 6, 1941.

+ SPRUCE, FAIRVIEW, VANCOUVER   *M. KLUCKNER 1988*

manufactures the implements of his hobby, and in another section he keeps the rabbits and gold fish who act as his stooges. Upstairs we went into a small room, lavishly painted in yellow, gold and Chinese red, colours dearly beloved by every magician, and here are stored hundreds of gadgets, including a small mahogany box. This was put together by Mr. Shelly and the trick, which consists of placing a playing card in it, closing the lid, and then opening it to reveal no playing card, has consistently fooled every visiting wizard. I should record that when Mr. Shelly does the trick he says 'poochie poochie poochie,' and that, of course, explains it. Next door is a small theatre, complete with stage and theatrical lights, and this is where he and his visitors have their fun, trying to out-illusion each other. Across the hall is another room where Mr. Shelly stores larger apparatus, including the floating table, and on the main floor of the house is a library of volumes on magic."[6]

Two years later, Shelly gave a performance at a Christmas party for about 300 children from Gordon Neighbourhood House: "Bill pulled rabbits out of hats and made things come out of everywhere for a solid hour. Then, it happened. He put a big empty dish on the table — and he waved a big, magic silk shawl over it. And then, there it was — candy — piled in the dish until it spilled over onto the table."[7] The unveiling caused a sensation, the more so as there had been sugar rationing for a year and a half.

Shelly died in August, 1951, at the age of 73. His yacht, the *Cora Marie*, built in 1929 by Hoffar's in Coal Harbour and said to be one of the finest on the coast, became a shuttle vessel for Alcan executives. It had been named for his wife, the daughter of one Burton Snure. She survived Shelly, as did his four sons and two daughters. One son, Leon, was a film producer, and had produced the first "Beautiful B.C." film in colour in 1940.

The house at 1104 West 15th Avenue in Fairview originally occupied four lots — a 132-foot by 120-foot property. It was built in 1911-1912 by a carpenter named Thomas Pledger, resident at 675 West 12th Avenue, who probably worked from mail-order architect's plans of Craftsman houses such as those on pages 24 and 25. William Curtis Shelly bought the house soon after its completion[8] and lived there until he was able to move "up" to Shaughnessy Heights in the late 1920s. The house is notable for its exceptional woodwork and leaded glass, as well as for an attached garage-cum-carport on the west side, with carved posts and brackets in the same style as the main house.

7 *Vancouver News-Advertiser*, December 21, 1943.

8 Pledger signed the water-connection application, and the house appeared in next year's city directory as a "new house."

WILLOW STREET NEAR DOUGLAS PARK

M. KLUCKNER 1990

The MacKey house at 19th & Willow in the Douglas Park area, shortly before its demolition in the spring of 1990.

The area south of Vancouver General Hospital is undergoing a steady redevelopment, the old houses being replaced by townhouses and apartments (see page 2). Most of the houses between the hospital and 16th Avenue are small and relatively insignificant from a historical standpoint; however, they provided various levels of affordable housing, and have been replaced with more luxurious and expensive accommodation.

A slightly different situation exists in the blocks south of 16th Avenue between Oak and Cambie streets, in the Douglas Park area. A well-established residential area, it has a mixture of housing from the 1910s, 1920s and 1930s, and is zoned for duplexes. Many of the houses have been renovated and modernized, while the most modest and least expensive of them are candidates for demolition and replacement by new construction.

The Craftsman house illustrated above stood at the northwest corner of 19th and Willow, with a street address of 807 West 19th Avenue. It stood out from most of the Douglas Park houses as it was very large and well-built; a notable feature of its construction was the unusual bevelled glass in the panels above its triple-paned sashes. It was one of a group of three old houses on that block, the earliest of which, at number 837, dated from 1912. At the end of the First World War, a roofer named George MacKey built for himself the house to its east at 821 West 19th; in 1922, he built 807 West 19th Avenue.

The city recognized the heritage value of 807 West 19th Avenue and, when its owner sought a demolition permit, the city heritage planner offered density bonuses and easements that would have allowed him to restore the house profitably and make additional money on a backyard coachhouse. But the owner was not interested, and demanded a demolition permit and the "outright use" — two quickly constructed duplexes — guaranteed by the area's zoning. Thus, 807 West 19th Avenue was demolished on March 26, 1990. In addition, all of the trees on the heavily landscaped property were cut down (see the photograph on page 199).

KITSILANO

The great feminist Mary Ellen Smith lived in the unusual gabled apartment building at 2456 Point Grey Road. The first woman elected to the British Columbia legislature following the passage of women's suffrage in March, 1917, she assumed the riding held by her late husband Ralph, and was reelected subsequently in 1921 ("by the largest majority in the Dominion") and 1925; she was also the first woman cabinet minister in a provincial government. Calling herself an Independent Liberal, she refused to toe the government's line; although part of its caucus, she campaigned against it on matters of women's rights and social welfare. She was instrumental in the passage of a Minimum Wage Bill for Women and Girls, a Deserted Wives' Maintenance Act, an Equal Guardianship Act, and a Mothers' Pension Bill. Before emancipation, she had been active in the Suffrage League of Canada, and had been a regent of the Imperial Order Daughters of the Empire and president of the Women's Canadian Club.[1]

Two of the fine houses from the early years of Kitsilano, photographed about 1914-15 for the booklet Beautiful Homes.[2]

(Above) The 1912 house of Harry L. Jenkins, president of the Vancouver Lumber Company, at 2831 Point Grey Road, just west of the foot of Macdonald on the waterfront. Following Jenkins's death in the early 1920s, the house was bought by grain-elevator-owner E.A. Woodward. Known for years as "Seagate Manor," by 1974 it had been divided into eleven suites which were occupied by fourteen people, mainly seniors. However, it was now owned by the city on behalf of the parks board, which had been sporadically pursuing a plan to clear the water side of Point Grey Road of houses, presumably to make the view better for motorists.[3] The active Kitsilano citizenry wanted the house preserved, and it received a reprieve late in 1973 when the city's Community Development Committee, chaired by Alderman Jack Volrich, questioned the value of razing it in the midst of a housing crisis.[4] The reprieve was only temporary, however, and "Seagate" was demolished in April, 1977. The site was redeveloped as a grassy but featureless park.

(Below) The Craftsman house of Matthew Sergius "Sea Wall" Logan (1866-1952) at 2530 Point Grey Road. Born in Morrisburg, Ontario, Logan arrived in New Westminster with his family in 1875, but they soon returned to Ontario; Logan came himself to settle in 1899, and went into the lumber business. As a parks commissioner from 1916-19, he was an advocate of a Stanley Park seawall, something that was not completed until years after his death.[5] He built the Point Grey Road house in 1909, the year that a group of local residents bought five acres of the former Greer's Beach as a park. For several years, the beach area had been crowded in the summertime with tenters, but it was the commencement of streetcar service from downtown to the newly named Kitsilano on July 4, 1905, that opened the area to settlement.[6] Visible in the background is the back of the Roy MacGowan house at 2575 Cornwall, built in 1904 and one of the very few houses left in Kitsilano which predate the commencement of streetcar service (the three MacGowan brothers — Alexander, Max, and Roy — ran a shipping and insurance business under their own name). Logan's house survives today in excellent condition, although it has been extensively modified since this photograph was taken.

1 Information from *Who's Who in Canada*, 1930-31 edition, page 1609. Obituaries published in Vancouver newspapers on April 4, 1933.

2 CVA, pamphlet Und-831.

3 The city's "Ocean Boulevard" schemes attracted their most vociferous protests in the winter and spring of 1957, and again in August, 1966. See J.S. Matthews news clippings 7439, CVA. The proposal surfaced again in May, 1990.

4 *Around Kitsilano* community newspaper, January, 1974.

5 Obituaries published in Vancouver newspapers on July 2, 1952.

6 The agreement giving the B.C. Electric Railway Company the use of the Canadian Pacific Railway Company's "English Bay" tracks was signed on July 9, 1904; *that* was the real beginning of the neighbourhood's development. The text of the agreement is in Ewert, *The Story of the B.C. Electric Railway Company*, page 53.

Ever since the late 1960s, the World War One-era architectural character of Kitsilano has been steadily eroded. The old rooming houses that were so much a part of the district's character have in many cases been demolished, converted into expensive strata-titled condominiums, or reconverted into single-family houses. Highrise apartment construction on the slope north of Fourth Avenue and east of Larch Street was stopped by citizen protest in the early 1970s, and redevelopment since has been mainly with lowrise townhouses. West of Larch and north of Broadway, new construction has been mainly duplexes, some of which have been designed quite sensitively to fit into the neighbourhood, but all of which have occupied more of their lots and subtly changed the nature of the neighbourhoods. Many of these new front-back duplexes, and the double garages built at the rear of lots, shade adjoining backyards, and create fortresslike "dead spaces" in what had been one of the most neighbourly and open urban landscapes in the city. An active residents' association has been working through a city-sponsored local area planning process to fight these development trends, and to preserve and renovate the existing housing stock; as in other areas of the city, such as Second Shaughnessy and Kerrisdale (see pages 114 and 122), the organized residents see the control of demolitions as the way to retain the neighbourhood's established character and adapt it to changing times. The issue is not so much the preservation of heritage housing per se, but the preservation of character, which includes family housing, affordable rental accommodation, and landscaping.

Good examples of this established neighbourhood character are the blocks of builders' houses — the Vancouver Boxes, Craftsmans, and California Bungalows — in the area west of the old CPR land boundary at Trafalgar Street. The Craftsman houses illustrated on pages 26-27 are probably under little threat of redevelopment under the current duplex zoning, as they are large buildings on small lots; that is not the case with the California Bungalows on pages 28-29, which are "underbuilt" by contemporary standards, and could be profitably demolished and replaced by new duplexes that would put more built square-footage on the lots, but would not necessarily provide accommodation for more people. Although the trend of new development in Kitsilano, as in other areas of the city, is towards bigger buildings, the actual result is a depopulation, as the variety of small and affordable suites in older buildings is removed, and the new housing is far more luxurious and spacious than what it replaced.

Another consistent area of old houses in Kitsilano occupies the blocks between Arbutus and Cypress streets along the tracks of the Vancouver & Lulu Island Railway. The old V&LI line ascends from False Creek on the double curve known as "the Horseshoe" before heading south from Broadway towards Marpole. Incorporated by the Canadian Pacific Railway in 1891, the V&LI was a spur line branching from the CPR's "English Bay" tracks at the south end of the Kitsilano trestle (page 62). The company saw the economic potential of joining its main line in Vancouver with the distant, utterly separate sawmill town of Eburne (now Marpole), the Lulu Island farms, and the fishing and canning centre at Steveston. Accordingly, the V&LI began clearing the line's right-of-way in February, 1900, and established stations at Magee (49th Avenue) and Eburne in the modern city of Vancouver, and at Cambie (modern Cambie Road), Brighouse (Minoru Park), Lulu (about Number Two Road), and Steveston in Richmond.[1] The company later established the so-called "CPR gardens" at what is now Kerrisdale Field near the corner of 41st Avenue and West Boulevard, to provide produce for its many operations. The first steam passenger train ran on the line in June, 1902, but three years later the V&LI decided to lease its track to the B.C. Electric Railway Company, which started an electric interurban service in 1905. *That* rapid transit system lasted until 1958, but the private right-of-way still survives, in use since then as a freight route by the B.C. Electric and B.C. Hydro railways, and since 1986 by the CPR again.

In the watercolour opposite, the railway tracks cross Cypress Street; the blocks to the south and west were developed before 1910, as residents found transportation convenient on the interurban, and on the Fourth Avenue and Broadway streetcar lines after they commenced service in 1908 and 1910 respectively. The Vancouver Boxes on the left were built late in 1907; the block on which they stand and the adjoining block to the west are more or less intact, with Edwardian-era houses. Little redevelopment has marred the area's consistency, as many of the houses there are owned by the city and the parks board; the long-term plan is to redevelop the blocks in

1 Ewert, *The Story of the B.C. Electric Railway Company*, pages 58-59.

2 This "Arbutus corridor," using the railway right-of-way, is the cheaper alternative; a potentially more desirable but more expensive one would be a line on Cambie Street, which would connect City Hall, Vancouver General Hospital, the high-density housing already built around the hospital, the new shopping complexes at Broadway, 12th Avenue, and 16th Avenue, and Oakridge with the centre of Richmond and the downtown.

599 STREET AT 6TH AVENUE, LOOKING NORTH   *M. KLUCKNER 1988*

some manner as an extension of Delamont Park at 7th and Arbutus. However, lacking maintenance by the landlord, the houses are subsiding into genteel decay.

At the time the city bought the land, it was considering the construction of the Burrard-Arbutus connector, a scheme whereby southbound automobile traffic from the Burrard Bridge would be quickly funnelled through upper Kitsilano along the path of the old railway line, away from the curving streets of Shaughnessy Heights (and its influential residents). With a freeway orientation dominating City Hall in the late 1960s, the Burrard-Arbutus connector looked like an inevitability, but the reform council headed by Mayor Art Phillips voted in late 1973 to postpone the project for two years; by the time it resurfaced, freeways had been discarded as a means of solving Vancouver's traffic problems — at least, in that part of town.

However, the future is far from secure for this little Kitsilano backwater. The area is completely surrounded by apartments, and the railway line may well become the right-of-way for a rapid-transit line to Richmond.[2] Unless the city decides to invest in the restoration of the houses and some very creative infill, the land may become park or the city may decide to place the land on the market; the economics of Kitsilano housing make it unlikely that any of these buildings, including the quaint Arbutus Grocery at 6th and Arbutus, could survive.[3]

Looking north down the hill from the corner of 6th and Cypress in Kitsilano, towards the cloud-shrouded mountains, in late October.

3 Grocery stores often survive because of the "grandfather clause" that allows them, as a commercial use, to operate on a piece of property with residential zoning as long as they are not physically changed. See also page 121.

Rock-clearing and grooming operations along Kitsilano Beach about 1914, photographed from the old pier at the foot of Balsam Street. Clearly visible is the low-lying, undulating land, all of which has been filled and levelled in the decades since, and the two BCER streetcar passenger shelters, one each at the bottom of Vine and Yew streets. On the left, in the middle distance (indicated by the arrow), is the odd duplex at 2146-2148 Cornwall. In the extreme left-distance is Henry Hudson school at Cypress and Cornwall.

PHOTOGRAPH BY WILLIAM J.L. GIBBONS

Kitsilano Beach, looking north to the downtown skyline, about 1960. Visible on the skyline from left to right are the pointed top of the 1929 Marine Building, the 1955 Burrard Building, the 1929-39 Hotel Vancouver, the 1957 B.C. Electric building (with St. Paul's hospital visible in front), and the 1912 Vancouver Block. The swimming pool in the left foreground is the old, tidal-filled (and free!) Kitsilano Pool, replaced by a more modern one in the early 1980s; the rambling Kitsilano Beach bathhouse, built in the 1920s, was demolished soon after this photograph was taken. The parks board, which has earned quite a reputation over the years for flattening anything that casts a shadow, can count this bathhouse and "Seagate Manor" (page 103) among its victims. However, it has belatedly recognized the landmark status and charming, rustic architecture of some of its remaining park structures, including the 1911 Stanley Park Pavilion, the 1925 Connaught Park fieldhouse on West 10th, and the 1930 Memorial Park South fieldhouse on Prince Albert Street, and has restored and designated them as heritage buildings. The fate of the Comox-Pendrell (pages 76-7) and Delamont Park (pages 104-5) houses owned by the parks board is uncertain.

The odd duplex at 2146-48 Cornwall (in the foreground), and the fine old house at 2152 (the blue one), were among the last really old buildings on Cornwall Avenue opposite Kitsilano Beach. Both had to be approached by walkways, visible in the watercolour, as they were built before the beach and Cornwall Avenue were filled and levelled, raising the land level at the sidewalk by about eight feet. The blue house was the older of the two, having been completed at the beginning of 1908 by a builder named C.W. Mathers. In the spring of the same year, the duplex was completed for its owner James Simpson, a printer, who took up residence in its west half. At that time, there were no houses on Cornwall east of Arbutus Street; Cornwall dead-ended at Chestnut Street, on the edge of the Kitsilano Indian Reservation. The duplex, which had become decrepit in recent years, stood on one side of quite a large property; there was a basement suite with a side door, visible on the extreme left, and to reach it from the sidewalk, one opened a gate and descended a flight of steps to the lawn below. Since the early 1970s, the other old buildings along the beach, including cottages and quaint little apartments, have been gradually demolished and replaced, so that now there exists only one infill apartment building in the lane behind Cornwall. Tenants of the duplex and adjoining houses received their eviction notices for the beginning of January, 1989; the buildings were torn down in March, but a year later nothing had happened on the site.

SHAUGHNESSY HEIGHTS

Two of the fine houses in First Shaughnessy, as they appeared around 1914. On the left is ''Glen Brae'' at 1690 Matthews Avenue,[1] built in 1910 for the lumber company owner and developer William Lamont Tait and for most of the last sixty years a nursing home. ''Glen Brae'' and ''Hycroft'' (now the University Women's Club on McRae Avenue) are the only two houses in Shaughnessy Heights that are designated heritage buildings and thus safe from demolition or catastrophic renovation. On the right is the monumental Neoclassical Revival house at 1350 The Crescent,[2] built in 1912 for Pacific Great Eastern Railway executive George F. Macdonald. Known for years as ''The Hollies,'' the house was fashionable for wedding receptions until served with a ''cease and desist'' injunction by the Shaughnessy Heights Property Owners Association.[3] It has recently been renovated extensively and has been featured in home design magazines.

1 Photograph from *Vancouver Today*, a 1912 booklet in CVA, pamphlet number 1912-19.

2 Photograph from *Beautiful Homes*, a c.1915 booklet in CVA, Und-831.

3 *Sun*, February 1, 1951.

4 See "Shaughnessy Heights Is Almost Ready For The Many Handsome Homes Soon To Grace It," *Province*, July 17, 1909.

The First Shaughnessy district, developed by the Canadian Pacific Railway Company and laid out and landscaped by F. Todd of Montreal, is one of the great heritage assets of Vancouver. Although the house designs in the neighbourhood include all the styles popular in the period around the First World War, the boulevard trees and curving streets contribute a gracious air and a consistency which unites the disparate houses and their large, irregular properties. Shaughnessy belongs to an era that gave society the *Titanic* ocean liner and Mahler symphonies; in the depression following the booming 1920s, when the area was dubbed Mortgage Heights, many of the biggest houses were subdivided into rooming houses, and more modest houses were built as infill on the former multi-acre properties and on the vacant lots unsold during the prosperous years between 1909 and 1929. Nevertheless, its Edwardian streetscapes survive.

The company logged and cleared the area in the first few years of this century, then laid out a network of curving streets and boulevards, installed concrete sidewalks, curbs, and sewers, and even carted in soil (from the worked-over Marpole midden) for gardens.[4] The 250-acre First Shaughnessy (between 16th Avenue and 25th Avenue, Arbutus Street and Oak Street) was subdivided in 1907 and, with the exception of the above-mentioned infill buildings, was largely established by the beginning of the First World War. In the seventy-five years since, the heavily planted gardens and boulevard trees have flourished and almost engulfed the large houses. To the south, Second and Third Shaughnessy were subdivided in the 1920s (page 114).

Recent changes to the area have been mainly restorations and strata-conversions, coupled with discreet and well-designed infill buildings, which have to a great extent preserved the streetscapes and historical quality of the neighbourhood. The key to success has been the city's First Shaughnessy Official Development Plan, which uses the area's rigid single-family zoning as a lever for a conditional zoning process, whereby owners and developers of large properties are encouraged to preserve streetscapes and restore houses in return for permission to build complementary infill. The negotiations between city and developer include the review of new construction by a design panel, whose intent is to maintain the area's character. So far, the system has worked quite well, allowing massive houses such as John West's Mission-Revival-style mansion at 3290 Granville to be converted into condominiums, and the nearby Brydone-Jack house to be used as the embassy for the People's Republic of China. However, the use of residential property in the city for a single-family house is an "outright" one, not a conditional one, so anyone with the money to buy a house, demolish it, and replace it with a new one is entitled to do so under the city's zoning, without requiring the blessing of the First Shaughnessy Design Panel on the new plans. Only two houses in the whole of Shaughnessy are effectively protected from demolition by existing legislation (see the caption above).

The comparatively modest house at 1727 Cedar Crescent was a classic example of "demolition by neglect" — the watercolour shows its untended garden, overgrown wisteria, collapsed front fence, missing shingles, and broken porch roof. Nevertheless, it was a solid, well-built house, with hexagonally cut granite foundations and porch posts, occupying the eastern half of a hundred-foot-wide lot. Its porte-cochère almost touches the porte-cochère of the house on the right, at 1703 Cedar Crescent, which was restored in 1988-89.

This sort of deterioration began in Shaughnessy in the Great Depression, when many of the neighbourhood's high-flying residents had their wings clipped. Although known then as "Mortgage Heights" or "Poverty Hill," it was ruled by the litigious hand of the Shaughnessy Heights Property Owners Association, empowered by provincial legislation[1] to control and police the area's single-family status through good times and bad. The SHPOA zealously pursued owners who were indiscreetly renting rooms or dividing their houses, but even its influence was not equal to the wartime housing crisis that prompted passage of legislation allowing conversion of Shaughnessy homes into rooming houses and apartments.[2] Following years of such hard times, many influential people in the city during the forties, fifties and sixties, including the chairman of the Town Planning Commission,[3] considered the area to be an anachronism, ripe for redevelopment. In anticipation, absentee landlords, such as the former owners of this house, were free to conclude that renting out Shaughnessy houses remained a profitable enterprise, but that maintenance was a waste of money. One resident who devised a more interesting way to turn a profit on a Shaughnessy house was Anne McCormack, aged 28, at the house called "Greyston" at 1638 Angus, who was arrested in 1951, along with nine of her customers, for operating a gaming house.[4]

The circa-1912 Craftsman house at 1727 Cedar Crescent in Shaughnessy Heights, as it appeared in January, 1989. After years of deterioration as a third-rate rooming house, it was sold for "lot value" of about $600,000 and appeared to be slated for demolition; then, at the end of March, 1989, it was put back on the market with a prominent "will build to suit" sign in the front yard. It sold quickly and the tenants were evicted, but contrary to all expectations, the new owners began to restore it.

1 An Act Relating to Shaughnessy Heights, March 4, 1914, also known as The Shaughnessy Settlement Act.

2 J.S. Matthews news clippings, CVA.

3 Prof. F.E. Buck, quoted in *Sun*, April 2, 1948.

4 See *Sun*, May 21, 1951.

NEAR CEDAR CRESCENT, SHAUGHNESSY HEIGHTS

Francis Edmund Burke

The Burke house at 1612 Cedar Crescent occupies an elongated, spacious lot with a long driveway and a gateway at the corner of Fir Street and Cedar Crescent, "down the street" on the right of the watercolour above. It is a late example of the Queen Anne style, seen more often in Vancouver in comparatively modest dwellings, such as the Strathcona houses on page 87. Although this house is more impressive, by virtue of its hexagonally cut granite foundations, curved glass, wide porch and unusual dormers, than such little wooden builders' houses, it has the asymmetrical lines and corner turret typical of the Queen Anne style.

Francis Edmund Burke had the house built in 1913, probably by the contractor Grover Lloyd, at the time of his marriage to Jessie Wallace.[1] Born in Americanus, Georgia, in 1878, Burke went first into banking in Macon, Georgia, then into employment with the Cotton Seed Oil Company in Texas, and finally into accountancy. He moved to Canada in 1910 to work for the

The house at 1612 Cedar Crescent, painted in September from Fir Street looking north to the corner of Fir and Cedar Crescent. The house is unusual for its Queen Anne design, as well as for being immaculately maintained, and for its unusual landscaping, including one of the rare ponderosa pine trees in the city.

Canadian Western Lumber Company and attracted the attention of Major-General A.D. McRae, whose business investments included Burke's employer. In 1914 Burke was appointed managing director of Wallace Fisheries — owned by his father-in-law — which later amalgamated with B.C. Packers.

He was president of the Vancouver Board of Trade in 1926-27, and maintained a long-time involvement with the Alexandra Children's Home, where he was president from 1916-38. During the war, he served as the head of the Priorities Branch, Construction Control Division of the Department of Munitions and Supply. He was still living in this house on Cedar Crescent when he died in 1947.[2] It subsequently became a rooming house, and was known locally as "the cat house" due to the menagerie of about forty felines owned by one of the tenants. The current owner has restored the house during the past twenty years.[3]

1 In 1913, Grover Lloyd built an almost identical, slightly more elaborate version of the same house at 1979 West 19th Avenue, for a man by the name of J.A. Wallace, who owned a carriage-building firm. It is possible that J.A. Wallace was a relative of Burke's father-in-law.

2 Obituaries published in Vancouver newspapers on October 28, 1947.

3 Conversation with Hugh MacNeil, 1990.

Shaughnessy Heights is more than just a collection of grand houses; the people who have lived there over the years include, not surprisingly, many who had a significant influence on the development of the province. The houses, and the intact neighbourhood they form, are a tangible, impressive commemoration of these people's achievements.

In the house at 1389 The Crescent lived John William Fordham Johnson (far left), the province's lieutenant-governor before Eric Hamber. Fordham Johnson had emigrated from Lincolnshire to British Columbia in the 1880s, but was transferred by his employer, the Bank of British Columbia, to Portland, where he spent the ten years until 1898. Transferred back to Vancouver, he soon found himself an employee of the Toronto-based Canadian Bank of Commerce when it took over the Bank of B.C. His new local manager, William Murray, was a friend of B.T. Rogers, owner of the B.C. Sugar Refinery; the following year, Fordham Johnson resigned from the bank and joined the refinery as its accountant. He soon became a close associate of Rogers, accompanying him on lengthy trips to the South Pacific in 1905, during which they decided to enter the sugar-growing business in order to stabilize the refinery's source of supply. The result was the establishment of the Vancouver-Fiji Sugar Company, and the creation there of the Tamunua plantation — a major source of sugar for Rogers's company through the First World War years. Fordham Johnson took his young family to Fiji and stayed until 1907 as resident manager. That year, he was appointed secretary of B.C. Sugar and returned to Vancouver. Upon the death of B.T. Rogers in 1918, he became vice-president; the new president was Rogers's eldest son Blythe, who had just turned twenty-five, but whose frail health brought him to an early grave in May, 1920. Fordham Johnson then became president, as Rogers's second son Ernest had just been demobilized from the Royal Air Force and had no experience with sugar refining; he remained in the position, earning the nickname among his associates of "Can't Afford'em Johnson" for his expensive tastes,[1] until August, 1931, when he was appointed lieutenant-governor of British Columbia. He died in 1938 on his seventy-second birthday. One of his daughters, Bea, was an actress who collaborated with and married Frederick Wood, the namesake of the theatre on the U.B.C. campus.

The unusual, imposing Queen Anne-style house at 1927 West 17th Avenue was built in 1912-13 for and by John C. Hawkins, a carpenter who in 1910 had built the similar home at 1020 Victoria Drive. Hawkins was still living in the latter house when he signed the water connection permit for 1927 West 17th. During the twenties and thirties, the house was occupied by Irene Helen Moody (left), who had moved to Vancouver from Ontario following the death of her husband in 1905, and entered public life in 1916 (the year of the successful provincial referendum on women's suffrage). She was a member of the board of education from 1916 to 1920, and her service as chairman of the board in 1917 and 1919 was said to be the first such by a woman in Canada; in 1918 and 1919, she served as education editor of *Woman's Century*, a magazine published in Toronto; in 1920, she became president of the British Columbia School Trustees' Association.[2]

The house at 3450 Osler Avenue was home at different times to two of the prominent Liberal politicians of British Columbia. The photograph is of The Hon. Malcolm Archibald Macdonald (right), who lived there during the 1920s. Yet another Ontarian, he received his legal education at Osgoode Hall and moved to Cranbrook in 1907 to become a partner in a legal firm. Soon, however, he was devoting his time to Liberal politics. Although an unsuccessful candidate in the provincial election of 1909, he had risen to the presidency of the provincial Liberals in 1913. He and another prominent Liberal were picked to contest two by-elections called for February, 1916, to gain voter approval (as was the law at the time) for two cabinet appointments by Conservative Premier William Bowser. Macdonald ran against C.E. Tisdall, the minister of public works, in the Vancouver City riding and defeated him by a two-to-one margin, but rumours soon surfaced that the Liberals had hired "gangs of pluggers" from Seattle, who were paid ten dollars each to vote using either fraudulent names or names supplied by a janitor in the legislature who had been paid by Macdonald to produce a list of dead voters. The sensational testimony riveted public attention through the subsequent months, and although one Liberal organizer eventually served nine months in jail and another fled the country, there was a general election in September before any of the mud could be affixed to Macdonald personally. In the new Liberal government elected that September, Macdonald became attorney general, but following the revelation that a Canadian Northern Railway executive had given him $25,000 for his by-election campaign, he resigned from cabinet and returned to private practice.[3] He retained his seat in the legislature until 1921, when he made an unsuccessful bid for federal office. Premier John Oliver rewarded him for his long service to the party by elevating him to the bench as justice of the court of appeal, in May, 1924. He was appointed chief justice of the Province of B.C. in May, 1940,

1 Interview with Bea Wood, 1986. Fordham Johnson prospered sufficiently that, in the late 1920s, he and his second wife — the former Alice Ridley — moved into "Rosemary" at 3689 Selkirk Avenue, one of the grandest houses in Shaughnessy Heights. John Schreiner, in his book on B.C. Sugar entitled *The Refiners*, offers the opinion that Fordham Johnson earned the nickname due to his parsimony. Whatever the reason, there was a definite cooling of relations between the Rogers family and Fordham Johnson. A plausible explanation for this — in addition to the question of finances — was that Mrs. B.T. Rogers had been a close friend of Fordham Johnson's first wife Helen, who died in 1916; in Mrs. Rogers's eyes, Fordham Johnson remarried with unseemly haste, and did not even inform his teenage daughters of his intentions. Information from family interviews and from *M.I. Rogers*, pp. 63-65, and *Who's Who in Canada*, 1930-31 edition, page 1653.

2 *Who's Who in Canada*, 1930-31 edition, page 808.

3 Castell Hopkins, *Canadian Annual Review of Public Affairs*, 1916 and 1917 editions, pages 772-74 and 814 respectively.

but died eighteen months later.[4] A later occupant of the house was the future Liberal premier John Hart, during the period that he was managing director of Gillespie, Hart & Todd, Limited. Hart had entered politics in the September, 1916, provincial elections that brought the Liberals to power for the first time. Appointed whip in his first session, he was promoted to minister of finance in 1917 and held the position until 1924, when he resumed private life.[5] His financial ability led him back into politics with Duff Pattullo's Liberals in the thirties; it was Hart's orthodoxy and businesslike reputation, by contrast with Pattullo's perceived radicalism, that caused him to be chosen over Pattullo in the Liberal convention of December, 1941. Hart continued as premier until his death in 1947.[6]

The house at 1837 Matthews Avenue was home to the lawyer Leon Johnson Ladner (far right), a son of the founder and namesake of that community. He attended primary school in Ladner and high school in New Westminster, before heading to Toronto, where he read law with the firm of Sir Charles Hibbert Tupper. At the age of thirty-five, he was elected to the House of Commons as a "Liberal-Conservative," and was reelected twice before defeat and retirement from politics in 1930.[7] Known as "the grand old man of the Conservative party in B.C.," Ladner was a great believer in physical fitness and a central banking system. Late in life, he wrote and published his autobiography[8] as a platform for his very conservative views on life and politics.

The house at 1289 Balfour Street belonged for a time to William George Murrin (far left), the president of the B.C. Electric Railway Company and B.C. Power Corporation from 1929 until Dal Grauer took over in the mid-1940s. A Londoner trained as an electrical engineer, he worked for the London Electric Lighting Company and the London United Tramways Company before immigrating to Vancouver in 1913. His great service to the community was in maintaining the electric street-railway and utilities system through years of unprecedented demand during the Second World War. In addition to his career with the BCER, he was a director of a variety of companies including Union Steamships, Dominion Bridge, and the Bank of Montreal, and served terms as president of the Vancouver Little Theatre Society and the Vancouver Art Gallery.[9]

The large house known as "Duart," which stood at 3741 Hudson Street until 1977, was the long-time home of Harvey Reginald MacMillan (left), co-founder of the MacMillan-Bloedel forestry empire. Born in 1885 in Newmarket, Ontario, he attended the University of Toronto and earned a master's degree in Forestry at Yale in 1908. His achievements in British Columbia, beginning with his appointment as chief forester in 1912, ran the gamut from lumber to banking, shipping, and shipbuilding. For his unpaid services as president of Wartime Merchant Shipping Limited, he was made a C.B.E. in June, 1943.[10] Following his death, the Hudson Street house was razed and the property divided into three lots, but portions of the old stone wall and gates, incised with the name "Duart" — conferred on the property by the first owner, Hugh McLean[11] — survive at the corner of Hudson and Balfour.

The lawyer John Wallace de Beque Farris (right) lived in the fine Maclure and Fox Tudor house at 3351 Granville Street. A Liberal, he successfully entered politics in the 1916 election that brought H.C. Brewster to the premiership after the thirteen years of Conservative regimes led by W.J. Bowser and Sir Richard McBride. The following year, Farris became attorney general, and to him fell the task of sorting out the mess of Prohibition, which had been in force in the province since September, 1916, but was clearly not working; in February, 1921, after years of prosecuting citizens for petty liquor violations, Farris introduced the Liquor Act that established government liquor stores, but denied organizations such as the Legion and businesses such as hotels the right to sell liquor by the glass. He was pilloried by both wet and dry interests, and in frustration made this classic statement on politics: "What is there in political life in this province good enough to have to stand for this sort of thing?"[12] Early in the following year, he resigned as attorney general, and did not seek reelection. Returning to his private practice with the firm Farris, Farris, Stulz & Sloan, he had a distinguished career as solicitor for clients such as the B.C. Electric Railway and the Bank of Toronto. For his years of service to the Liberal party, he was appointed to the Senate by the Mackenzie King government in 1936.[13]

J.W. de B. Farris's brother, Wendell Burpee Farris (far right), lived in the house at 3638 Pine Crescent. Born in New Brunswick and educated in St. John (his brother received his law degree at the University of Pennsylvania), W.B. Farris moved to British Columbia in 1909, avoided political entanglements, and in addition to his legal work was the director of about a dozen companies, including Canadian Forest Products, Harrison Hotspring Hotel Company, and Home Oil. In 1942, he was appointed chief justice of the Supreme Court, succeeding M.A. Macdonald.[14]

4 *Who's Who in Canada*, 1930-31 edition, page 1008. Obituaries published in Vancouver newspapers on October 14, 1941.

5 *Who's Who in Canada*, 1930-31 edition, page 782.

6 Ormsby, *British Columbia: A History*, pages 469-475.

7 Information from *Who's Who in Canada*, 1930-31 edition, page 1284, and *Who's Who in British Columbia*, 1944-46 edition, page 144. Obituaries published in Vancouver newspapers on April 12, 1978.

8 Autobiography called *The Ladners of Ladner, By Covered Wagon to the Welfare State*, Mitchell Press, 1972.

9 Information from *Who's Who in Canada*, 1930-31 edition, page 241, and *Who's Who in British Columbia*, 1944-46 edition, page 196.

10 *Who's Who in British Columbia*, 1944-46 edition, page 177; photograph from *Who's Who & Why*, 1921 edition, page 141.

11 Kalman, *Exploring Vancouver 2*, page 268.

12 Castell Hopkins, *Canadian Annual Review of Public Affairs*, 1921 edition, page 880.

13 Information from *Who's Who in Canada*, 1930-31 edition, page 250, and *Who's Who in British Columbia*, 1944-46 edition, page 80. Obituaries published in Vancouver newspapers on May 15, 1970.

14 Information from *Who's Who in Canada*, 1930-31 edition, page 575, and *Who's Who in British Columbia*, 1944-46 edition, page 81. Obituaries published in Vancouver newspapers on June 17, 1955.

1 See the advertisement in the *Province,* February 21, 1926.

2 The reason often given for this is a general feeling of revulsion towards modern life following the First World War, and towards the giddy pace of social change in the twenties. The architectural historians David Gebhard and Robert Winter, referring to the Spanish Colonial Revival of the 1920s, certainly thought so: "Here was a style which reflected the storybook romance associated with Californians — one into which Americans, tired of the nastiness of war and modern life, could retreat" (Gebhard and Winter, *Architecture in Los Angeles,* page 17).

3 Following intense public pressure at public hearings in March, 1990, city council agreed to consider specific zoning for Third Shaughnessy to make demolitions and redevelopment there "economically unattractive," in order to preserve the area's character. See *Vancouver Sun,* April 6, 1990.

The two later, southward subdivisions of Shaughnessy Heights, called Second and Third Shaughnessy, contain comparatively modest houses, built during the twenties and thirties when incomes were lower and tastes less ostentatious than they had been in the boom years before the First World War. The servant situation had also changed: the upheaval of the First World War and concurrent social changes, such as women's suffrage and increased opportunities for education, reduced their availability, making the large houses of previous generations less practical to maintain. Life had in most ways become simpler, less constrained by the rigid conventions of Victorian and Edwardian manners. Instead of servants there were new "consumer durables" and labour-saving devices, such as automobiles and vacuum cleaners, on which the middle classes wanted to spend their money. Second Shaughnessy, which was subdivided and placed on the market by the Canadian Pacific Railway soon after World War I, comprises the area between King Edward Avenue and 37th, bounded by Oak Street and Arbutus. The parklike Third Shaughnessy, which went on the market in 1926, is the area between Maple and Granville streets, and extends south from 37th Avenue to 41st.[1]

There are two distinctive features of these two Shaughnessys: firstly, the 1920s and 1930s were, in domestic architecture at least, a period of great nostalgia, reflected in the "revival" architectural styles — mainly Tudor and Georgian — of the houses on the curving streets;[2] secondly, these comparatively modest houses were built on large suburban lots (sixty to a hundred feet wide), further reinforcing the image of suburban Vancouver as a garden city. The Kerrisdale-Granville area adjoining Third Shaughnessy south of 41st Avenue is quite similar, except for the grid system of its streets; it, however, has in recent years fallen victim to the developers of so-called monster houses, a fate that is only now beginning to threaten the houses of Second and Third Shaughnessy.[3] The old houses are in jeopardy mainly because the zoning in these parts of the city allows a much bigger house to be built on the lot than was originally there.

The two houses on these pages (the one below in Third Shaughnessy and the one on the next page in Second Shaugnessy) and the house on page 116 were demolished so that bigger homes could be built on their lots, with the results shown on pages 199 and 200.

The house that stood at 5669 Angus Drive just north of 41st Avenue was a classic Georgian Revival ''CPR Box,'' distinguished from the dozens of others in that part of the city by the quality of the carved arches, sunbursts, and other decorations above the windows and around the front doorway. Built in 1935 for Henry Kohlman, it was quite small by today's standards, with only three bedrooms upstairs, but it had exceptional woodcarving and panelling inside.

5669 Angus Drive, Vancouver.

ANDRA + 29TH VANCOUVER.   M. KLUCKNER 1989

One of the finest Tudor Revival houses in Second Shaughnessy stood on a large lot at the northwest corner of Alexandra and 29th Avenue. Built in 1922 for the businessman David J. Christie, it was one of the early houses erected after the CPR subdivided the land south of King Edward Avenue. In keeping with contemporary style, it had a comparatively small living room, but a huge dining room with chest-high wainscotting and a beamed ceiling. On the second floor were four bedrooms and a steep staircase that ascended to two more on the third floor, probably originally intended as maid's and cook's quarters. The master bedroom, at the west end of the house (farthest away in the watercolour), opened onto a covered sleeping porch. There were four fireplaces — in the den, living room, master bedroom, and basement family room (which had a slate floor).[1] In short, it was a large, well-built house, on a well-landscaped lot, and was comparatively well maintained.

An advertisement, giving no address, appeared in the *Real Estate Weekly* early in February, 1989; it read: "90 x 150 lot in Shaughnessy. Builder is ready to plan new 8,300 square foot home. To customize to your specifications call now." Early the following month, a large sign appeared on the front lawn, stating: "on this site will be built this luxury residence" beneath a coloured rendering of a new house. The realty company, Sutton, held an agent's open about March 15, and a day or so later the sign disappeared from the front lawn. In October, the Christie house was demolished.

The corner of Alexandra and 29th Avenue in Second Shaughnessy, looking west at the Christie house, in March, 1989.

1 Conversations with Bruce Stratton and Joan Anderson in March and April, 1989. Their parents bought the house from the CPR in 1942, probably following a foreclosure, and lived there until 1967.

C.B.K. VAN NORMAN

The exquisite little Van Norman chateau at 1308 West 47th Avenue, shortly before its demolition in the summer of 1989.

Although both the houses on these pages are in revival styles, they are unusual for the Kerrisdale/Shaughnessy area, where most of the buildings in the twenties and thirties were variations on the Tudor and the Georgian, with the occasional Dutch gable and Spanish hacienda thrown in for good measure. Both houses were designed by the same architect, Charles Burwell Knight Van Norman, one of the more active members of his profession in residential work in the city during the 1930s.

Van Norman quickly established a large residential practice in the city after his arrival here in 1930; born in 1907, he had grown up in Meaford, Ontario, and received his architectural training at the University of Manitoba.[1] The two houses here, both designed while he was still in his twenties, are representative of his skills. In addition, he and his associates had a flair for the *business* of architecture, and managed to involve themselves in some of the downtown ventures into the International Style in the 1950s. Their efforts included the 1950-54 Customs Building at 1001 West Pender Street and the 1955-56 Burrard Building at the corner of Burrard and Georgia, as well as some of the big land-development projects, such as the monumental Beach Towers on Beach Avenue for Block Brothers, and Park Royal Shopping Centre.[2] Like many architects, Van Norman also did alterations and renovations, including ones at "Duart" for H.R. MacMillan between 1936 and 1953, and for the Foleys at 1389 The Crescent. Among his more modest designs were prefabricated houses for the Veterans' Land Act.[3] An entrepreneurial streak revealed itself in the proposals drawn for a large number of projects, very few of which were ever built.[4] His own radically modern house, built in 1939 at 1840 West 61st Avenue, anticipates mobile home design.

Van Norman designed the house above, at 1308 West 47th Avenue, in 1936 for Mr. and Mrs. J. Lamprey. In the same year, he designed the house next door at 1320 and the one across the street at 1307. The Lamprey house is a modest example of the French Norman style, using the hipped, steep roof, wall dormers and tall chimneys typical of farmhouses in Normandy and Brittany. "Knowledge of this image developed in the teens, as an outcome of the First World War, and on into the 1920s through the publication of numerous illustrative books and articles."[5] The house on West 47th lacked one of the distinctive features of the French Norman style as practiced elsewhere in North America — a conical-roofed tower, placed at the junction of the two parts of an L.

The blocks of Vancouver around 1308 West 47th Avenue — in fact, the entire area bounded roughly by Granville, Oak, 41st, and 57th avenues — has been largely rebuilt in recent years

1 *Who's Who in British Columbia*, 1944-46 edition, page 262.

2 Kalman, *Exploring Vancouver 2*, page 292.

3 City of Vancouver Archives, VAN files.

4 Conversation with architectural writer Sean Rossiter, 1989.

5 Gebhard and Winter, *Architecture in Los Angeles*, page 484.

ANGUS DRIVE, VANCOUVER

M.KLUCKNER 1989

by developers buying houses for "lot value," demolishing them, and erecting much larger and more lavish structures. Most of the houses in the area will not be missed, as they were cheaply built wood and stucco bungalows and split-levels from the forties and fifties. The Lamprey house at 1308 West 47th was an exception, but quality was no defence. The house was sold in the spring of 1989, flipped a few months later, and stood empty until its demolition in July.

Van Norman also worked in the Cape Cod Revival or Colonial Revival style, a good example of which is the house above at 5391 Angus Drive at 38th Avenue. It was designed in 1937 for a man named C. Halterman. Although its design hearkens back to houses along the northeastern American seaboard, the house attracts attention more because of its dramatic siting, the fine stone wall and landscaping, and the framing of mature cedar trees around the side and back — not Cape Cod features, but a stylish example of the garden city of the 1930s. Although it looks dramatic from the outside, it is a curious house, obviously designed from the outside in, with large principal rooms on the main floor, but a cramped and almost windowless upstairs. The original plans allowed for only three small gabled dormers at the rear to illuminate the three upstairs bedrooms.

Another, more modest Van Norman Cape Cod, designed the year after the house on Angus Drive, stood at 2615 Point Grey Road,[6] but was demolished recently for a townhouse development. In the same style is his 1938 Bell-Irving house at 2995 Rosebery Avenue in West Vancouver.[7]

Angus Drive at 38th Avenue in the summer — a classic example of the 1930s Vancouver landscape.

6 See Kalman, *Exploring Vancouver 2*, page 199.

7 Foundation Group Designs, *West Vancouver Heritage Inventory*, page 30.

KERRISDALE

The house that stood at the southwest corner of 49th Avenue and West Boulevard until the mid-1970s was designed in 1911 by the architect Thomas Hooper for Chris Spencer, son of the founder of the Spencer's department store chain, who had moved to Vancouver to manage the company's Vancouver branch. Spencer lived there until his death; subsequently, Dominion Construction bought the house, renovated it, and sold it to Athlone Boys School.[1] It was demolished in the 1970s, and the site redeveloped with townhouses. The photograph here was taken about 1915.[2]

The photographs and watercolours on the next several pages illustrate some of the former landmarks on what used to be one of the great streets of the city — 49th Avenue and its continuation onto South West Marine Drive. Originally called Magee Road, 49th connected the Southlands farms of the McCleerys, Hugh Magee, and Henry Mole with the 1889 "mile-long peephole" through the forest (later Granville Street), and after 1902 with the Vancouver & Lulu Island Railway tracks (later the B.C. Electric's interurban tracks). On the original railway line, Magee station was the only stop between downtown and the lumber mills at Eburne.[3] Marine Drive was the old River Road, cleared in the 1860s by a group that included Fitzgerald McCleery, who purchased District Lot 315 at the foot of today's Macdonald Street and there established the first farm within the modern boundaries of Vancouver. A small cairn in McCleery Park at Marine Crescent and 49th Avenue marks a corner of the old McCleery property, but the family's 1873 farmhouse, the first building in the city, was demolished in the 1950s because it interfered with the layout of a golf course (page 145).

Forty-Ninth Avenue west of Granville Street descends gradually through an arch of fully grown boulevard trees towards the railway tracks at West Boulevard, then drops quite sharply to the west and Southlands; there are sweeping views of the Gulf of Georgia and the distant mountains of Vancouver Island. Not surprisingly, a number of prominent people established homes there, and even some of the more suburban houses of the 1920s had a half-acre or more of grounds. It was all quite grand, in the woodsy, overgrown style of Vancouver. Although it has not been a consistent streetscape since the 1930s, until recently one could look only for the landmarks, and, ignoring the generations of infill housing between, see the "bones" of the old Magee Road.

At Marguerite Street, there was the Crandall house (page 123); a few blocks west, there is the landmark façade of Magee High School, and the site of the Kerrisdale Grocery (page 121); next come the ghosts of the Royal Nursery,[4] the railway tracks (now only a freight line), and the wall which once surrounded the Arnold-Spencer house (above); farther west, as the road descends the hill towards Marine Drive, are the Tudor-Revival house at Balsam Street (page 125), the houses of Ben Cunliffe and Harry Stone, and the beautifully landscaped Tudors along Marine Crescent (page 124); on Marine Drive, there was the Malkin's "Southlands" estate, to name just one. On the Southlands flats, the traces of the early farms that were the raison d'être for Magee Road and the River Road are difficult to locate: the McCleery, Magee, and Mole farmhouses, all older than the City of Vancouver itself, were demolished in the 1950s, coincidentally within a few years of each other; the 1891 farmhouse of Sam McCleery, which stood at 2610 South West Marine Drive, was torn down in 1977 and replaced by a new house.[5]

1 Conversations with Chris McGregor and Cathy Barford, 1990.

2 From the booklet *Beautiful Homes*, pamphlet Und-831, in CVA.

3 Ewert, *The Story of the B.C. Electric Railway Company*, page 58.

4 "Royal" was a forty-acre property on the south side of 49th Avenue between Laburnum and the railway tracks that operated for about a decade after 1908. It was said to be the largest botanical garden and nursery in the province, and had its own railway siding at 51st Avenue.

5 There is a photograph of the house in Kalman, *Exploring Vancouver 2*, page 263.

The photograph above is from the booklet *Beautiful Homes*[1] and shows "Southlands," the estate of the wholesale grocer and mayor W.H. Malkin, at 3269 South West Marine Drive. As originally developed around 1910, it occupied the land bordered by Balaclava and Blenheim between Marine Drive and 43rd Avenue. The house had its own well until 1926.

"Southlands" had one of the most splendid gardens in the city, as recorded by an anonymous newspaper reporter advertising a "Gardens Beautiful" fundraising tour one May during the Second World War: "Beyond the white gate, the drive winds through spacious lawns, dotted with spreading maples and fir trees, with English ivy climbing far up their trunks. Following the drive to the right of the house, there are sweet briar roses in shades of yellow, red and orange, also a 'Napoleon's Heart' rose just coming into bloom. Here there is a bed of fragrant English heliotrope. A path between hedges leads to the greenhouses, vegetables and fruit gardens. Very interesting are the pear and apple trees, growing in 'espallier' fashion. Beyond a cedar hedge there is the formal garden, with a broad, velvety lawn on one boundary, and a flowing stream, spanned by rustic borders, that widens into pools at intervals . . . . Flowering shrubs and perennials grow along the stream, with some rare varieties, such as *Ixia*, a South African plant, with very brilliant flowers. A magnificent perennial border forms another boundary of the lawn. Far down is the rose garden, the climbers trained to pillars along a flagged walk. There are many beds of roses showing their first lovely bloom. The conservatory may be seen, where there is a showing of giant *schizanthus* and *clueraria*."[2]

Two years before this description was written, Malkin had donated the six undeveloped acres on the north side of his estate to the city as a park.[3] His only stipulation was that springs rising on the vacant land not be diverted from his property. Although the land became known as Malkin Park, it has never been developed. Malkin died in 1959, and his estate was subdivided in the spring of 1960 by Warnett Kennedy for the real-estate firm of Macauley, Nicolls & Maitland; "Southlands" itself was demolished in May, 1960. Southlands Place is one of the little streets winding through the old estate.

The fate of Malkin Park was not so neatly resolved. A fight began in 1964 between the parks board and the school board for the northern half of the park, which the latter wanted as the site of an annex to Kerrisdale elementary school. When Malkin gave the land to the city, he had insisted that the land be used for park, and the wording of the gift was such that the city could not find a convenient loophole. The issue was resolved in an extraordinary way: the city bought a fourteen-foot-wide strip at the extreme southern end of the Crofton House School property north of 43rd Avenue, and closed 43rd Avenue between Balaclava and Blenheim; on the resulting piece of land, it managed to insert the new Kerrisdale school annex, whose southern wall sits right on the boundary of Malkin Park.[4] The annex's playgrounds are in fact on parkland, and the bushland to the south — all part of a fifty-year-old bequest — has never been developed. There is no commemoration of Malkin there for his gift to the city.

1 Pamphlet Und-831, in CVA.

2 *Sun*, May 21, 1940.

3 *Province*, August 9, 1939.

4 See *Province*, August 15, 1964, and *Sun*, September 9, 1964.

MAGEE HIGH SCHOOL

Magee High School in 1914. Originally, the school's entranceway was underneath a portico, with classical columns framing the front door. Some years later, the portico was bricked in around the columns, new front doors were installed, and the east wing was added to the building, creating the façade familiar to recent generations of students and nearby residents.

1 They were effectively forced into that position due to provincial school financing policy: to save the building, the Vancouver School Board would have had to pay the full cost and await 60 percent reimbursement by the province; with a new building, the provincial government pays 100 percent, and the school board pays back a percentage over thirty years. Information from Robert Smith, chairman, Vancouver Heritage Advisory Committee.

2 A similar question is confronting St. George's School (page 158), and a number of other old schools in the Vancouver area, mainly due to the earthquake question.

At the corner of 49th Avenue and Maple Street, Magee High School and Kerrisdale Grocery formed an odd couple: the one a large, brick, Edwardian educational institution, the other a little gabled corner store, probably modified by the builder from a standard house plan. The school and the candy and cigarette store — the inseparable duo of modern education.

Booming residential growth in Kerrisdale before the First World War prompted the planning of the area's first high school. There had been an elementary school at the corner of Wilson Road (41st Avenue) and Carnarvon since 1908, but senior students travelled to King Edward School at the corner of 12th and Oak (demolished by fire, 1973). School authorities chose a site on Magee Road just east of the Magee station, and selected this design by the architects Jones and Beatson. Opened in 1914, the new school building was a combined elementary and high school, and carried the names King George V High School (after the king who had ascended to the throne following Edward VII's death in 1910) and Magee Public School. A new elementary school was erected to the northeast in 1926, and named Maple Grove School; by then, only the high school was known as Magee.

Although the original school is a neighbourhood landmark, and one of the last of the significant buildings along 49th Avenue, its interior had been shoddily altered and the rest of the school was a rambling, poorly built, overcrowded assemblage that needed replacement. Discussions on its future became public early in 1989 (coincidentally as the school prepared to celebrate its 75th anniversary), and acquired some urgency that October following the San Francisco earthquake and the subsequent publicity predicting a massive subduction quake in Vancouver — the school building, of brick and reinforced concrete, was not up to current seismic standards. The school administration and school board were in favour of demolition and replacement,[1] a course supported by many parents, who voiced concerns at public meetings in November about their children's safety, and the disruption of the educational process. As a solution that would answer both concerns, they favoured a new school being built behind the old one, which would be demolished when the new one was completed. The option of restoring and upgrading the original main building and constructing a new school behind it received little support, as this would entail dislocating the students for a couple of years. In February, 1990, the school board voted unanimously to demolish the old school buildings.

Magee is an old school, by Vancouver standards, and many of its students from the surrounding, well-established Kerrisdale neighbourhood aspire to settle there themselves (if they can afford it) and to send their own children there, for the school has a "spirit" that seems to endure from generation to generation. But the fate of the old Magee school building, and the status of other school buildings everywhere in western Canada, raises the question of whether the spirit of the old school can be successfully transferred to its new incarnation. Will the school, operating in a new building, still be Magee?[2] The venerable schools of eastern North America and England hang tenaciously onto their old buildings, whether they "work" or not in the modern educational context, in the belief that the buildings themselves exemplify the institutions, their spirit, and the permanence of the educational values they hope to impart.

M·KLUCKNER 1989

Is it only Vancouver, which would rather replace than restore most of its landmarks, that sees no permanence and little value in the best efforts of previous generations? Or are buildings such as the original Magee High School indeed shoddy by modern standards, to be replaced without regret when society changes and the city grows?

• • •

Although it was probably the most jerry-built and modest of the historic buildings on 49th Avenue, the Kerrisdale Grocery might well have outlasted all the others. Due to the zoning curiosity generally known as the "grandfather clause," grocery stores such as this can continue to operate as non-conforming uses in residential areas, as long as they are not substantially altered. Although there was always a possibility that it would be stuccoed or otherwise defaced, or that it would gradually lose business and close due to changing shopping habits or the arrival on a nearby commercial site of a "7-11," the Kerrisdale Grocery was a venerable institution and something of a neighbourhood landmark for seventy-five years. Only a few of the big houses several blocks to the west and the razed Arnold-Spencer house (page 118) were older.

At the time Kerrisdale Grocery was built, the future Magee High School, then called King George V, was approaching completion across Maple Street. Forty-Ninth Avenue was narrow and unpaved, with ditches on each side, and was still known as Magee Road; a few houses had been built in splendid isolation on lots between Granville Street and Marine Drive. However rural this part of Kerrisdale may have been, the downtown terminus of the interurban railway — at the north end of Granville Bridge — was only an eighteen-minute trip from Magee Station,[3] regardless of the time of day. The new grocery building was hooked up to the municipality's water system in March, 1914, for a confectioner named J. Farr.

On May 12, 1989, a fire started in the back of the adjoining butcher shop, and quickly spread through the frame building. The old store's blackened ruins stood until October, when they were taken down.[4]

Kerrisdale Grocery and the Quality Meat Market, at the corner of 49th Avenue and Maple Street, gutted by fire in May, 1989, and demolished that October. In the right distance is Magee High School.

3 B.C. Electric 1908 timetable reproduced in Ewert, *The Story of the B.C. Electric Railway*, page 77.

4 With the destruction of the old store, the "grandfather clause" has lapsed and the property has reverted to a straight single-family zoning, but there is a possibility that the city might allow a new grocery store to be built on the property as a service to the neighbourhood. The property went on the market in the winter of 1990 for $660,000.

THE CRANDALL HOUSE

In the late 1980s, one of the battlegrounds between developers and established residents has been the Kerrisdale-Granville area, the blocks on either side of Granville Street south of 41st Avenue. Two factors combined to make the area such a popular place for new home building: firstly, the houses were "underbuilt" on their lots, and under present zoning new houses could be much bigger, thereby justifying the very steep prices that wealthy prospective residents were willing to pay; secondly, Kerrisdale was perceived as a stable and safe neighbourhood, close to a number of good schools. The neighbourhood organized against the onslaught, partly because many of the new houses clashed with the more modest Tudors and Georgians built there in the twenties and thirties, and stood out from the subtle, English-influenced, soft-edged streetscapes. Some of the new houses looked like fortresses, and a few speculative builders drew the ire both of neighbours and city council for their habit of clear-cutting the heavily landscaped lots before starting construction; "Save Our Trees" became the cry, and it echoed around the city in an environmental and aesthetic chorus for the preservation of the city's greenery.[1]

Many of the new houses were staggering in their luxury and scale. An advertisement from the *Real Estate Weekly* during the summer of 1989 described a representative new spec-built dwelling, built in an area where the typical house had been about 2,000 or 2,500 square feet:[2] "Archit. design. resid. sit. on 60x134' lot in one of Van.'s most prestig. neighbourhoods. Home offers 5000 sq.ft. of LUXURIOUS and UNCOMPROMISING QUALITY. Total of 17 spac. rms, a warm fam rm, den, spac. kitch, sunken liv rm, grac. din rm. Up the elegant staircase to 5 BDRMS (2 enste) includ. beaut. MASTER SUITE W/GAS F/P & vaulted ceilings. This one of a kind resid. incl. nanny suite down, skylights, u/g sprinkler system & spec. lighting features. Offers to $1.148 million."

An illustration of what used to constitute prestige in Kerrisdale is the story of the name change of Sperling Street, between Angus and Marguerite. By the late 1940s, east Vancouver had become built up and formed a continuous suburban sprawl into Burnaby, where there was already a through street called Sperling. Kerrisdale's Sperling Street needed a new name. Magee Street was suggested, and briefly adopted, but a number of home-owners objected that the street would become known as "Maggie," with detrimental consequences to property values. City council agreed to change the name to Wiltshire Street on August 30, 1950.[3]

One of the most historically significant, well-built, and elegant of the houses in the Kerrisdale-Granville area stood at the northwest corner of Marguerite Street and 49th Avenue, on a three-quarter-acre lot. A unique three-storey Craftsman building, it had stone porch piers, porte-cochère, wraparound porch, beamed ceilings, wainscotting, leaded glass, four bedrooms on the second floor with sleeping porches, and a matching garage with upstairs living quarters. It was connected to the municipal water supply in June, 1914, for a manufacturer's agent named Elmer E. Crandall, who sold "stoves, ranges and furnaces, and the Lundy shovels and tools, axes, etc." from his offices at 1052 Homer Street. Perhaps due to the economic doldrums in Vancouver in 1913-14, Crandall lived there only briefly, if at all, and the house was subsequently occupied for years by Albert M. Johnston, director of a firm known as Johnston Bros.[4]

Originally, it stood on an even bigger property, incorporating the lot to the west (the left side of the watercolour, behind the hedge); that side of the garden was a private tennis court,

1 One of the most notorious tree-destruction episodes, which was widely reported in the media, occurred on April 4, 1990, when the land developer Jack Eng ignored the protests of neighbours and cut down a pair of 70-year-old sequoias in front of his recently purchased Georgian Revival house at 6425 Marguerite Street. Some members of city council also protested, but lacked the legal ability to stop him; proposed amendments to the Vancouver Charter by the provincial government will give the city the ability to protect trees.

2 This advertisement (with abbreviations and punctuation as written) is for the new house at 2179 West 36th Avenue, another part of Kerrisdale drastically redeveloped in recent years (see page 129). A petition of about seventy home-owners, organized by a group on the 2100-block West 34th, sought to change the zoning in their area to allow two houses to be built on the sixty-six-foot lots, to protect the street from the "large boxy" houses being built in the area. A man named Rae Coates, who supported the proposal to split the lots, said: "the larger houses are out of keeping with the neighbourhood feeling we've been accustomed to." See *Vancouver Sun*, "Lot Division Scheme Sparks Feud" by Gillian Shaw, April 28, 1989. When houses went on the market in the area, they sold for "lot value" (such as one mentioned in the above newspaper article: $570,000 for a sixty-six-foot lot with a worthless house); the old, "small" houses with their big gardens were demolished and cleared, replaced by looming, ostentatious houses with small "gardens."

3 Matthews, "Notes on Streets and Place Names," CVA.

4 No relation to Johnston Terminals.

5 *Who's Who in British Columbia*, 1944-46 edition, page 216. Obituaries published in local newspapers on November 3, 1961.

"Randallcroft," at the southwest corner of 49th Avenue and Adera Street (razed in the 1960s), was one of the first houses built on the south side of 49th Avenue in the blocks just west of Granville Street. It was owned by Sam Randall, one of the important figures in horse breeding and racing in British Columbia. Randall (1882-1961) built Lansdowne Park on Lulu Island in 1924, and was the long-time operator of Exhibition Park in Vancouver and the Willows in Oak Bay. He was the first Canadian race-track operator to install a camera finish and the first one in the world to install an electric starting gate on a race-track. In addition to his 49th Avenue home, where he lived from about 1915 until his death, Randall owned the Ascot Stock Farms on Lulu Island and the Goodwood Dairy and Stock Farm, where he raised Jersey and Holstein cows. He was the builder, in 1930, and the owner of the Gothic Revival Randall Building at 535 West Georgia Street.[5]

SAM RANDALL
RACING CHIEFTAIN, HASTINGS PARK.
MAY 24 1947

1701 W 49TH AVE. AT MARGUERITE   M. KLUCKNER 1989

with a gazebo at the back. The beech tree dominating the front yard is evidently one of three English beeches imported around the First World War for the old Shaughnessy golf course at 41st and Oak Street; there turned out to be room on the course for only two, and the third one somehow ended up in front of this house.[6] Such a grand property was not out of character with the early years of 49th Avenue; it is still possible to see how the bungalows between the few big houses on 49th are infilled on what were once sideyards, tennis courts and gardens.

The house's long-time occupant sold it in 1986 to a man who promptly set about trying to subdivide the 148-foot by 191-foot lot.[7] Failing to gain permission for that, partly due to objections by neighbours, he put the house on the market late in the winter of 1989. It sold quickly for about $750,000, and was unceremoniously demolished that summer. A new, larger house, which presents its brick sidewall to 49th Avenue, has since been built on the lot (see page 200); only the seventy-five-year-old beech remains. Houses such as this one, although listed on the city's heritage inventory, have no protection against demolition. The issue here was not one of a heritage building making way for higher density housing or a different land use; it was just a case once again of a fine old building in the city being perceived as lacking the prestige and value of the brand-new.

The Crandall house at the northwest corner of 49th Avenue and Marguerite in Kerrisdale was erected in 1914 and remained as a neighbourhood landmark until its demolition in the summer of 1989. The watercolour was painted in April, just before the huge beech tree in the front yard came into leaf.

6 Interview with Doris Dennison, who lived in the house until 1986. There is an equally large beech tree in Van-Dusen Gardens, the successor to the golf course.

7 Conversations with Doris Dennison and Eric Watt, 1989.

THE MUNICIPALITY OF POINT GREY

Nearly all of Kerrisdale is built on Canadian Pacific Railway land — the southern portion of the company's huge District Lot 526. The southwestern boundary of District Lot 526, near the corner of 49th Avenue and Marine Crescent, is notched around Fitzgerald McCleery's District Lot 315 (see page 7). It was divided into large properties which became attractive home-building sites when municipal water mains were laid along 49th Avenue in 1912.

Kerrisdale, and indeed all of Vancouver west of Main Street, developed in an orderly fashion because of the residents' desire for modern civic services, and their willingness to pay for them. All of Vancouver south of the city boundary at 16th Avenue had been part of the Municipality of South Vancouver, founded in 1891 (page 166), whose penurious and ill-organized administrative ways caused the residents west of Main Street to secede in 1908. They formed the Municipality of Point Grey, with headquarters at 43rd and West Boulevard — an independent political entity until its amalgamation with Vancouver in 1929. One of the strongest advocates of strict zoning and controlled planning was the Canadian Pacific Railway itself, which wanted to create a separate municipality of Shaughnessy Heights, presumably to preserve its exclusivity. The proposal was rejected by Frank Bowser, who was reeve of Point Grey (he lived on a ten-acre property at 6000 Macdonald Street) and had the ear of his brother William, the province's attorney general. The proposed municipality was to include all the CPR land grant from 16th Avenue to Shannon (57th) Avenue — in all, nearly five thousand acres.[1]

The new Municipality of Point Grey set out aggressively to provide services such as water, electricity, and transit to prospective homebuilders. Its water-connection records[2] detail the development of that part of Vancouver. The earliest permits were issued in 1908 for connections in new houses built just south of the city boundary on 17th and 18th avenues between Laurel and Heather. Four years later, the municipality was still connecting water for logging and clearing camps, such as the one in April, 1912, for a logging camp at the corner of 29th and Dunbar, employing forty men, or the one in October, 1912, issued to Alfred Markham, superintendent of land clearing for the Canadian Pacific Railway, "for use by donkey engine" at the corner of Hudson and Magee (49th Avenue). Although utterly pro-development, the Point Grey municipal council was aware that the rapid change in the muncipality was obliterating all traces of the past, and voted in 1913 *not* to remove the old first-growth stumps from Maple Grove Park, "so that children, years hence, would have an idea of the great stands of timber that once covered Point Grey."[3] The stumps are still there today.

The clearing camps were still operating when the first houses were built in the area of 49th Avenue and Macdonald Street. A number of houses were connected to the water mains in March and April of 1912: in order from the earliest, they are 2587 West 49th (either razed or modified beyond recognition) for Boyd Stewart Easton, 6550 Marine Crescent (razed) for Grace Gilmer, 2443 West 49th Avenue by the builder Jonathan Harrison for Benjamin Cunliffe, 6489 Macdonald for Arthur Blackwood, and 6674 Marine Crescent (razed) for R.W. Errington. A slightly later arrival was the rambling Italianate house at 2537 West 49th Avenue, built for Henry A. Stone, the president of Gault Brothers and one of the founders of the Vancouver Art Gallery (see page 182-83). Also living on that block around that time, although it is impossible to determine exactly where, as the street numbers did not appear in the city directory, was the Walter Scrope-Shrapnel family; he was the grandson of the inventor of the shrapnel shell.[4]

The finest house remaining from those days is 2443 West 49th Avenue; set well back from the road on a beautifully landscaped piece of property, it retains the look — or at least the *intended* look — of the gracious homes of old Magee Road. The house originally stood on a five-acre property bounded by Larch Street, uncleared 47th Avenue, uncleared Balsam Street, and Magee Road,[5] and was built for Ben Cunliffe, who was reeve of the Municipality of Point Grey in 1916.[6] In conversations with Charles Bayley in the early 1950s, Cunliffe and his wife recounted the time a bear tried to open the meat cooler underneath the porch of their house, and gave a graphic description of political life in the wilds of Point Grey: "One night, a knock came to Mr. Cunliffe's back door and there was [chairman of the board of works] Richardson, with waders and lamp. A workman on the Dunbar Street sewer had just come up to his house and claimed that the big seven-foot sewer under construction had already started to sink. Charlie Richardson, as upright as a steel post, had to investigate immediately. At nine o'clock at night, he and Mr. Cunliffe walked down to Dunbar Street, entered the sewer, and trekked all the way down to the Fraser River right inside the sewer. They were satisfied that the sewer seemed on the level . . . at least it wasn't sinking."[7]

1 Newton J. Ker, former CPR land agent, March 9, 1938, quoted by J.S. Matthews, in file "CPR Land Grant," CVA.

2 Preserved in CVA.

3 Cited in Bayley, *The Kerrisdale Story*, page 31.

4 City of Vancouver 1917 directory and *Who's Who in British Columbia*, 1944-46 edition, page 233.

5 *Goad's Atlas* 1912, CVA.

6 See "Kerrisdale Pioneers Celebrate Golden Wedding," *Kerrisdale Courier*, February 14, 1957.

7 Bayley, *The Kerrisdale Story*, page 31.

M.KLUCKNER
1988

One of the casualties of Kerrisdale's redevelopment saga was the fine Tudor Revival house at 2383 West 49th Avenue, at the "T" with Balsam Street. The house stood on a large property of about a half acre, 100 feet wide and 209 feet deep, the extra depth occurring because 48th Avenue was never put through.[1] The house was built early in 1924 to the design of the architect Ross Lort by Hope and Ridley contractors, of 1994 West 14th Avenue. The owner Randle Knowles was also listed in city directories as a builder. Subsequently, it was either owned or occupied by a building contractor named William Harrison Snowball, the proprietor of Carpentry Services of 6592 Yew Street. From the 1930s, it was owned by yet another building contractor, a man named W.J. Read. Perhaps because of all these cooks and only one broth, it was an odd house, seemingly put together from builders' samples — some of the windows were standard rectangular wooden sashes, while others were leaded with curving, pointed, "Moorish" tops.

In 1988, following the death of Mrs. Read, the house went on the market for $650,000 — lot value. It was purchased by a builder-renovator named Carter Maitland, who sought support from the neighbours to subdivide the lot front to back, so that an infill house could be built on the spacious back lawn, but received little. He was left with the unpalatable option of subdividing the lot from side to side, creating two 50-foot by 209-foot lots, as the house could not be economically modernized and still be sold at a profit; therefore, to save the house, he had it lifted off its foundations, turned sideways on the lot, and dropped onto a new foundation. He then sold off the adjoining 50-footer to finance the renovation and modernization of his Tudor. He rebuilt the side façade to look like the old front, utilizing the curved gable ends and triangular "flying buttresses" of houses of the period and incorporating windows removed from similar houses. The renovation works quite well, although the total effect is spoiled by the new house next door, which was allowed to be built seventeen feet farther forward on its lot than the existing houses on the block.

A classic example of a Tudor Revival house in an English garden — the house at 2383 West 49th Avenue, in October, 1988. It stood on a half-acre lot, with a very deep, parklike backyard with large flowerbeds around its perimeter and an extensive rose garden.

1 The typical depth for city lots in that part of town is about 120 feet.

R.P. S. TWIZELL

Robert Percival Sterling Twizell (whose directory advertisements listed him sometimes as Robert P.S. Twizell, and other times as R.P. Sterling Twizell) was born in Northumberland in 1879, and attended the Science College of Durham University before apprenticing with the architectural firm of Hicks & Charlewood in Newcastle. In the period of 1903 to 1908, he worked as a lecturer at Durham University, then came to Vancouver, started into practice by himself, and was joined by his brother in 1917. He was president of the Architectural Institute of British Columbia and of the Art, Historical and Scientific Association of Vancouver. In 1920, he married Mabel Akroyd Denness of Vancouver; they had two daughters.[1]

While the ghosts of many Vancouver architects must look on askance at the fate of their greatest achievements, R.P.S. Twizell and his brother George would be pleased that so many of their buildings still stand. Their survival owes much to the fact that Twizell and Twizell were the great church and institution architects of the city, and these are the types of buildings which tend to be maintained and preserved for generations.

In order of their construction, R.P.S. Twizell's major designs include the following: St. George's Anglican Church, 2960 Laurel, 1910; McBride School, 1300 East 29th, 1912; Queen Mary Elementary School, 2000 Trimble, 1914; Prince of Wales School (now Shaughnessy Elementary), 4250 Marguerite, 1919; Kerrisdale School, 5555 Carnarvon, 1921; Vancouver College, 1356 West 38th Avenue, 1924; Lord Kitchener School, 4055 Blenheim Street, 1924; Talton Manor Apartments, 1886 West 15th, 1925; Canadian Memorial Chapel, 1810 West 15th, 1927; Mount St. Joseph's Oriental Hospital, 238 Campbell Avenue, 1928; St. Andrew's Wesley United Church, 1012 Nelson, 1930; Provincial House for the Oblate Fathers, 2015 West 8th, 1930; St. Augustine's Church, 2015 West 8th Avenue, 1931; Christ Church Cathedral chancel, 690 Burrard, 1934; St. Phillips Anglican, 3737 West 27th, 1941; West Point Grey United Church, 4595 West 8th Avenue, 1941; extensions to St. Mary's Anglican church, 2498 West 37th Avenue, 1947; Fathers of the Blessed Sacrament Church, 3050 Heather, 1948; and St. Giles United Church, 305 West 41st, 1949.[2]

Two of the best Twizell & Twizell churches — Canadian Memorial at 15th and Burrard and St. Andrew's Wesley United at Nelson and Burrard — demonstrate their ability to adapt traditional forms to modern materials. Both churches are built of reinforced concrete, concealed by stone veneers inside and out.[3] Both are in the Gothic Revival style, as is the red-brick St. Augustine's — still one of the landmark buildings of Kitsilano. R.P.S. Twizell favoured the Gothic Revival style from a deeply held conviction of its appropriateness for church architecture (as did the English philosopher John Ruskin); in the 1950s, he described modern church design as "chaotic," observing that "for 3,000 years architecture meant showing the strength and stability of the building."[4]

R.P.S. Twizell practiced architecture in the city from 1908 until his retirement in 1954. He died in 1964.

1 Information from *Who's Who in Canada*, 1930-31 edition, page 882.

2 Plans for most of these buildings are preserved in CVA, plan file "Twizell."

3 Kalman, *Exploring Vancouver 2*, page 130.

4 Newspaper interview published on August 31, 1957, J.S. Matthews' news clippings, CVA.

An early Twizell school: Queen Mary Elementary on Trimble Street in West Point Grey, photographed about 1915.

VPL 16976

st SUN AFTER A WEEK OF RAIN, NOVEMBER   M KLUCKNER 1989

The Twizell house at 6450 Cedarhurst, in late November, 1989.

In 1928, R.P.S. Twizell bought a lot near the southern end of the newly opened Cedarhurst Street, designed this house for himself, and engaged a builder named Archibald Sullivan. Set well back from the street, on a large, parklike lot, it is a classic example of informal Vancouver landscaping, and the aesthetic and philosophical values embodied in the small house on the big lot. The only other house on semi-rural Cedarhurst Street in 1930 was the one at 6410; even today, the large properties, mature trees and hedges, and lack of curbs give the street a casual, picturesque look.

After arriving in Vancouver in 1908, Twizell lived at 1201 Pacific Street, and moved about 1911 to the duplex (which he possibly designed) at 3036 West 8th Avenue in Kitsilano. In 1919, he built a new house for himself at 2001 West 37th Avenue (now demolished), in anticipation of his marriage. He lived there until 6450 Cedarhurst was completed in 1928-29. Upon retirement, he moved to 6188 Mackenzie Street.

B.C. HYDRO

The photograph shows Strathcona station, at the corner of 37th Avenue and West Boulevard, looking northeast, in 1916. The station was the highest point above sea level on the B.C. Electric Railway's Vancouver-Marpole-Steveston interurban line. The photograph shows the extensive development of the blocks of 36th and 37th avenues with "Swiss cottage" Craftsman houses. Most of the houses seen here survive today. In the late 1920s, the Municipality of Point Grey established Point Grey School on the property on the extreme right of the photograph, and at that time the little superintendent's bungalow on the property was moved across the street and inserted sideways onto the lot at 2057 West 37th Avenue. The houses in the right centre of the photograph face 37th Avenue. From left to right, they are 2063, which is still in good condition; 2049, which is very dilapidated; 2033, which has an ugly 1950s renovation on its front; and 2025, a California Bungalow with original shingles on the house but stucco on the porch. The houses in the middle of the photograph in the distance face 36th Avenue, and were built in the spring of 1912. The one with double dormers is 2031 West 36th Avenue, and to its right are 2027 and 2019; all three are in excellent condition today. On the extreme left of the photograph is 2071 West 36th Avenue.

This area, and the one a few blocks to the west around the splendid St. Mary's Church, built in 1913, had an established, *finished* look — rare for Vancouver — that lasted until the disruption and redevelopment of the late 1980s. The architect of St. Mary's, G.L. Thornton Sharp, built two of the houses directly across the street from the church, at 2403 and 2437 West 37th Avenue, the latter for himself. Two other houses that reinforce the neighbourhood character are the Armstrong house, kitty-corner from the church (page 8), and the McCleod house on the next page.

2194 WEST 36TH, VANCOUVER

M.KLUCKNER '89

The house at the southeast corner of 36th Avenue and Yew Street is a representative of the combination of house, garden, and street that once was so typical of the established older neighbourhoods of the city. That block of 36th Avenue is lined with magnificent plane trees, and most of the houses there are set well back from the sidewalk and almost buried in their shrubbery. This house, built in 1922, is an excellent late example of the California Bungalow style, with its broad front porch, low-pitched roof, double eave brackets, and clinker-brick chimney. As it appears above, with its mature landscaping, it is a Vancouver version of the "bungalow in its garden" envisioned by the originators and promoters of the style. By comparison, the row of bungalows on 5th Avenue, illustrated on page 28, is visually interesting because of the repetition of similar elements, but they cannot be said to have the house-and-garden combination idealized in Los Angeles or even elsewhere in Vancouver.

Although it was well maintained, and by no means a small house (probably between 2,000 and 2,500 square feet), this bungalow was in jeopardy because it stood on a large corner lot, and a bigger house could be built there. When it came on the market in the spring of 1989, it was advertised as "What a Lot!" It sold at the beginning of July, but was leased out to tenants, presumably until the new owner is ready to build his new house. There have been a number of demolitions in the area, and the new houses built there have been, in the main, well-constructed and reasonably attractive, but all are very large, and the discreet house-and-garden style of the neighbourhood is changing.[1]

The California Bungalow at 2194 West 36th Avenue, in the summer of 1989.

1 See footnote number 2 on page 122.

PANEL ABOVE MANTELPIECE IS VERY FADED CLAUDIAN LANDSCAPE ON WALLPAPER.

PANELS OF WAINSCOTTING BORDERED BY HALF-ROUND "COLUMNS"

LIVINGROOM

CUP RAIL

BUILT-IN CHINA CABINET

DEN

DINING ROOM

ARCH

LIVING ROOM

FIRE PLACE

ONE SIDE OF ARCH BETWEEN LIVINGROOM + DININGROOM

DININGROOM WAINSCOTTING WITH LEATHER PANELS

A Craftsman Interior 2049 W. 36th Vancouver 1912

M. KLUCKNER 1989

M.KLUCKNER 1989

The Craftsman house at 2049 West 36th Avenue, built in 1912.

Occasionally, a house survives for seventy-five years without any renovation or modification. The Edwardian Builder house on Lakewood Drive owned by the Harris family (page 162) is one; this house, at 2049 West 36th Avenue, is another. It owes its remarkable state of preservation to Mrs. Aletta King, who moved into it in 1918 with her husband — the first head of the department of animal husbandry, now called animal science, at the University of B.C. — and stayed for seventy years. As she never had the inclination to modify it, features such as the built-in china cabinets, wainscotting, kitchen cabinets and sink, and even some of the original wallpaper with leather insets have survived. The King house was built at the pinnacle of the Craftsman movement in Vancouver, when the quality of woodwork even on modest suburban houses reached unsurpassed levels. It is one of a number of houses, the easternmost of which had panoramic views northward to the mountains and southward across Kerrisdale to the Fraser River and the gulf, built near the Strathcona interurban station in the years just before the First World War. Recent demolitions have destroyed the continuity of the block.

As it stood, the house was too small for all but the most determined modern occupant, as it had only two bedrooms and a small den. Using plans by the architect Richard Fearn, the new owners have modernized and expanded the house but have kept many of its features intact. In this case, because the house was listed (as a "B") on the city's heritage inventory, the single-family zoning strictures were relaxed in order to encourage renovations and expansions that retained the character.

THE BEEMAN COTTAGE

The Beeman cottage at 5775 Macdonald Street is one of a handful of cabins left in Vancouver that were built without the blessing of municipal building inspectors. Its major infraction of the building code is its lack of a foundation — it is built flat on the ground, with neither basement nor crawl space, like a summer cabin or guest house. The watercolour also shows the jog in 42nd Avenue at Macdonald Street, due to the fact that the Canadian Pacific Railway's District Lot 526 ended a half block to the east, and the DL 526 surveys did not line up with the earlier ones in District Lot 321 west of Macdonald Street (see map, page 7).

The cottage stands on what was the rear of a long lot extending from the corner of Wilson Road (41st Avenue) and Kaye Road (Macdonald Street) south to 42nd Avenue. The family house, built about 1911, faced 41st Avenue until its demolition a number of years ago; two "Vancouver Specials" now occupy the site. Halfway down the long back yard, a third "Vancouver Special" was built, so now only the old cottage, built at some time prior to 1920, survives.[1] The year 1920 was the last that the Beemans spent in their big house; thereafter, they lived in the cottage, having either rented out or sold the house.

Herbert Beeman was born in England and came to Vancouver in 1898. He worked as a clerk at the Badminton Hotel and as a brewer's helper at the old Stanley Park brewery on Chilco. Upon marriage, he and his wife moved to Kamloops, where they lived until 1907. The following year, he was appointed the first clerk and assessor of the Municipality of Point Grey. Several years later, he joined the real-estate and insurance firm of Ceperley and Rounsefell, then worked as assistant secretary to the board of trade for the thirteen years prior to his death in 1931.

His wife, the former Miss Elsie Machin, was a community worker, church leader, librarian, and the first organist at St. Mary's Church in 1910, when the church there was only a tent. She was the daughter of James Edwin Machin, the second librarian of the Vancouver Public Library. Writing in the 1930s of her father, city archivist J.S. Matthews noted that "in the early days of Vancouver's history, Mr. Machin has been one of the human landmarks. Mr. Machin was a walking encyclopaedia, able to speak several languages. All questions of difficulty were referred to him and he was seldom applied to for information in vain."[2]

Herbert Beeman was something of a character, as witnessed by this poem, written about 1920, called "How To Pronounce Burrard."[3]

> On Prospect Point in the evening glow
> Of the sunset's mirrored glory,
> I glanced above where an ancient crow
> Was telling a bedtime story.
>
> Perched on a bough, this jolly old bird
> Recalled — for a young relation,
> What a hundred years ago he'd heard
> And seen from his lofty station.
>
> "June, ninety-two, Ah, then I was young
> As I sat in this tree in the gloaming.
> A queer sort of fish, with fins outflung,
> In from the sea came roaming.
>
> "I know better now, for the fish was a boat,
> And the fins were the oars to move her.
> There jumped ashore in a bright blue coat
> A man they called Captain Vancouver.
>
> "I flew quite near as he spoke to the mate,
> Or, as sailors say, came furrard,
> He'd name the place I heard him state
> For his friend Sir Harry Burrard.
>
> "Now, I'm getting old and my hearing's hard,
> So it may be I'm mistaken,
> But you'd better look out if you say Burrard
> Or George from his grave will awaken."[4]

1 There is no record of when the cottage was built, but it must have been between 1911 and 1920, when it was connected to the municipal water supply (permit 2780).

2 Matthews, Add.Mss.54, "Beeman" file, CVA.

3 Ibid.

4 On the same subject, it is interesting to note that Jasper Stembridge, "the well-known (English) geographer and map-maker, whose books have sold well over a million copies in recent years," in his 1943 *A Portrait of Canada* (Oxford University Press), consistently misspelt Burrard Inlet as "Burrad." Perhaps this was the way he heard it pronounced here.

BEEMAN COTTAGE

M.KLUCKNER 1989

Following Herbert Beeman's death, his widow and sister lived on for years in the little cottage; they are remembered in the neighbourhood for the kindergarten they ran there. The cottage has been owned for the past two-dozen years by Mr. Bill Nesbitt, who bought it at the time he was purchasing and moving houses from the nearby apartment area onto lots such as this one that contained poorly built little shacks. He had intended to move a house from Balsam Street onto this lot, but someone else bought the house and moved it to Chilliwack. Although this cottage contained neither a bathtub nor a furnace, he upgraded it enough to rent it to a "honeymoon couple," as he described them, and has been doing so ever since.[5]

The corner of 42nd Avenue and Macdonald Street in Kerrisdale, looking west in late September, showing the little Beeman cottage buried in the trees at 5775 Macdonald Street.

5 Conversation with Bill Nesbitt, November, 1989.

GARDEN AT 45th·MACDONALD, VANCOUVER

1 Named after Alexander Kaye, an Englishman who in 1903 bought ten acres along its west side from F.M. Chaldecott, at one hundred dollars an acre. See Matthews, Notes on Names and Places, CVA.

2 All that survives of the transaction is a microfilm of a portion of the original transfer in the Vancouver Land Titles Office, containing Joly de Lotbinière's signature, and a cover page indicating that it was a crown grant.

3 See Add.Mss.54-110 in CVA. His son, Alvah Ernest Foreman, was a noted civil engineer as well as chief engineer of the provincial works department. As a private consultant

Only a few blocks south of the little Beeman cottage and suburban builders' houses, such as the one on page 20, are some of the biggest properties remaining in the city of Vancouver. They owe their existence to the Canadian Pacific Railway's District Lot 526 boundary line along the right-of-way of Trafalgar Street. Around the turn of the century, Trafalgar Street was called Boundary Road and was little more than a logging trail running south from English Bay to Wilson Road — today's 41st Avenue. Between Wilson Road and the River Road — now Marine Drive — beyond which were the long-established farms of the McCleerys and the Magees, there was a trail which became known as Kaye Road.[1] It ran along the boundary line between District Lot 2027 and District Lot 321 (see map, page 7); the right-of-way of Trafalgar Street south of 41st Avenue was not opened.

The southern end of the "finger" between District Lots 321 and 526, properly known as Block One of District Lot 2027, was bought from the crown by a man named Christopher F. Foreman, sometime between 1900 and 1905, during the term of Lieutenant-Governor Henri Joly de Lotbinière.[2] Foreman, who came to Vancouver in April, 1890, operated a grocery store from the brick building at the northeast corner of Main and Pender; he was a city alderman from 1898-1902.[3] In 1909, Foreman filed a subdivision plan for his nine-and-three-quarter-acre block,

The huge garden at 45th and Macdonald in Kerrisdale, established in the 1920s and 1930s by George Smellie and John Crawford.

and on the strength of its approval the municipality opened, graded, and laid water mains along Kaye Road the following year.

Christopher Foreman's subdivision plan for the land south of 45th Avenue included seventeen very deep lots, running all the way from Kaye Road to the CPR boundary at the still-uncleared Trafalgar Street. Most of the lots were 66 feet wide, and all were 315 feet deep, almost three times the depth of a standard Vancouver lot. The earliest house built there, in 1912, occupied two of the 66-foot lots, at 6238 Macdonald. The house at 6350 followed, then the house at 6288.

The biggest of all the properties is the one-and-a-third-acre one above, at 6120 Macdonald, occupying three lots, with a frontage on Macdonald of 180 feet.[4] It was bought by George L. Smellie, the manager of the Canada Permanent Mortgage Corporation, who built a rather modest Georgian Revival house there in the spring of 1921. Smellie lived there until 1934; the next owner was John Crawford, the president of Macdonald Consolidated. The latter was a gardener, and probably laid out much of the parklike garden, with its lawns, orchard, herbaceous borders, and semi-wild woodlot. Its contemporary layout, retaining many of these old plantings, has been maintained since the early 1950s by the current owner, Arthur Ross.[5]

to the city, he enthused over the potential of the parking meter for relieving downtown traffic congestion (see *Province*, November 23, 1940) and then, as the Vancouver agent of the Dual Parking Meter Company of Oklahoma, sold the city 1,000 meters at seven dollars apiece. It being wartime, the shipment of the meters and the transfer out of the country of Canadian funds was halted by a federal import ban (*News-Herald*, February 6, 1941).

4 The northernmost of the three lots is only 48 feet wide, due to a road allowance along 45th Avenue.

5 Conversation with Joan Paterson, daughter of Arthur Ross, 1987.

The Stewart house in late November.

Another of the very fine properties on Block One of District Lot 2027 is the house built in 1920 for A.M. Stewart at 6200 Macdonald Street. It stands on one and a half of the block's big lots, with a frontage of about one hundred feet on Macdonald Street. This house, the one next door at 6190 Macdonald, and the Smellie house at 6120 Macdonald form one of the most dramatic streetscapes in the city — an almost English "manor house" scene, with the large houses set well back from the street behind hedges, and completely surrounded by the lush, west-coast urban forest. This mature combination of natural cedars and Douglas firs, combined with introduced species such as oaks, chestnuts, the two splendid copper beeches that flank the view of the house above, holly hedges, rhododendrons, and Virginia creeper, is the new "natural Vancouver landscape" — having gradually replaced the original forest over the past century.

"SHANNON"

The "Shannon" estate in the 1940s, looking north from a position above 60th Avenue. (Along the estate's near boundary is 57th Avenue; running towards downtown on its right-hand side is Granville Street.) Visible are the main house, the garage and outbuildings to its north (demolished), a fenced paddock for livestock, and its parklike grounds, since infilled with townhouses. Directly north of the line formed by the garage and outbuildings is a wooded quarter block that was not part of the estate — it was subdivided by the Canadian Pacific Railway and developed with housing in the late 1950s. The photograph shows the postwar bungalow housing on the blocks surrounding "Shannon," distinguishable from the 1920s and 1930s developments by the absence of trees. Also visible are some of the landmarks of old Vancouver: in the left middle distance, Quilchena Golf Course and the bushland that became the Arbutus Village development; in the right middle distance, Shaughnessy Golf Club; and in the centre distance just to the right of Burrard Bridge, the old Granville Street Bridge, demolished in 1954.

One of the largest estates ever completely landscaped in the City of Vancouver,[1] which has retained some of its original character to the present day, is B.T. Rogers's "Shannon," at Granville and 57th Avenue. In the 1970s, following the death of the estate's second owner, Austin Taylor, it was converted into a townhouse development; the main house and gatehouse survive, as does most of the surrounding stone wall, the front garden and rose garden, but the kindest thing that can be said for the new townhouses is that they are relatively unobtrusive, for they certainly do not blend with the Beaux Arts style of the old mansion and gatehouse.

Benjamin Tingley Rogers was a restless and adventurous man, who rarely was content for long with any possession, be it a car, a yacht, or a house. Such was the case with "Gabriola," his West End house completed in 1901 (page 70). Following an extended trip to England in 1911, he started to dream of building a large, semi-rural estate. He found the piece of property he

1 The Johnson-Von Alvensleben property at 41st and Blenheim in Kerrisdale, later owned by *Sun* publisher Robert Cromie and now Crofton House School, was originally about 20 acres, but much of that was probably bush; W.H. Malkin's "Southlands" (page 119) was about twelve and one half acres, but the northern part of it was bush, and nothing remains of the house or gardens today. There were larger estates elsewhere in the Lower Mainland, most notably Alfred St. George Hamersley's in North Vancouver (page 180), and A.J.T. Taylor's "Kew" on Marine Drive in West Vancouver.

The rose garden, to the south of the main house; the photograph looks east. The two children are Janey and Peter Cherniavsky, grandchildren of B.T. Rogers.

wanted on November 13, 1912, when he went with his friends "Puffy" Campbell and Richard Marpole — the latter being the western superintendent of the Canadian Pacific Railway — to look at a ten-acre block of land at Shannon Road (57th Avenue) and Granville Street, near the extreme southern end of the CPR's District Lot 526. There were very few houses south of 25th Avenue on Granville Street at that time; the area had been logged, and was starting to grow up again in vine maples, alder, and berry thickets. South of the Shannon Road was the dairy farm of William Shannon. The acreage was an excellent site for his dream estate, as the land fell away gradually to the south and west, offering panoramic views over the Fraser delta and the Gulf of Georgia. Late in November, 1912, he bought it.

A clearing crew went to work early in the new year, but Rogers did not sign the contract with architects Somervell & Putnam until November, 1913. Rogers, who was an adept gardener, began planting trees and arranging the garden before that Christmas, and early in 1914 Dominion Construction started work on the foundations. Mrs. Rogers's diary noted the progress on the estate they had come to call "Shannon": in early June, 1914, they gathered their first crop of strawberries; that autumn, they fenced part of the property for pigs and chickens; in December, they had a lamb, seven piglets, and a Jersey cow; the following spring, they hired a landscape gardener named Coles. As it was wartime, a labour force was difficult to obtain, so the actual construction went slowly. The garage was completed first, and its upstairs suite occupied as a "home away from home" early in 1917 by the two eldest daughters, Mary and Elspeth, who nicknamed it "Bohemia." By the spring of 1918, the exterior of the main house was finished, and Rogers had begun to plan the interior decoration with L. Alavoine & Company, a Paris firm with a New York outlet,[2] when he died suddenly on June 17. His ashes were placed in a vault in the rose garden on July 15, 1917 in a private service attended only by his widow, three older children, and sister Emma.

His widow had little desire to finish "Shannon." Family members have since speculated that her inaction was due to the fact that it was so much her husband's dream, and that she found it all a bit too grand and ostentatious — in her diary, she referred to the house as "the lodge." Nevertheless, while she continued to live at "Gabriola," she allocated money for staff to maintain and develop the beautiful gardens at "Shannon." Her diary notes the use she made of the grounds there: "The Strathearn Chapter's (I.O.D.E.) fete at 'Shannon' a huge success. The gate was almost rushed, and considerably over a thousand people were there. Elsie did splendidly at lavender stall. Receipts came to $950" (August 11, 1920); "Went to 'Shannon' to see the calf, born yesterday" (December 7, 1921); "Moore [the head gardener] reports fifty hens stolen" (February 10, 1921); "(Dame Nellie) Melba came to lunch, and I took her to 'Shannon,' gave her a big bunch of roses" (July 7, 1921). She finally prepared to finish and move to the estate after making the decision in January, 1925, to convert "Gabriola" into an apartment building (page 70). Over the next several months, with architect Bernard Palmer and Charles Bentall of Dominion Construction, she chose fixtures and decor to complete "Shannon."[3] With her three

2 From B.T. Rogers's private papers, cited in Schreiner, *The Refiners,* page 69.

''Shannon'' interiors, about 1930. (Top left) The main hallway, looking from the back of the house to the front door. The door on the left in the foreground leads into the dining room; the door on the right leads into the drawing room; the doorway on the right, one-third of the way down the hallway, leads into the great hall; in the distance, on the right, another doorway leads into the library. (Top right) The drawing room, with Jan Cherniavsky (a son-in-law of Mrs. Rogers) playing the piano. (Bottom left) The great hall, with its hideous Beaux-Arts decoration and flocked wallpapers, probably by the firm of L. Alavoine & Company of Paris and New York; the left doorway opens through into the drawing room; the right doorway opens onto the main hallway; the French doors on the left open onto the rose garden. (Bottom right) The dining room.

unmarried children, the oldest of whom was seventeen, Mrs. Rogers moved in on August 31, 1925.

"Shannon" in its heyday had a sizeable staff: indoors were a butler, cook, kitchen maid, upstairs and downstairs maids, and a laundress; outdoors were the head gardener, four or more assistants, and a cow man named Ozzie; as well, there was Hathway the chauffeur, who worked for Mrs. Rogers for almost forty years. The estate was a splendid venue for entertaining, sometimes for as many as 300 during garden parties for charity, including her favourite — the symphony. But Mrs. Rogers, who turned sixty-five years old in 1934, was losing interest in such an extensive property. In June, 1934, two doctors named Hatfield and Haywood came to tea "to discuss my proposition as to 'Shannon.'" Perhaps she thought to convert it into a hospital, although no one in the family has any recollection of this. Instead, she was approached in September, 1935, by the financier Austin Taylor, who purchased "Shannon" the following June for $105,600 — slightly less than ten times the annual property taxes. At that time, the total assessment of house and ten acres was $270,400. Mrs. Rogers moved to 3637 Angus Drive, where she lived for the rest of her life.[4]

3 Kate Reed, the CPR's interior decoration expert who had executed, among other commissions, the Empress Hotel in Victoria, visited Mrs. Rogers at "Shannon" on August 20; one wonders what impression she had of the interior furnishings and decoration seen in the photographs on these pages.

4 Information unless otherwise noted from *M.I.Rogers*, and from conversations with Mrs. E.H. Gudewill (Janey Cherniavsky), one of Mrs. Rogers's granddaughters, who spent part of her youth at "Shannon."

OAKRIDGE

The Vancouver Gun Club, on Oak Street near 45th Avenue, in the 1920s. The photograph looks north to the ''Oak Street ridge'' at 41st Avenue. The club eventually moved to a more remote location, at Number Five Road and Westminster Highway in Richmond, in the early 1950s.

Although the Oakridge area was only developed forty years ago, many of its original houses — and the Oakridge shopping centre — have already been demolished and replaced by more lavish ones. Development pressure is so strong in this part of the city that some of the luxurious houses built around 1960 are no longer considered to make the best use of their large lots and are thus prime targets for sale at "lot value." As in Kerrisdale, many houses built here in the last couple of years easily command prices above the million-dollar mark.

Before the Second World War, the Oakridge area was bushland — one of the last undeveloped sections of the Canadian Pacific Railway's 1886 land grant. Most people knew the area for the Vancouver Gun Club, opened in 1923 on the east side of Oak Street at 45th Avenue. Local parents had the club's gunshot to worry about, as well as the sewage-filled ditches in the area, which until the early 1950s was still on a septic tank system. A streetcar line ran along Oak Street between Marpole and Fairview; it had been established in 1910 to service the subdivision of the Eburne district south of the CPR's District Lot 526 boundary at Park Drive. By the late 1940s, it was reckoned to be the worst teeth-rattler in the entire B.C. Electric system, and pressure to replace the streetcar with buses, and the tracks and granite blocks with a paved road, grew after the end of the War.

As a preliminary to organized settlement, the area received the name "Oakridge" in January, 1949, and the first major building erected was appropriately at the Oakridge Transit Centre at

Looking north from 45th Avenue along Cambie Street in the early 1950s. The site of the Oakridge Shopping Centre, on the left, was still bushland (Howard Severson photograph).

41st and Oak Street, opened to serve the city's new trolley bus fleet. At that time, the area east of the Transit Centre was the abandoned parade ground of the Little Mountain army camp; to the west of Oak Street north of 41st Avenue was Shaughnessy Golf Course, now VanDusen Botanical Gardens.

Cambie Street was graded, but uninhabited from 33rd Avenue to 49th Avenue, and had not even been cleared from there to 63rd. Motorists driving south along Oak Street in 1950 found the road concrete-paved to 33rd Avenue, then asphalt-paved "so primitive a caveman could have done better," with six-inch-deep potholes pockmarking the road as far south as 41st Avenue. From 41st south to 57th Avenue the road was so dusty and bumpy that "no Saskatchewan road could be worse." It received a facelift in 1952.

Meanwhile, the Canadian Pacific Railway was developing a scheme for an Oakridge subdivision, on 276 acres bounded by Oak, Cambie, 41st and 57th avenues. The plan, announced on March 10, 1955, included a shopping centre "similar to West Vancouver's Park Royal," apartment blocks, single family homes, parks, a community centre, and school sites. Dead-end streets and crescents were designed to eliminate cross-traffic in the area. In May, 1957, eighty-foot-wide housebuilding lots went on sale, and were snapped up at an average price of $7,125. That July, construction began on the $10 million Oakridge Shopping Centre, with Woodward's as the major tenant.[1]

Oakridge opened on May 6, 1959, and brought the world of automobile-oriented mall shopping to the City of Vancouver. In the ensuing years, new malls opened throughout the region, and Oakridge lost its novelty and paled by comparison with the flashy "fashion malls" in downtown Vancouver. To recover its share of the marketplace, Oakridge's owners completely rebuilt and expanded the old mall, adding office space and multilevel parking garages; the new Oakridge opened in the autumn of 1984.

[1] Information and quotations from newspaper clippings by J.S. Matthews, "Oakridge" files, CVA.

MARPOLE

Marpole has a handful of impressive houses, and many blocks of more modest ones from the period before the 1930s. Perhaps more than any other area outside the neighbourhoods of east Vancouver, Marpole has been extensively redeveloped with garish, tile-roofed "Vancouver Specials." Developers have correctly perceived the area as desirable to new-home buyers, and have accordingly mowed down the comparatively low-priced older houses that lined the area's quiet streets.

J.M. McCallan's 1912 house at 8264 Hudson Street is one of the more impressive ones left in the area. The community generally known as Eburne Station — Marpole since 1916 — was separated from developing Shaughnessy and Fairview by miles of bushland; there was no transit system on Granville Street, but Eburne Station residents bound for downtown could catch the convenient Oak Street tram, or walk to Eburne Station itself, where the Vancouver-Steveston interurban stopped. In the old street system, Hudson Street for a time was called Bridge Road (because at its foot was the swingspan, built in 1901 and demolished in 1957, connecting Eburne Station with Eburne on Sea Island), and in 1912 was called 4th Street. The first address for McCallan's house, on its Point Grey water connection permit, was "East of 4th." A shopping district had developed near the foot of Bridge Road, but the area was too remote, in pre-automobile Vancouver, to benefit much from the 1908-13 building boom.

McCallan rented his house in 1920 to William Adams, who owned a hardware store at the corner of Hudson and Marine Drive; in 1926, he moved back, but in December, 1927, he agreed to rent the property to the newly formed Crippled Children's Hospital Society. The group had formed as a result of an appeal made in 1922 to the Women's Institute, seeking aid for a child named Othoa Scott of Hornby Island. There was little government involvement in, or feeling of responsibility for, health care at that time; thus, the Women's Institutes of British Columbia, under the direction of their provincial secretary, Mrs. C.S. MacLachlin, set out to raise money to provide specialized care for children. After a couple of failed attempts, the Central Park Women's Institute subscribed the basis of a fund — twenty-five dollars — and the other institutes soon joined in, raising money and disseminating information about crippled children in the province. By February, 1924, they had collected $1,303; meanwhile, children needing care were overflowing a ward in Vancouver General Hospital, and others were being attended to at Dr. F.C. McTavish's office in the Vancouver Block on Granville Street downtown.

One of the finest Colonial Revival houses in the city stood at 1591 South West Marine, just east of Adera Street. It originally occupied a five-acre piece of property purchased by William Charles Bunnett from George E. Magee in April, 1890. At some time between then and about 1910 this house was built, probably as the farmhouse for a small dairy operation. Mr. T.C. Usher, an employee of the Pacific Steel Works, lived in the house with his family after about 1915 (city directory information for that area, which was then "way out in the country," is almost non-existent before about 1920). The house was in a convenient location, as the Marine Drive crossing was the site of Townsend Station on the BCER interurban train system. Reduced eventually to a very large lot, the property was sold and subdivided in 1982; the house itself was moved by truck and barge to Lasqueti Island.

1591 SW MARINE VANCOUVER

M. KLUCKNER
1981-1985

In 1925, the women's group incorporated itself as a society, with Mrs. F.H. Barber as president, and in December, 1927, they rented McCallan's house on Hudson Street and converted it into a sixteen-bed hospital. Almost immediately, they began raising funds to build a permanent hospital, and in 1933 were able to erect the first unit of the present 100-bed building at 250 West 59th Avenue. Patients were transferred from the Hudson Street house that November.[1] McCallan's old house was converted yet again, this time into apartments.

In the modern Vancouver real-estate market, 8264 Hudson Street was not a historic building with heritage designation and protection from demolition: it is an old house on two duplex lots, one of which is on a desirable corner. The property was put on the market for $750,000, the advertisements appealing to "Builders" and noting the potential for subdivision of the property. A consortium of developers purchased the house with the intention of demolishing it and building two duplexes, but the city, responding to lobbying from the neighbourhood, stepped in and purchased it from the developers, then leased it to the Abbeyfield Housing Society for use as a seniors' housing project. When restored, it will provide housing for nine seniors and a housekeeper; the city will also build a "coachhouse" on the southeast corner of the lot, which will provide accommodation for nine more seniors.[2]

The city's first Children's Hospital, built in 1912 as the home of farmer J.M. McCallan, stands at the northeast corner of Hudson Street and 67th Avenue in Marpole. The watercolour was painted at the end of the memorable cold snap of February, 1989, by which time the sky had been blue for so long it had begun to fade in the sunshine, the grass had turned brown, and even the laurel hedges atop the stone walls were showing signs of frost damage. The stone walls, hedges, mature perennials, porte-cochère on the north (left) side, and the surrounding boulevard trees, all contribute to yet another classic Vancouver scene.

1 Information from a Children's Hospital handbill distributed at a Marpole Neighbourhood Network meeting in May, 1989.

2 *Vancouver Courier*, April 11, 1990.

FARMHOUSES

Vancouver and its environs used to be dotted with little farms, some producing vegetables for the local market, others milk or beef. The fertile soil along the Fraser River supported a great number of produce farms, while dairy operations were scattered more widely, the cows grazing amid the stumps and scrub of the growing city. The key to the success of such operations, in the days before portable refrigeration, was access to transportation, and many of the oldest roads in the Vancouver area were opened to link farmers with their customers. Kingsway, connecting Vancouver with New Westminster, was lined with dairy farms. Marine Drive was originally the McRoberts Trail, connecting McRoberts' farm called "Richmond" on Sea Island with New Westminster.[1] Both Granville Street and Fraser Street were cleared and opened due to the lobbying of Lulu Island farmers, whose efforts were also responsible for the construction of the Eburne and Granville Street bridges in 1889, and the Twigg Island bridge in 1894.[2] Another boon for farmers in the years just before the First World War was the B.C. Electric Railway's interurban system. Although most of the farms have vanished with scarcely a trace, it is still possible to pick out the network they formed and their transportation links around the city.

1 Thomas R. Weir, "Early Trails of Burrard Peninsula," *B.C. Historical Quarterly*, Vol. IX, No. 4 (October, 1945), page 274.

2 Richmond was incorporated in 1879. Its reeve, Thomas Kidd, sought the support of Vancouver city council and Mayor Oppenheimer for a request to the provincial government in 1888 for financing of the Eburne Bridge; Vancouver's cooperation included the erection of the first Granville Street Bridge, and the clearing of Granville Street from False Creek to the Fraser River. The erection of the Twigg Island or Number Five Road Bridge by James McGhie followed a similar request in 1892, by the farmers of east Richmond. See Ross, *Richmond, Child of the Fraser*, pages 54 and 56.

CVA BU. P.641

Looking northwest to what was then the oldest house in the city — Hugh Magee's much-renovated 1860s farmhouse, known as ''Spruce Grove,'' at 3250 West 48th Avenue, as it appeared in November, 1958, a few months before its demolition. It was then used as the office for the Hyland Barnes nursery.

An aerial view of the McCleery farm in the 1950s, shortly before its demolition, photographed from above the corner of South West Marine Drive and Macdonald Street. The 1873 farmhouse is the building just south of (above) the line of houses facing Marine Drive. The eleventh tee of McCleery golf course now occupies the house's site, and the prominent poplar trees visible in front of the house survive.

OLD MARKET GARDEN AT 57ST + BALACLAVA, VANCOUVER

1 Fort Langley dates from 1827, but it was a Hudson's Bay Company trading post, a semi-military operation that, like the Colony of Vancouver Island, did not encourage the intrusion of settlers.

2 Magee's sale in 1891 of the northern half of District Lot 321 to his solicitor, Francis Chaldecott, precipitated the first settlements in the Kerrisdale area — the 20-acre Byron Johnson property that is now Crofton House School, and the MacKinnon's "Kerrysdale."

3 Municipality of South Vancouver tax assessment rolls, 1893, CVA.

4 The cannery began to purchase water from the Municipality of Point Grey in April 1913, indicating that water mains were laid through DL 194 early in that year, probably in anticipation of subdivision and housebuilding.

The earliest settled part of the modern City of Vancouver is the Southlands flats, near the mouth of the Fraser River. Occupied since the mid-1860s, the area is only a few years younger than New Westminster, the first civil settlement by Europeans on the British Columbia mainland.[1] Fitzgerald and Samuel McCleery, Henry Mole, and Hugh Magee were the first farmers in the Southlands area now occupied by the Marine Drive, McCleery and Point Grey golf courses, and an equestrian enclave of semi-rural properties between Macdonald and Blenheim streets. Fitzgerald McCleery owned the 180-acre District Lot 315; his brother Samuel owned 182-acre DL 316 and 117-acre DL 317. Hugh Magee owned District Lots 194 and 321.[2] And Henry Mole owned District Lot 314, the area now occupied by Point Grey Golf Course, to the west of Magee's DL 194 (see map, page 7).[3]

Following Hugh Magee's death in 1909, portions of District Lot 194 were sold off, under the terms of his complicated will. One of the first of the new occupants was the Celtic cannery of the B.C. Packers' Association, on the riverfront east of the foot of Carrington Avenue, about 1911-12.[4]

The last vestige of the old market gardens on the Southlands flats, at the corner of 51st and Balaclava, looking north, in late March.

    A number of small properties split away in the 1920s and 1930s operated as nurseries and English-style "market gardens"; most have gone, the properties have been further subdivided and the cheaply built clapboard and stucco dwellings replaced by stables and the lavish, sprawling homes of Southlands' wealthy horse-owners.

    The watercolour shows the sole remaining piece of a market garden, at the southwest corner of 51st Avenue and Balaclava, preserved in its Wordsworthian state by the current owners, Mr. and Mrs. Lawrence Young. The field was established in the late 1920s by Mr. and Mrs. Archie Irwin, who planted the King Alfred daffodils and the fruit trees. Each February, the field is dotted with snowdrops, which as they fade are replaced in March by splendid drifts of daffodils. The Irwins sold daffodils to Superior Produce on West 41st Avenue in Kerrisdale, the venerable Chinese greengrocer that closed its doors and ceased business in the summer of 1989. Later in the summer, the fruit was picked and went to market, too. Although the fruit trees are now old and gnarled, the hosts of daffodils continue to thrive in the soft springtime air of this very English place, in its most English season.

1 As part of its agreement with the CPR's Vancouver & Lulu Island Railway, the BCER operated it, but the CPR built it. See Ewert, *The Story of the B.C. Electric Railway Company*, page 66.

2 1893 Assessment Roll for the Municipality of South Vancouver, CVA.

3 Chaldecott, born in Surrey, England, and the son of a physician, came to Vancouver in 1890 and bought 107 acres in the Municipality of South Vancouver, the north half of DL 321 from Hugh Magee, and a half interest in 50 acres in DL 2027 in Point Grey. He did all the legal work to obtain the charter of incorporation for the Municipality of South Vancouver. The meeting was held in the barn, he recalled, as it was near the corner and "I think the house was a little way off," probably across muddy fields, as it was early April. Information is from a letter he wrote to J.S. Matthews in 1948: from Matthews Add.Mss.54, file "South Van," CVA. Block 80 of DL 2027 was named Chaldecott Park by the Point Grey council; Chaldecott Road was an early name for King Edward Avenue.

4 Hastings Townsite had a western boundary of Nanaimo Street and a southern one of East 29th Avenue; see page 167.

5 W.H. Gallagher, in *Early Vancouver*, volume 3, page 168, CVA.

The old South Vancouver schoolhouse, which used to occupy the site of the Blue Boy Motor Hotel at Fraser and South East Marine Drive, photographed in 1912.

Although it is now one of the least prepossessing corners in the city, the junction of Fraser Street and South East Marine Drive is one of the most historically significant in the old Municipality of South Vancouver. It is the junction of the River Road — the trail cleared in the early 1860s by the McCleerys to connect the colonial capital, New Westminster, with the McRoberts farm on Sea Island and the Musqueam village of Mahly at the foot of Camosun Street — with the North Arm Road. The latter was cleared in 1875 to connect the Fraser River flats with the 1861 military trail that had become the Westminster Road and since 1913 has been called Kingsway. At the bottom of Fraser Street, in 1894, the Twigg Island Bridge was completed across the north arm of the Fraser River (it was dismantled in 1974). In 1907, the B.C. Electric Railway Company completed its interurban line between Eburne Station and New Westminster along the north side of the Fraser River.[1] Thus, the area at Fraser and Marine was strategically located for the transportation of farm produce to the urban areas of Vancouver and New Westminster.

The earliest surviving tax assessment roll for the area shows that a man named J.W. Lawson owned 166 acres of District Lot 313 to the west of Fraser Street; the land to the east, in District Lot 327, comprising properties varying in size between five and twenty-five acres, had a large number of owners.[2] In the early 1890s, some parcels were occupied and farmed, while others were just vacant land held for speculation.

One of the farmers there was Peter Cordiner, whose property extended south and east from the corner of the future Fraser Street and South East Marine Drive. In his barn, on April 10, 1891, a group of property owners in the rural area south of the Vancouver city boundary (16th Avenue) met to discuss the incorporation as a municipality of their area. The group included W.H. Rowling, a corporal of the Royal Engineers; J.W. Lawson; S.K. Twigge; a Mr. Campbell; Mr. Bodwell, whose holdings in the Mackenzie Heights area led to the naming of Bodwell Road, now West 33rd Avenue; William Shannon, the Cariboo freighter and dairy farm operator south of Shannon Road, now West 57th Avenue; Peter Cordiner; William Rowling; and Francis Millar Chaldecott, the group's solicitor, and the namesake of Chaldecott Park at the western end of King Edward Avenue.[3] At their next meeting, on April 29 at the Gladstone Inn at 2219 Kingsway, this group chose the name "South Vancouver." The vast area, including all of the land south of 16th Avenue and the Hastings Townsite, between Point Grey and Boundary Road, became a self-governing municipality the following April 13.[4]

Directly across River Road from Cordiner's barn, on the site of the Blue Boy Hotel, stood the old North Arm or South Vancouver school, built in 1886 for the handful of children within walking and rowing distance. It was the site of a meeting of local electors during the 1886 provincial election campaign.[5] Not long after the photograph on this page was taken, the little schoolhouse was moved south on Fraser Street to a spot between Marine Drive and the Twigg Island Bridge, where it served as the office for a meat packing firm. It has since been demolished.

CVA SCH. P.24

The old farmhouse at 8220 St. George Street survived for decades after the area had ceased to be agricultural. Built sometime around the turn of the century, it presided over what was likely a vegetable and produce operation on the Fraser River flats south of the old River Road. Not only was the soil there fertile, but transportation to market was relatively straightforward via the North Arm Road (Fraser Street), and later by the BCER's interurban line to New Westminster and Marpole. Before its demolition in April, 1989, for a "New Commercial Development," the house was a last reminder of the community of farms and the network of wagon roads, railway lines, and bridges along the Vancouver bank of the Fraser River that provided Vancouver with food and milk in the years before this area became industrial.

Early records of the house are scanty, as it was a mere farmhouse in the country. The 1912 *Goad's Atlas* shows the house, with land not yet subdivided to the west and unoccupied to the south; aside from a few other houses, the map shows the two local landmarks: the old North Arm School on the site of the Blue Boy, and the North Arm Road station of the B.C. Electric Railway at the foot of Fraser Street. The 1953 *Insurance Atlas of Vancouver* illustrates how industrial the area had become, and remains to this day: a sash and door factory on Kent Avenue; the Fletcher's and Gainer's meat packing plants, and the cattle pens of the B.C. Livestock Producers Co-operative at the bottom of Fraser Street; and the rolling mills of the Western Canada Steel Company to the west of St. George Street.

The house had gingerbread brackets identical to those on the 1900 Dixon house in Strathcona (page 90). It had its own well until 1919.[1] Probably the best illustration of what the property looked like in the early years of the century is the photograph overleaf of the bottom of Main Street.

The rear view of 8220 St. George Street, the oldest farmhouse in South Vancouver, in December, 1988, shortly before its demolition. The point-of-view of the watercolour is the lane south of Marine Drive and east of St. George Street, looking west. The few old stucco and clapboard houses around the farmhouse dated from decades later; all were surrounded by litter and junk cars, rats ran among the morning glory and blackberries, and a huge flock of starlings twittered and wheeled above the houses and roosted on the television antenna and willow tree.

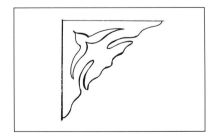

The gingerbread brackets on the porch posts at 8220 St. George Street.

1 South Vancouver water permit 0667, CVA.

The photograph looks in a southwesterly direction from the porch of the Grimmett house on East 64th Avenue, about a hundred yards east of Main Street, in May, 1911. Mrs. John F. Grimmett, her son Jack, and her daughter Grace are standing on 64th Avenue; in the background are the buildings that stood at the northeast corner of River Road (Marine Drive) and Main Street, including Boswell's Grocery and Hardware store. Beyond are the Chinese market gardens on the Fraser River flats and the river itself. The Grimmett house had a hipped roof and was painted white; it has since been demolished. The family were among the pioneers of that area, before the arrival of the single-track streetcar that terminated at the corner of Main and Marine, and operated "Grimmett's post office" on Main Street.

SOUTH VANCOUVER
AUTO CAMP
ON MARINE DRIVE
ABOUT 1 MILE EAST OF
FRASER ST.

An early auto-camp on South East Marine Drive, in 1926, looking south towards the Fraser River. The rural character of South East Marine Drive, with patches of bush separating the farms on the flat land and the shanties and docks along the riverfront from the encroaching city suburbs, remained until recent years. A few years ago, travellers eastbound along Marine Drive proceeded through southeast Vancouver and Burnaby into New Westminster along the escarpment above the Fraser River flats. Once past Boundary Road, South East Marine Drive became a winding, little two-lane road, and the houses flanking it were like the roadside country buildings of a forgotten corner of the province. Occasionally, views opened onto the Chinese vegetable gardens and patches of bushland below. Both South East Marine Drive in South Burnaby and the flats below were a backwater — an anachronism on the edge of the metropolis. The bank above the river in southeast Vancouver, where this auto-camp once stood, has recently been redeveloped with townhouses that, with fine views of the river traffic and the poplars and Richmond flats, have found a ready market.

THE AVALON DAIRY

LEE CROWLEY

Looking north in the 1920s across the Avalon Dairy's hayfields to the Crowley family house at 5805 Wales Street, built in 1908 and still standing today as the centrepiece of the dairy's operations.

1 Everett Crowley's lifetime of community service is commemorated in the park that bears his name, on the site of the old Kerr Street dump. His achievements included the organization of the Killarney Community Centre, terms on the parks board and the town planning commission, and the presidency of the B.C. Dairy Council and the South Vancouver Lions. His refusal to pay the $5 poll tax in a civic election earned him three days in jail, but the satisfaction of seeing the city drop the enabling by-law in 1950.

2 The most historically significant farm to be taxed out of existence was the McCleery's in Southlands, which fought a battle with the city for decades, finally capitulating in the 1950s. Taxes there rose from $413 in 1908 to $5,533 in 1923, three times what the farm's competitors were paying. The city wanted the property for a golf course, and finally got its way in 1954, when the Logan family — a daughter and son-in-law of Fitzgerald McCleery — sold the property.

3 Information about the Crowley family and Avalon Dairy from a promotional newspaper published in November, 1987, by Barb Nielsen and Rod Raglin of the *South Vancouver Review*, and from conversations with Lee Crowley.

One remaining piece of Vancouver's rural past is the Avalon Dairy on Wales Street just south of 41st Avenue. The oldest continually operating dairy in the province, Avalon Dairy got its name from Newfoundland's Avalon peninsula, the birthplace of Jeremiah Crowley. Lured west by news of the Klondike gold rush, Crowley arrived too late to profit from the diggings, but decided to bring his family west and settle in Vancouver. He and his family, eventually to include thirteen children, arrived in the city on March 17, 1906, and rented a house on Wales Street near Kingsway. Six cows came with the house, and Crowley was soon contemplating a career as a dairyman. He found a more attractive property, comprising two and one-half acres of District Lot 336 on Wales Street south of 41st Avenue, in an area of small farms, orchards, and bushland. In 1908 he started to build his farmhouse, which survives today, still with its long, tree-lined driveway, weeping willows, and board fencing — a pastoral scene amid the gaudy, barren "Vancouver Specials" of the surrounding streets.

As the years went by and the area became more settled, demand increased and Crowley's delivery routes expanded; by 1915 he owned thirty cows and was leasing pasture for them on the site of Norquay Park at Wales and Kingsway and on land surrounding Trout Lake. Gaily painted, horse-drawn carts and sleighs carried the milk through the streets; until 1916, when the company introduced bottles, milk was sold by the dipperful into any container the householder provided. The wagons and sleighs were replaced by trucks after the Second World War.

Jeremiah Crowley died in 1951, and the business was taken over by three of his sons, most notably Everett (1909-1984),[1] who had started developing milk delivery routes during the Great Depression when he lost his wage-paying job elsewhere. Nearly every food business — butchers, bakers, greengrocers, as well as dairies — delivered door-to-door, and the housewife truly spent her days in the house, but changing attitudes towards shopping, and post-Second World War prosperity and car ownership, gradually eroded the business of companies like the Avalon Dairy. Moreover, the city's policy of taxation of agricultural property made it very difficult for farms to survive,[2] and Crowley sold off his adjoining pastureland, choosing instead to have milk trucked in and bottled there. By the mid-1970s, when Everett Crowley and his brothers reached retirement age, it looked increasingly as though the dairy had outlived its time. However, the 1970s saw the return of neighbourhood shopping, the rise of the health food store, and a concern for conservation and recycling. Everett's son Lee took the company over, and has piloted it to a pre-eminent reputation among dairies. The company still markets its milk in bottles, and delivers it throughout the city to homes and stores. Although the raw milk is now delivered to Avalon Dairy in tanker trucks from the Fraser Valley, the property still has the air of a rural dairy. Even the front of the original 1906 barn is still standing.[3]

M. KLUCKNER
1988

Just north of the Avalon Dairy, at the corner of 41st and Wales, stands another reminder of South Vancouver's agricultural past. Sheltered by trees on its north and east sides, the old farmhouse there was built about 1913 for Samuel Gunning, the operator of a hardware store at 41st and Victoria Drive. It stands on a large piece of property owned since the 1950s by the First Lutheran Church, which has the intention of building a seniors' housing complex on the site and so has put little effort into this house's maintenance. Although in dilapidated shape, the house still retains its fine leaded glass and woodwork, and has an unusual hipped roof with bellcast eaves and dormers. It *could* be restored, and certainly there is enough land around it not to affect the density of any social housing complex that might share the property.

One of the many heritage issues yet to be properly addressed in Vancouver is the role and obligation of churches in the preservation of the city's history. On occasions such as this, where the church's intention to erect social or seniors' housing threatens to destroy a significant piece of the community's roots, it behoves them to consider whether heritage and social demands cannot be reconciled in such a way as to promote both. This should be especially so as the city has, at least in theory, a policy supporting the preservation of its heritage, and churches benefit from another of the city's policies — to allow religious institutions to occupy tax-free land. A recent example in North Vancouver, which illustrates the ambiguous attitude of church authorities towards community roots, was the desire of the elders and congregation of St. Andrew's Presbyterian (now United) at 10th and St. Georges to have their 1912 church designated as a heritage building; the bid was thwarted by the church's senior authority, the Vancouver-Burrard Presbytery. Besides its desire to preserve the church building, the congregation sought heritage designation in order to qualify for provincial heritage funds; the congregation was divided on the issue of accepting the funds, as they are the government profit from gambling (the lotteries). The Vancouver-Burrard Presbytery was opposed to designation evidently because of its difficulty preserving the designated Chalmers United Church at 12th Avenue and Hemlock in Vancouver.[2]

The 1913 farmhouse with the splendid wraparound porch at the corner of 41st and Wales is gradually subsiding into the landscape. The watercolour looks north from the rear of the property to 41st Avenue, in mid-November, 1988. At the time the house was built, the area was bushland dotted with little farms, including the nearby property for which the street was named, demolished a few years ago. The nearest transportation was the streetcar on Kingsway several blocks to the north; even 41st Avenue, now a busy crosstown through street, dead-ended a block east of Wales Street.[1]

1 *Goad's Atlas*, 1912, CVA.

2 Information from Cliff Green, a church member.

Looking south on Trafalgar Street, then known as Kaye Road, from about 18th Avenue, in 1912. Between the city boundary at 16th Avenue and the Kerrisdale community south of 37th Avenue, there was nothing except the Playfair house at 31st Avenue. The roadway was planked because the ground was so wet that gravel merely sank and, regardless, teams could not turn around in the mud off the roadway. The plank road soon rotted, but the roadway was eventually stabilized with fill from the Imperial Street sewer construction, which was dumped on top of the rotted planks. Visible in the distance on the hill, just south of 25th Avenue, is the original dirt road. Too steep for any practical use, it was rerouted along the line of today's Puget Drive. The flatland in the foreground, extending as far south as 25th Avenue, was built up as a ''trolley-bus suburb'' in the late 1930s.[1]

CVA STR. P.207

1 Photograph and information from W.B. Greig, the municipal engineer of Point Grey.

2 The real-estate agent was so certain that the house was only of interest for the lot on which it stood that he had not even bothered to prepare a sheet of taxes or utility consumption for the existing house.

3 Between the beach and the city boundary at 16th Avenue, the CPR's old Boundary Road had been renamed Trafalgar Street in 1907. Trafalgar Street's continuation south of the city boundary was called Kaye Road; at Wilson Road (41st Avenue), Kaye Road took a jog to the west. Its continuation to the south is today known as Macdonald Street.

The oldest building in Mackenzie Heights was the fine, two-and-a-half-storey Craftsman house that stood at 4707 Trafalgar — the southwest corner of Trafalgar and 31st Avenue — behind a tall laurel hedge. Built in 1911-12, and connected to the Municipality of Point Grey's new water mains in April, 1912, the house had a commanding view over the vast, empty Canadian Pacific Railway lands to the northeast, and the bush to the north, undeveloped all the way to the distant rooftops of Kitsilano. The view from any of the three floors was panoramic — in 1987, it was possible to see with one turn of the head through 180 degrees, from Point Atkinson in the northwest all the way around to Point Grey School in the southeast. The house was very solid structurally, and the exterior was in excellent condition; some shoddy renovations had been started in the interior, and the wood floors had not been maintained, but the magnificent interior panelling, pocket doors, and built-in fixtures were all intact. The old kitchen had been replaced by a modern one, connected by French doors to a sundeck. It was not an old wreck waiting to fall down; its doom lay in the fact that it stood on two legal lots. It sold for "lot value" at the beginning of 1988 and was demolished, and two houses were built on the site.[2]

Trafalgar Street was the CPR lands' western boundary, and at that time that stretch was known as Kaye Road;[3] the house's first address was "west of Kaye." It would have been a very isolated house in the spring of 1912, and difficult for the owners to reach in muddy weather

VIEW OF HOUSE FROM TRAFALGAR STREET, JUST SOUTH OF 31ST AVENUE.
JANUARY, 1988

4707 TRAFALGAR STREET

VANCOUVER

1912 – 1988

DINING-ROOM
FIREPLACE
AND
BUILT-IN
SIDEBOARDS.
OTHER FIREPLACES
IN DEN
+ BASEMENT.

BEVELLED
& LEADED GLASS
WINDOW
ILLUMINATING
MAIN
STAIRCASE

M. KLUCKNER

on the steep hills. Probably they owned a car, but it would have been useless in the wintertime. The nearest transportation was the Bodwell Road (33rd Avenue) stop of the interurban railway, several blocks to the east on the other side of a steep dip into "Consumption Hollow."

The water application for the house was signed by Harriet S. Playfair, but there is no one named Playfair in any city directory of that period. A later resident, between 1916 and 1925, was John Reginald Davison, the manager of the Vancouver Publicity Bureau. Born in Florence, Ontario, he moved to Alberta in 1907 and spent several years in publicity work with the Alberta Development League before moving to Vancouver in 1913. He was appointed industrial commissioner for the city, "responsible to publicity campaigns. During the war, together with his associates of the Industrial Bureau, (he) succeeded in bringing to Vancouver and districts a high class of settler, and has developed the tourist traffic to one of large proportions."[4] He quit his job in 1925, following "bitter opposition from certain quarters in the city," and returned to Toronto.[5]

4 Who's Who and Why, 1921 edition, page 1550.

5 Obituary published in local newspapers on February 16, 1945. Information on his ups and downs as Vancouver publicity manager are in the J.S. Matthews news clippings in CVA.

The old Craftsman house at 2880 West 28th Avenue, just east of Mackenzie Street, on the steep slope of Mackenzie Heights. The watercolour looks south, and was painted in the middle of the cold, sunny February of 1989; the low sun could not reach the hard frost on the north-sloping portions of the lawn.

Like its nearest early neighbour at 4707 Trafalgar, the large, beautifully built Craftsman house at 2880 West 28th had a spectacular view to the north and east — in the easterly direction, it was possible to see over the treetops of distant Shaughnessy even from the bay window of the dining room (at the rear of the house in the watercolour), as no building ever occupied the sideyard.

Built early in 1912, probably for a man named J.T. Stephenson of Red Deer, Alberta, it stood on a triple lot on the cleared but vacant Mackenzie Heights hillside. It was a house in a location that required an automobile for easy access — a suburban house, rather than a farmhouse, from which the owner went to work elsewhere. The nearest public transportation was about a mile away: either the streetcar line on Dunbar or the interurban east of "Consumption Hollow." In 1912, 28th Avenue did not exist between Cambie and Macdonald streets, and this house was the first one on its continuation to the west.

By comparison with craftsmanship in this era of housewrap and nail guns and imitation-brick veneer, the quality and scale of construction of a *Craftsman* house such as this boggles the imagination. Visible in the watercolour are the heavy, hexagonal-cut granite foundations, and the semi-circular windows underneath the porch, typical of expensive houses of the time. Every piece of wood was massive and solid, and even the decorative brackets between the walls, porch posts and roofs were several inches thick. The living-room fireplace was faced with hand-painted tile, and there was extensive use of leaded glass in windows and doors. All of the matériel had to be brought to the site by horsedrawn wagon, up the steep hills on dirt roads.

In the mid-1930s, 2880 West 28th was purchased by Gordon Wood Scott (1893-1966), a lawyer who was the assistant city prosecutor. A controversial and outspoken advocate of law enforcement, he returned to private legal practice in 1938, but resumed public service in 1948, when he was hired as city prosecutor; subsequently, he became magistrate in 1953 and senior magistrate in 1962. During his career, he fought with Mayor McGeer over the need for inquiries into police activities, prosecuted stores for violating the Wednesday closing by-law, and at various times recommended jail as "shock treatment" for juvenile delinquents.[1] He quit in 1965 when he was denied either a raise or a pension, and died the following year.[2]

Following his death, the house remained in the family, but no maintenance was done on it for years. By early 1989, every bit of paint on the front porch was peeled and curled; even the furnace had broken down, and the house had about it an abandoned air.[3] With its spectacular view, it was a desirable commodity and sold quickly to a developer, who demolished it in the spring of 1989 and built three houses, each with four bathrooms and a nanny suite, on the three lots (the old house had occupied one-half — the western one — of the old triple lot). When asked about the intrinsic value of the old house, the developer said that he had bought it for $800,000, and because of its condition it was uneconomic to restore: "People had walked all over the hardwood floors wearing golf spikes," he said. He also claimed that city hall would not guarantee the permits necessary to complete a restoration.[4] The question is purely academic now, but perhaps it could have been restored, the restoration financed through a bonus that would have added density onto the sideyard, *if* the city and surrounding neighbours had recognized the house's historical value to the neighbourhood and had been willing to bend the rules to ensure its preservation. However, the Vancouver real-estate mentality, supported by city zoning, taxation and permit-approval practices, ensures that it is only the view and the location that are valuable. The specific case of this house demonstrates that preservation is not necessarily always straightforward; unlike the house at 4707 Trafalgar, this one was in terrible condition, and no building in the Vancouver climate can survive the prolonged indifference of its owner.

• • •

At about the same time as the houses at 2880 West 28th Avenue and 4707 Trafalgar Street were under construction, the Convent of the Sacred Heart was nearing completion in the bush a dozen blocks to the west. The photograph below shows the unfinished state of the roads and the partially cleared vacant lots that were characteristic of much of Vancouver in the years just before the First World War. At the time of the photograph, a logging camp employing forty men was operating near the corner of 29th and Dunbar, a block to the east of the photographer.[5]

The convent was built by the Religious of the Sacred Heart, a Catholic educational order modelled on the Jesuits, which had been founded in France in 1800 by Saint Madeleine Sophie Barat, and operated as a girls school. It was one of several such convents in North America; elsewhere in Canada, the order operated schools in Winnipeg, Montreal and Halifax. Its location, and the multi-acre property surrounding it, allowed the sisters to develop a small farm, playing fields, and winding paths through its own forest. The convent building itself was a superb edifice in the Gothic Revival style, designed by the Seattle architect Charles G. Badgley and erected by a Seattle-based contractor.[6] Its 300-foot-long façade of granite and terra cotta is four storeys high for much of its length, with a five-storey central tower. The corner stone of the building is

1 See the news clippings by J.S. Matthews, "G.W. Scott" file, in CVA.

2 Obituaries published in Vancouver newspapers on August 22, 1966.

3 One of the residents, when asked how she felt about leaving a house that had been in her family for fifty years, replied, "Oh, it's a lot easier now that the place is falling apart."

4 See "A Very Fine House," by Nancy Knickerbocker, *Heritage Canada* magazine, Summer, 1989.

5 Municipality of Point Grey water records, in CVA.

6 *Vancouver Heritage Inventory Summary Report*, page 61.

Looking west on Buckland Avenue (now West 29th Avenue) from Alma Road in 1912, at the Convent of the Sacred Heart as it neared completion. The forest in the distance is the University Endowment Lands. The house in the left distance, at the modern address of 3954 West 29th Avenue, was evidently built by a Mr. Gosse around 1910; in 1930, it became the first St. George's School.

CONVENT OF THE SACRED HEART, VANCOUVER

dated 1911, and the convent celebrated its anniversary each year early in May. Even a decade after it was built, the convent's location was sufficiently isolated that it could be threatened by a forest fire: in July, 1919, a fire devastated 500 acres in the vicinity, before being brought under control by backfilling along Sasamat Street.[7]

As the years passed, fewer women were interested in a religious life, and it became more difficult to continue to operate and maintain the Convent of the Sacred Heart. The sisters made plans to close the convent and school, and late in 1978 announced that it had sold the building and its grounds to St. George's,[8] the private Anglican boys school that had been founded in 1930 in a converted house a block to the west. The latter announced that it would use the old building, its outbuildings, and grounds as its junior school, and sell off a three-and-one-half-acre block of the old convent property, bounded by Crown, Wallace, 29th and 30th,[9] presumably to finance the purchase. The final class of girls graduated from the Convent of the Sacred Heart in June, 1979.

The old building had more than its share of maintenance problems, including leakage in its concrete-tile roof[10] and the need to refinish its terra cotta and granite façade, as well as

7 *Sun*, July 16, 1919.

8 *Province*, December 22, 1978.

9 Ibid.

10 A replacement about twenty years ago of the original slate roof.

M.KLUCKNER 1990

The old Convent of the Sacred Heart, now in use for the junior grades of St. George's school, at 3851 West 29th Avenue in Dunbar.

operational problems, most stemming from the school's use of a building that had been designed as a convent. In the summer of 1989, St. George's school engaged the architect Robert Lemon to assess the building and to examine options for the school's long-term future. His report, which was given added urgency by the San Francisco earthquake of October, 1989, pointed out that the building was extremely poorly built — being constructed of load-bearing clay bricks with little reinforcing. The combination of construction materials and the building's long, narrow, and tall shape would likely perform very badly in almost any earthquake.

Lemon developed three options for the school to consider. The least expensive was to upgrade the building seismically and restore its façade and roof, and while so doing to reconstruct the interior bearing walls and partitions in such a way that would improve the operational efficiency of the school. A more expensive option was to raze the old building and erect a new school on the site, which would give the school the most efficient and modern operation possible but might undercut the school's reputation as an upholder of traditional values and community continuity. The most expensive option was to build an entirely new school behind the historic façade.[11] At this writing, no decision has been made.

11 Conversations with Robert Lemon, and with construction company president Stanley Wales of the school's building committee, in April, 1990.

3517 W. 30TH VANCOUVER

M.KLUCKNER
SEPT. 88

The real-estate speculator Charles Trott Dunbar, born in Newport, Rhode Island, in 1861, had a background in real estate and stocks in St. Paul, Minnesota, in the boom years there in the 1880s.[2] He moved to British Columbia in 1889, but according to city directories lived here only sporadically over the ensuing twenty-five years. His longest-term residences were at 839 West Hastings and in the Hotel Vancouver.

1 Charles Henry Wilson, Add.Mss.54, "Wilson" file, CVA. The original line branched southwest off the Tenth Avenue hill onto Crown, east on 16th, then south on Dunbar to 41st.

2 *Who's Who and Why*, 1913 edition, page 214.

Dunbar Heights, like many other Vancouver districts, was a real-estate speculation. Each district is distinct, but all have shared a similar fate — they have never been completed in the consistent way that was intended, due to Vancouver's roller-coaster economic fortunes. Even First Shaughnessy is dotted with cheap stuccoed bungalows from the 1940s and 1950s.

Dunbar Heights was the brainchild of C.T. Dunbar, a speculator in mines, timber, and real estate. He used his accumulated capital, and the opportunity presented by the booming real-estate market of the years before the First World War, to buy up undeveloped land on the western side of the city, and to pay the B.C. Electric Railway Company $35,000 in 1913 to run a streetcar line into the area.[1]

The house illustrated above, at 3517 West 30th Avenue, and the one to the west at 3537 West 30th, were built on hundred-foot-wide double lots after the First World War, several years after the abandonment of the original subdivision promotion. Property was cheap, and these suburbanites bought such big lots to maximize the size of their gardens. The latter house, built in 1919 for M.G. Haigler, is a fine Craftsman in the Swiss Cottage style, with granite foundations, a granite boundary wall, and a cottage garden occupying the entire front yard — it survives today in excellent condition (see page 31). Unfortunately, the same cannot be said for the house above, an interesting transition between the Craftsman and the Tudor Revival styles, built in 1923 for the Elliott family. It was not well maintained in recent years, and was sold for about $600,000 in October, 1988, and demolished the following spring. A very large house now occupies each of the fifty-foot lots created from the original property.

GRANDVIEW

Grandview is similar to Dunbar Heights in that it is a hodge-podge of the old and the new, the well-built and the shoddy. But Grandview, the older district, attracted, in addition to the speculative builders, a number of wealthy individuals who built very fine houses in the area, including the Odlum house on Grant Street and J.J. Miller's "Kurrajong" on Salsbury Street. All have been converted either to suites or institutional purposes such as private hospitals. One of the finest remaining from that period is the William Miller house at 1020 Semlin Street, designed and built by the firm of Beam and Brown and connected to the city's water system in April, 1909. In use since the early 1920s as the St. Francis Friary, the house has been drastically altered since its erection.

The photograph above shows the house in about 1915,[1] when all its decoration was intact. Since that time, the entire wraparound front porch has been filled in with brick and windows, obliterating the splendid grouped columns. The curved gable screens on the third floor have been removed, and the decorative cresting is gone from the roof line. Only the precast concrete balusters on the two staircases and the interesting fence survive.

1 From the anonymous booklet *Beautiful Homes*, Und-831, in CVA. The booklet identifies the house as the residence of Thomas Evans, whereas directory information of the period shows it to have been occupied by its original owner — the realtor Miller. Evans lived nearby at 1859 Napier Street, a fine house that still stands behind its stone wall; he was one of the best-known printers in the city, having founded the firm of Evans & Hastings, and served as an alderman in 1913-14.

(Left) James Henderson Falconer, the general manager of the British Columbia Vinegar Works, lived in the house at 1848 Venables Street. Born in Scotland in 1867, he came to Canada in 1885, and was first employed in a vinegar company in Toronto. Five years later, he moved west and established a vinegar factory in Victoria, but was lured away by the Klondike gold rush and spent ten years as a merchant and manager of a soda works and wood business in Bennett and Dawson. Upon his return to Vancouver, he established the B.C. Vinegar Works, "manufacturers of vinegar, sweet apple cider, boiled cider, apple syrup, pectin and evaporators of apples and apple waste, pickles, sauces, ketchups, high-class dills and sauerkraut."

(Right) At 2036 Kitchener Street lived Lieut.-Col. John Weightman Warden, D.S.O., O.B.E., a distinguished veteran of the First World War. Born in New Brunswick in 1871, he apprenticed to a piano manufacturer in Boston until the outbreak of war in South Africa prompted him to volunteer for service. Subsequently, he joined the South African Constabulary, remaining there until 1906, when he moved to Vancouver and joined the staff of the Moortelius Piano Company as a salesman. Two years later, he jumped on the real-estate and insurance bandwagon, and worked as a salesman until the boom market collapsed in late 1914. War having been declared, he volunteered for service, was given command of "A" Company of the 7th Battalion of the Canadian Expeditionary Force, and went overseas with the first Canadian contingent. For his service on the Somme, he was awarded the D.S.O. (Information from Who's Who & Why, 1921 edition, pages 130 and 496.)

THE HARRIS HOUSE

1 During the First World War, Bismarck was renamed Kitchener.

2 The house at 1230 Lakewood was purchased before it was completed by a bricklayer named Arthur Gibbons, who subsequently lived there; since Ball's name does not appear on any of the documents relating to this house, it is speculation that he built it.

The eight almost identical builders' houses on Lakewood Drive south of Williams Street were built in 1909 and 1910 by two local carpenters. The four to the north (nearest the photographer) were completed in October, 1909, by a man named Storer J. Wing, who lived nearby at 1570 Bismarck Avenue.[1] The four houses to the north, numbered 1230, 1236, 1242, and 1248, were erected by a contractor and builder named James Ball, who lived just up the street at 1400 Lakewood Drive.[2] Of the eight houses, the one second along in the photograph, with a street address of 1210 Lakewood, has remained intact to the present day, faithfully preserved since 1918 by its owners, the Harris family.

KITCHEN OF HARRIS HOUSE, 1210 LAKEWOOD DRIVE

M. KLUCKNER 1990

The watercolour shows the kitchen of the Evelyn Harris house at 1210 Lakewood Drive, unchanged since 1919, when her father, Harford Harris, installed the Enterprise Monarch stove at a cost of $105. Visible on the stove's far side is the three-burner gas range installed soon after. Harris, his wife Viola, and two older children moved to Vancouver from Edmonton in May, 1919, and bought this ten-year-old house for $3,125. Harris was a barber, and owned a shop on Granville Street. His younger daughter Evelyn remained at home with her parents, eventually taking over the house when her parents died. In the years since, she has maintained it in its original condition; her efforts were recognized with a City of Vancouver heritage award in 1989.

Looking north on Commercial Drive to First Avenue about 1915. The old Grandview Theatre is advertising one of Mary Pickford's most famous potboilers — the first version of "Tess of the Storm Country" (when her career showed signs of flagging in the early 1920s, she remade it, again taking the starring role). The three buildings south of First Avenue survive to this day, although each has been modified. Vanished since the photograph was taken are the Vancouver-New Westminster interurban electric trains, one of which is visible in the left distance heading towards downtown, and the Canadian Bank of Commerce building with the prominent chimney at the northeast corner of First and Commercial. The vertical battens on that building indicate that it was a B.C. Mills, Timber & Trading Company prefabricated structure (page 19) — the Canadian Bank of Commerce was one of the BCMT&T's best customers, and bought so many bank buildings that the latter kept a stock of them in its warehouse.[1] Although this building has been demolished, there is another BCMT&T prefab — a model "LLL" house — still standing just behind the bank building site on East 1st Avenue.

The Grandview Heights hospital at 1090 Victoria Drive, as it appeared about 1918. The house in the background is the Queen-Anne-style Hawkins house at 1020 Victoria Drive; Hawkins later built and moved to the similar but more elaborate house at 1927 West 17th Avenue (see page 112).

1 Claude Douglas, "The Prefabricated Search Is On," *Heritage West* magazine, Winter, 1983.

6 VICTORIA DRIVE, VANCOUVER

M.KLUCKNER 1988

The commencement of the Westminster & Vancouver Tramway Company's interurban railway service in 1891 opened Grandview and Cedar Cottage to suburban development. But an economic depression during the middle years of that decade stalled all such activity, so that it was the turn of the century before housing began to appear around the Trout Lake area. One of the first residents to settle there was "Jack" Unwin, who, in March, 1899, purchased seven narrow lots in Cedar Cottage on Block 11 of District Lot 195 from Charles G. Major. At today's address of 3556 Victoria Drive, he built a charming little Vancouver Box which survived until 1990. The location was strategic because of its proximity to the interurban line and the easy access provided by train (at the Lakeview Station, a block to the southeast), as well as the nearby "Number Four" streetcar to the Commercial Drive shopping area and downtown Vancouver. Jack Unwin had been a storekeeper on *Empress* liners before becoming the assistant janitor at City Hall. His sudden death from heart failure at the age of forty-eight, leaving a wife and four children, attracted newspaper attention.[1] Ironically, the proximity of his house to the interurban's successor, the noisy SkyTrain, was to seal its fate, as the area promptly lost favour with most home-owners.

After being on the market for over a year, the house and the little infill bungalows to the north of it were sold, boarded up, and demolished early in 1990, to make way for a provincial government-sponsored social housing project. The project's budget did not allow for proper restoration of the house. While the construction of social housing is commendable, especially under the circumstances of Vancouver's housing market in 1990, it is also regrettable that the provincial and city governments — which claim to support the preservation of heritage — did not avoid the destruction of an old house listed on the city's heritage inventory by finding the money to incorporate it into the new project.

The Unwin house, on Victoria Drive just north of the SkyTrain right-of-way, was built at the turn of the century on newly subdivided land south of Trout Lake. It was an interesting little cottage, in a style combining some of the elements of the earlier Queen Anne style, such as the fish-scale shingles in the front gable and the ornate porch brackets, but with the symmetrical layout and simple lines of the developing Vancouver Box style. A number of the houses from that period in Strathcona, such as the one on page 90, were similar. The watercolour, painted in the summer of 1988, shows the house in considerable disrepair — it had not been painted for probably forty years, and even its main chimney had been removed. The elevated SkyTrain guideway is about fifty yards to the south — to the right in the watercolour.

1 *Province*, September 26, 1913.

CVA BU. P. 6

The man who put the Municipality of South Vancouver back on its fiscal feet was Francis Joseph Gillespie, who was close to retirement age when the provincial government, which had dismissed the elected council and police, asked him to become commissioner on May 1, 1918. A former schoolteacher and school trustee from Ontario, he had been a reeve, county commissioner and warden, and an employee of the grain dealer W.D. Matthews & Company, before moving to Vancouver. His major occupation was as provincial manager for the Excelsior Life Insurance Company. He had four sons and three daughters, and lived at 1323 Burrard Street.[1]

The stump house, at 4230 Prince Edward Street in the old Municipality of South Vancouver, was an extreme example of the kind of unplanned, "pioneer" development that, in the first instance, prompted the secession movement in the western half of the municipality, creating in 1908 the Municipality of Point Grey; and, in the second instance, kept property values low and attracted settlers who were often unable or unwilling to pay taxes for municipal improvements. The result was the bankruptcy of the municipality in 1918, due to its default on a bond issue, and the seizure of the municipality's administration by the province, which placed F.J. Gillespie in charge as a one-man government.

The stump house was reached by a short trail through the forest running north from Horne Road, now East 28th Avenue. It was built around 1910 by a man named Berkman. The notches in the large stump are for the springboards used as a sawing platform by the lumberjacks. The entire lower stump was kitchen; the lower part of the large stump was living room, above which was a doorless bedroom, reached by a ladder.

1 *Who's Who in Canada*, 1930-31 edition, page 260.

LES & 29TH AVE. VANCOUVER

M. KLUCKNER
1989

Some intersections, such as the one above at 29th and Earles in East Vancouver, manage to communicate visually that they are significant junctions for transportation systems. In the modern city, buses servicing this part of East Vancouver leave from the 29th Avenue SkyTrain station, a block to the west (right) of Earles Road. The area has been a transportation crossroads for eighty-five years, as indicated by the number of old wooden houses around the site of the "Earl's Road" interurban stop, established by the B.C. Electric Railway in 1904. It had the added attraction of being in the Municipality of South Vancouver, where taxes (when collected at all) were low, and building restrictions few. It first attracted the interest of an organized development company in February, 1908, when E.J. Clark, Christie & Company announced the opening of a subdivision, to be called Earlsville, at the "Earl's Road" station. The firm advertised 112 lots at prices starting at $200; according to the advertisement, all were less than a five-minute walk from the station. "Remember," it noted, "you don't have any bridges to cross to get to Earlsville."[1] North of 29th Avenue and east of Nanaimo Street was Hastings Townsite, a better-organized community that voted in 1910 to join the City of Vancouver, and thus to accept its higher taxes in return for better services. South Vancouver only voted to join Vancouver in 1929.

The oldest house in the area is probably the one on the left of the watercolour, at the southeast corner of 29th and Earles, with a street address of 3018 East 29th Avenue. The property it stands on was owned by a realtor named William O. Shrum of the firm Shrum and Lambert; he sold it in 1911 to a man named Scobey. Because of the style of the house, it is a reasonable assumption that Shrum had it built sometime around 1908, and the launching of "Earlsville." Houses such as this are rare in the area, as it was somewhat remote and industrial; one local landmark, dependent on the rail link, was the Vancouver Pipe and Foundry Company, which had its own spur line and stood on land to the southeast of the station, behind the Earles Road substation in the distance. Another indication of the area's isolation was the Isolation Hospital, occupying the blocks bounded by Kaslo, Slocan, 18th, and 21st avenues.[2]

The corner of 29th Avenue and Earles Street, looking south towards the old B.C. Electric substation and the SkyTrain line. Twenty-Ninth Avenue was the southern boundary of the old Hastings Townsite — thus, the houses in the watercolour were built in the Municipality of South Vancouver.

1 *Province,* February 14, 1908.
2 *Goad's Atlas,* 1912 edition, CVA.

BURNABY

The most significant enclave of historic buildings in Burnaby is on the south shore of Deer Lake, preserved and incorporated into the municipality's artistic and administrative centre. Its peaceful, sylvan setting is as attractive today as it must once have been for the wealthy, semi-retired Henry Tracy Ceperley and his neighbours. The area began to open up for suburban settlement in March, 1911, with the inauguration of the B.C. Electric Railway's Burnaby Lake line;[1] around that time, Ceperley completed "Fairacres," his magnificent stone and timber Tudor mansion on the gently sloping grounds above Deer Lake.

Ceperley was sixty years old when he moved to Burnaby. Born in Oneonta, New York, in 1851, he worked as a schoolteacher until 1875, when he decided to move west; he lived for a time in Minnesota and worked as a produce agent, then went to New Mexico as a cashier and bookkeeper, and finally lived in Montana as a cattle rancher, at the end of the storybook period of the American "wild west." Conforming to the popular image of a rancher, Ceperley was "cast in heroic mould, being six feet and three inches in height and weighing two hundred and forty pounds."[2] In Montana, he began to sell real estate, and when he came to Vancouver in 1886, having heard of the property boom in the newly incorporated city at the end of the transcontinental railway, he quickly became one of its leading property and insurance brokers.[3] Founded in 1887, his business was originally called Ross and Ceperley,[4] and in addition to selling real estate acted as Vancouver agent for a number of English and Scottish insurance companies. Ceperley's other significant interest was Vancouver's first street-railway company, of which he was secretary. In the summer of 1889, Ceperley and his partners made the fateful decision to establish a street railway using electrical power, rather than horsepower.

A barn to hold fifty horses was under construction at the corner of Main and East First Avenue in Vancouver, until Ceperley wrote in a letter to James Garden, the supervising engineer: "See the contractors for the barn and have them stop all work as regards interior arrangements until further orders as we will probably change to electricity, and will not need the stalls."[5]

In 1910, at the time Ceperley was building "Fairacres," he retired from active involvement in his firm, by then known as Ceperley, Rounsefell & Company. He stayed involved with the real-estate business as general manager of the British America Development Company, and retained the presidency of the Vancouver Milling and Grain Company, of which he was one of the organizers and incorporators.[6] He lived at "Fairacres" through the First World War years, but by 1921, when he was seventy years old, city directories listed his address as the Vancouver Club on Hastings Street. He and his wife are the namesakes of Ceperley Park, between Second and Third beaches on English Bay.

The house sold in 1922 to former Vancouver mayor Frederick Buscombe, who in the late 1920s proposed converting it into a "haven of rest for aged invalids" as a memorial to his son, who had been killed in the Great War. The province did not act upon his suggestion, or to a subsequent one in 1933 to convert the house into a tuberculosis sanatorium. In 1935, "Fairacres" was bought by Britannia Mines superintendent Alex Munro; he sold it four years later for $13,000. In 1940, along with the nearby house of W.J. Mathers and their combined twenty-two acres of grounds, "Fairacres" became the Seminary of Christ the King and the Westminster Priory of St. Joseph. In 1954, the house became the property of the Canadian Temple of the Universal Foundation of More Abundant Life. Finally, in 1966, the Municipality of Burnaby bought the buildings as its centennial project, and "Fairacres" opened the following year as the Burnaby Art Gallery.[7]

1 Officially known as the "Fourth District," the Burnaby Lake line branched away from the older Vancouver-New Westminster Central Park Line at 6th Avenue and Commercial Drive, and looped northeast until it reached First Avenue. It then proceeded east along First almost to Boundary Road, from whence it travelled in a southeasterly direction, more or less along the modern right-of-way of the "401" freeway between Deer and Burnaby lakes; at about Cariboo Road it headed south, still on its private right-of-way, and connected to Columbia Street and downtown New Westminster. The Burnaby Lake station provided easy access to the houses along Deer Lake. The line ceased operation in October, 1953. See Ewert, *The Story of the B.C. Electric Railway Company*, pages 94 and 276.

2 Howay and Scholefield, *British Columbia From The Earliest Times to the Present*, Volume III, pages 30-33.

3 *Who's Who and Why*, 1913 edition, page 135.

4 His partner, A.W. Ross, had connections with the Canadian Pacific Railway, and was the "CPR member of parliament" for the railway town of Lisgar, Manitoba. As a member of parliament, he was one of the influential lobbyists for the establishment of Stanley Park.

5 Document number Pho.2, CVA.

6 Howay and Scholefield, op.cit., page 33. His daughter Ethelwyn married J.E. Hall, who became the managing director (see page 88).

7 John Adams, quoted in "Heritage Houses Well Preserved," *Province*, January 20, 1980.

The Ceperley mansion at Deer Lake in Burnaby, photographed about 1914.[9] A magnificent gable-roofed example of the English Arts and Crafts style, it has the "Country Life manor house" look and, unlike most other examples of the style in the Lower Mainland, the expansive grounds to match. The photograph is from the southeast, and shows the rear of the house. Modern modifications to it include the raising of the hexagonal corner turret to the full height of the house, the removal of the iron conservatory, and the addition of a wooden fire escape from the second-storey balcony.

Henry Tracy Ceperley[10]

On the hillside overlooking the old mansions of Deer Lake is one of the few doomed historical landmarks of the Lower Mainland over which few will weep: the Oakalla prison on Royal Oak Avenue. The gloomy memory of nearly a century of prisoners will probably not linger on the site long after the buildings are cleared; however, the fine sweep of open, untrammeled hillside, framed along the skyline by alder forest, will be missed, as Burnaby intends to develop the lands with townhouses.

The original provincial jail for the Lower Mainland was in New Westminster and opened in 1887. As it became overcrowded, and the growing community crept closer to it, officials sought a larger site, and chose Oakalla at least partly for its remote location. The jail moved there in the 1890s, into a wooden building which is still in use as a motor shop. In 1914, the wooden jail was superseded by the brick prison building that still dominates the site.

Railway historian Henry Ewert described the effort required to build this solid brick structure in the middle of the Burnaby forest: "One of the most unusual projects ever undertaken by the [B.C. Electric Railway Company] came to fruition on May 1 [1914] with the opening of the 6,456-foot prison farm spur from Royal Oak on the Central Park line to the abuilding Oakalla prison farm buildings. Work on the $11,295.25 B.C. government-sponsored spur had begun a month earlier, the line running down the east side of Royal Oak Avenue. Despite the fact that the spur's northern half descended at an eight percent grade, and its last 620 feet were nine percent with a very sharp eastward curve at the steepest point, the company was able to deliver 115 cars of construction materials over the next five months, each car taken down singly by its locomotive! In wet weather there were no deliveries."[8]

Oakalla will shut down in March, 1991. Its male inmates will be sent to prisons in Surrey or Maple Ridge, while women will move to the new prison in South Burnaby on the Fraser River flats.

8 Ewert, *The Story of the B.C. Electric Railway Company*, page 102.

9 Photograph from the booklet *Beautiful Homes*, circa 1915, pamphlet number Und-831, CVA.

10 Photograph from Howay and Scholefield, op.cit., page 31.

"ESMOND"

"Esmond," Charles J. Peter's fine Tudor home at the corner of North Esmond and Trinity in Vancouver Heights, photographed about 1914.[1] In the years since the 1930s, first as the Seton Academy and now as Seton Villa, the house has been modified significantly — dormers have been removed, windows changed, and additions built — but it remains a commanding presence, clearly visible even from the Second Narrows bridge.

1 Photograph from the booklet *Beautiful Homes*, pamphlet number Und-831, CVA.

2 J.S. Matthews, Notes on Place Names, CVA.

3 Ibid. Matthews's source is Angus MacDonald, the namesake of MacDonald Street in Burnaby, an early settler in Vancouver Heights who owned the first automobile there, a 1909 Cadillac, and later was a member of Burnaby municipal council. MacDonald earned a reputation as an inventive electrician and contractor, beginning in 1893 when, as an employee of the Vancouver street railway, he demonstrated that the overhead wire for a streetcar line could be installed while fully charged, allowing it to be done by a moving electric streetcar. This evidently was a world "first" — see Ewert, *The Story of the B.C. Electric Railway Company,* page 22. MacDonald added to his reputation in 1905 by converting the Vancouver & Lulu Island steam railway to electricity for the BCER, a task which included setting the power poles into the boggy Lulu Island soil.

4 Ewert, *The Story of the B.C. Electric Railway Company,* page 80.

5 *Province,* April 19, 1912.

6 According to Seton Villa administrator Yvonne Cunningham, it was originally known as "Overlynn" — quoted in "Heritage Houses Well Preserved," by Aileen Campbell, *Province,* January 20, 1980.

7 Information from obituary, Matthews news clippings, CVA.

Vancouver Heights, also known as Beacon Hill or Capitol Hill, is east of Boundary Road and thus in Burnaby. Residents have some of the most spectacular views in the Lower Mainland, especially looking north and west over Burrard Inlet and the city. Regardless of its charms, however, it was a victim of the real-estate collapse of 1913-14, with the result that very few fine homes were ever built there. During the half century between that collapse and the mid-1960s, Vancouver was more often than not economically stagnant, and the prospective homebuilder had a tremendous variety of lots and locations to choose from. Land in most districts was quite cheap, and Burnaby was a remote location, so it is not surprising that an area such as Vancouver Heights ended up with so many cheaply built little stucco bungalows that do not take advantage of the view.

According to Vancouver archivist J.S. Matthews, "before settlement took place along (Hastings Street), Japanese and Indians cut shingle bolts in all the area known as Vancouver Heights and Capitol Hill, delivering them down a main skidroad near Willingdon Avenue to the inlet. A fine spring used to furnish water for their camps near Gamma Avenue and Albert Street. This was also the water supply for Mr. and Mrs. Goodridge, whose house at 4317 East Pender Street was the first in that neighbourhood."[2] Vancouver Heights got its name from Grant & McLellan, a firm of real-estate brokers, who cleared 160 acres, graded the streets, laid sewers and sidewalks, and put the property on the market early in 1909.[3] The agents organized excursions for prospective buyers to the remote new suburb: according to the *Province* of March 8, 1909, "an auto car leaves Hastings Street twice a day for East Vancouver Heights, the most promising subdivision on the market. Lots are only $300 each, the best snap in the city." Later that year, the B.C. Electric Railway Company obligingly extended its streetcar service east from Campbell Avenue through Hastings Townsite to Boundary Road; initially, commuters had to pay an extra fare at the Nanaimo Street boundary of Hastings Townsite, but, in the interests of attracting new settlers, the company soon dropped the fare to ten tickets for fifty cents.[4] Two years later, prices had climbed considerably, and the suburb continued to be touted by agents offering excursions, which probably included frequent stops for free liquor and food — one advertisement of nearly a full newspaper page declaimed "Special Saturday auto excursion to East Vancouver Heights — Tickets free at our office — Lots two blocks from Hastings Street and within five minutes of the car line for $450 to $750 — William & Murdoff Limited."[5]

One of the adventurous settlers in the area was Charles J. Peter (1865-1949), who commissioned Samuel Maclure to design the magnificent "Esmond," in the English Arts and Crafts style, at the southwest corner of North Esmond and Trinity streets.[6] Peter was the local manager of G. F. & J. Galt Company, "importers of Ceylon Teas, packers of Blue Ribbon and Monsoon Teas." He lived on Davie Street in the West End until 1910, when "Esmond" was completed. His wife was a well-known violinist, one of the founders of the Women's Musical Club, and active in the development of the Georgian Club. Upon his retirement in 1936, the Peters left Vancouver for Aberdeen, Scotland; evidently, Mrs. Peter died there, and her husband returned to the Pacific Coast and until his death lived in Ellensburg, Washington, with his son George.[7] "Esmond" became the Seton Academy, operated by the Sisters of Charity of Halifax; in recent years, the much-modified house has become part of a senior citizens' complex that also includes a highrise residence and other buildings on the site of the old estate.

NEW WESTMINSTER

The unique, turreted Galbraith house at 131 Eighth Street in New Westminster appears to exist as a kind of working laboratory, established to determine how long a landlord can avoid performing cosmetic maintenance, and how long a wooden house can remain standing in the west-coast climate without falling down. Not that this house is the only one in the Lower Mainland to be the subject of such treatment, but its case is especially sad, for the house is unique, nearly a century old, and a landmark in a city whose residents have preserved more of its heritage houses than has any other part of Greater Vancouver.

The Galbraith house has architectural details of the Stick style, so named by the historian Vincent Scully, as well as woodwork typical of the related Eastlake style, all mixed with Queen Anne elements. It illustrates the elaborate wood detail, including fish-scale shingles, friezes of drilled holes, elaborate cut-out crests, and brackets beneath the gables with a projecting turned knob, common in their profusion to all design of the late-Victorian period. The style was an appropriate choice for Galbraith, who owned a sash and door business on 10th Street that produced "sashes, doors, blinds, mantels, newel posts, balusters, mouldings, brackets, corner blocks, turning, scroll sawing, (and) shingles"[1] — everything a carpenter needed to decorate a building. The New Westminster historian Jack Scott has found a close resemblance between this house's design and plans in pattern books published in New York by William Comstock and Henry Hudson Holly, and available to carpenters by mail.[2] Most of the wooden decoration has somehow managed to remain attached to the crumbling house, although, as part of its shoddy conversion into a rooming house, it lost its open veranda, which probably was supported by beautifully turned posts and elaborate gingerbread trim.

The Galbraith house at the corner of Eighth and Queens in New Westminster, built in 1894, is in an advanced state of decrepitude and is something of a classic Western house — the type that one occasionally sees perched on hilltops near abandoned Nevada and California mining towns. Its air of "gothick" gloom brings to mind the works of Edgar Allan Poe, or the films of Vincent Price.

1 Scott, *Once in the Royal City,* page 49.
2 Ibid.

The sidewalk tile at 433 Carnarvon Street in New Westminster. ''Westham'' owes its name to the village in Essex, England, rather than the island in the south arm of the Fraser River.[1]

New Westminster is the Lower Mainland's proof of the adage that economic recession is the friend of heritage. Founded in 1859 as a statement of sovereignty over and centre of administration for the newly named colony of British Columbia, New Westminster was established at the mouth of the Fraser River — a strategic move to ensure the control of commerce between the open seas and the Cariboo goldfields. But what was strategic in 1860 had become a backwater by the 1880s, when the terminus of the transcontinental railway, and a harbour for the ships drawn to it, made the creation of a major city on Burrard Inlet inevitable. By then New Westminster was well established and quite prosperous, as witnessed by the fine houses from the decades since the 1880s that line many of the streets within a few minutes' walk of the downtown. Fortunately for their preservation, the slow economic growth of the city since the First World War has kept the downtown small and removed much of the population pressure that in Vancouver caused the replacement of most of the fine houses in old neighbourhoods such as the West End. Although more than 125 years old, New Westminster still has a significant amount of its architectural heritage intact. It is also comparatively affordable: a well-preserved heritage house, by a well-known architect such as Samuel Maclure — the sort of house that is rarely found and impossible to afford ten miles away in Vancouver — costs less than the price of a stucco box on a Shaughnessy lot.

In the six decades between 1891 and the early 1950s, New Westminster and downtown Vancouver were easily accessible to each other via the Central Park line — the interurban electric train run for most of that period by the B.C. Electric Railway Company. It is ironic that the interurban's successor — the SkyTrain — now represents one of the major threats to New Westminster's architectural heritage and quiet, almost small-town streetscapes. The office buildings of downtown Vancouver are suddenly just a few minutes away, even in rush hour, so the high-density apartment area of New Westminster is beginning to expand up the hill above the SkyTrain station. Thus, the long-term speculation of owners of houses such as "Westham" is finally paying off.

Built in 1905 by Captain W.H. Philpott, "Westham" was only a few blocks north of the New Westminster business centre. Philpott arrived in New Westminster about 1898, and worked as a cook, a fireman, and a dredge operator, before becoming a master mariner. He was also a businessman, and ran his Royal Ice Works from the rear of this property — 424 Victoria Street.

1 New Westminster Heritage Resource Inventory, supplement to Volume II.

The metal icehouse, built sometime before 1912, was still at the rear of the property, surrounded by motorcycles, until the property was redeveloped in 1990.

'Westham' is an example of the Eastern Shingle style,[2] with an odd combination of neoclassical details such as the porch columns and the symmetrical treatment of the front gable, Queen Anne details in the asymmetrical placement of the bay window and the fish-scale shingles in the gable, and Eastlake-style woodwork in the division of wall areas into panels surrounded by mouldings.

In the real-estate-based economics of the Lower Mainland, "Westham," like most of the houses in neighbourhoods where owners have speculated in anticipation of upzoning for high-density apartments, had outlived its time. Most of the neighbourhood was probably more than willing to have the property redeveloped in return for the disappearance of the tenants. But instead of being demolished, the house has been moved elsewhere and restored, an excellent use for it as its fine design and quality of construction are preserved. However, "Westham's" context — a house specific to Carnarvon Street — and the historic references of that New Westminster street have been lost.[3]

"Westham," on Carnarvon between Fourth and Sixth streets in New Westminster, painted in the summer of 1989. In recent years, it has been frequented by a group of bikers — the lawns and front porch were often crowded with people, sometimes numbering in the dozens, and the back of the house along Victoria Street resounded to the rumble of their Harley-Davidsons.

2 Ibid.

3 At the time of this writing, the house's destination is not known. The issue of moving old houses to enclaves and restoring them creates the spectre of "architectural petting zoos," such as Heritage Square in the Bunker Hill district of Los Angeles. If old houses are only examples of architectural styles, then they can be moved around at will, but if they are the visible evidence of a community's history, they should stay where they were built. See the discussion on pages 76-77.

NORTH VANCOUVER

1 A nickname for North Vancouver City, in use for years after its incorporation in 1891 — cited in Foundation Group Designs, *City of North Vancouver Heritage Inventory.*

2 Investors in North Vancouver were expected to believe that the Pacific Great Eastern Railway (now B.C. Rail) would make the city a metropolis to rival Vancouver once its line to the North and its terminus in North Vancouver were completed in 1915.

3 Information from John Stuart, North Shore Heritage Advisory Committee.

Like New Westminster, the City of North Vancouver still has a large amount of its architectural heritage, including its earliest office building (page 176) and cottages within a stone's throw of the commercial core of lower Lonsdale Street. But unlike New Westminster, it was an audacious real-estate promotion — "The Ambitious City"[1] — that, in the boom and bust market of the west coast, never really got off the ground.[2] Thus, buildings of historical importance that in Vancouver would be only memories still exist and have a chance of surviving the current boom — although the recent demolition of the 1911 Saint Alice Hotel at 2nd and Lonsdale demonstrates the difficulties of preservation. In that case, the city's planning department and heritage advisory committee considered buying the St. Alice and restoring it as social housing, but the anticipated cost of $3.5 million — of which only about $1.2 million would have come from the province — was too high. The developer, who wanted to build a tower on the site, offered to restore the hotel in return for a density bonus of a second tower; this was considered by the city to set an excessively generous precedent.[3]

The ferry service, operating from the wharf at the foot of Lonsdale Avenue, was North Vancouver's lifeline with Vancouver until the Second Narrows Bridge opened in 1925. This postcard, from the period before the First World War, shows two of the ferries of the North Vancouver Ferry and Power Company, an enterprise of former Vancouver city solicitor Alfred St. George Hamersley (page 180). The establishment of the service in 1903 was the beginning of the great North Vancouver land boom. The ferry on the right is the St. George, named for Hamersley. In one of the many instances of domination by the automobile that so marked the 1950s — most notably, the dismantling of the B.C. Electric Railway Company's interurban "rapid transit" system — the ferry service ceased operation in 1958. The last surviving vestige of the fleet is old Number Five, the 600-passenger, 30-vehicle ferry that has been the Seven Seas seafood restaurant since 1959. With the commissioning of the SeaBus fleet in the 1970s, ferry service resumed between the foot of Lonsdale and downtown Vancouver, and the Lonsdale Quay development has rejuvenated the North Vancouver waterfront.

In the early years of the century, the Hotel North Vancouver was a tourist destination for residents of Vancouver and New Westminster seeking an escape from the hurly-burly of summertime in the city. Located just west of Lonsdale on the Esplanade, it was a landmark of the North Vancouver waterfront from 1902 until fire destroyed it in 1929. A portion of its old garden retaining wall, at 166 Esplanade West, is all that remains of the property.

The Gill house, on Grand Boulevard near 17th Avenue, built in 1912 and photographed about two years later.[6]

One of the curious legacies of the "Ambitious City" era in North Vancouver is the 350-foot-wide Grand Boulevard, which, like so many of the real-estate dreams in Greater Vancouver, never lived up to the expectations created by its promoters. Like that other symbol of North Vancouver's future — the Pacific Great Eastern Railway — Grand Boulevard went "from nowhere to nowhere."[1] It begins above Keith Road, several blocks east of the city's commercial area along Lonsdale, and ends about a dozen blocks north, in the middle of what was bush and is today a residential area.

Conceived in 1906 as the centrepiece of the North Vancouver Land and Improvement Company's real-estate holdings,[2] it sought by its publicity to attract a high quality of resident, and by its building restrictions to keep out the riffraff. An example of the former is the NVL&I Company's "announcement" that Grand Boulevard would be "to North Vancouver what the Champs Élysees is to Paris, what Unter Den Linden is to Berlin . . . because it will not only be the principal promenade and drive, but also the finest residential avenue in the province . . . . As the expense of duplicating this boulevard in any large city would be prohibitive, North Vancouver is likely to retain the distinction of having the greatest residential boulevard on the continent. It will not only remain the premier avenue of the West, but, in a city which is already a health resort, as a reservoir of constantly renewed air, it will perpetuate through later time in the city's midst the salubrity of the surrounding country." In the same advertisement, the company advised of its building restrictions: "Property fronting on the Boulevard sells on the condition that for a period of twenty years no building other than residential and of $4,000 minimum cost can be built facing the Boulevard, unless a definite majority of the owners of the land fronting on the Boulevard register their signed consent to change of this condition. This Boulevard is thus *protected as an avenue, on which good residences can be built without fear that stores or depreciative structures will be erected next to, or near, them.*"[3] Another motive for making the boulevard so wide was that its promoters, having seen the carnage in San Francisco in April, 1906, thought that it would act as a firebreak.[4]

A number of fine houses did get completed there before the economic collapse of 1913-14. Most are in a woodsy combination of Tudor Revival and Craftsman styles, appropriate to Grand Boulevard's setting. The most unusual is the house in the photograph above, at 1617 Grand Boulevard, built in 1911-12 to the design of architect N.A. Kearns for former North Vancouver *District* reeve James C. Gill;[5] it is a formal, symmetrical, almost neoclassical design, executed in stone and shingles. On the left-hand (south-facing) side of the house is a sunroom.

Just as in Vancouver Heights, the boom collapsed before there was any consistency to the Grand Boulevard streetscape, and the later generations of little stucco bungalows and split-levels that filled up the vacant lots make a mockery of the monumental boulevard layout.

1 This expression was used to describe, among other things, the PGE's disconnected sections of track; until the 1950s, the railway ended at Whytecliffe, but began again at Squamish.

2 The Mahon brothers, who were the major financiers of the NVL&I Company, are the namesakes of Mahon Avenue two blocks west of Lonsdale.

3 Italics in original. Grand Boulevard advertisement in North Shore Museum and Archives, number 1908-2.

4 Foundation Group Designs, *City of North Vancouver Heritage Inventory,* page 11.

5 Foundation Group Designs, *City of North Vancouver Heritage Inventory,* page 41. The caption in the booklet from which this photograph was taken stated that the house belonged to C.S. Arnold, although there is no evidence in city directories that Arnold (1885-1955), a lawyer who was the founder of the Forest Lawn and Ocean View cemeteries, ever lived there. Arnold achieved a bizarre distinction when he was found dead on the site of his last project — the "Veterans' Field of Honour" at Forest Lawn Memorial Park.

6 Photograph from the booklet *Beautiful Homes,* pamphlet number Und-831, CVA.

The interior of the J.A. McMillan grocery store, in the Syndicate Block, about 1909. Note the electric carbon light hanging on the left.

One of the most historic buildings on the North Shore is still standing in relatively good repair at the northwest corner of Lonsdale and the Esplanade. Built in 1903, the Syndicate Block was the first commercial building in North Vancouver, the North Vancouver post office from 1903 to 1911, and the home of the *Express* — the first North Vancouver newspaper, which began publication in 1905. Like buildings in parts of Vancouver, such as Gastown and East Hastings, and in parts of New Westminster, the Syndicate Block has survived due to the sluggish economy in the Lower Lonsdale area, and the consequent lack of pressure for redevelopment. When the North Vancouver ferry service ceased operation in 1958, business both in Gastown and Lower Lonsdale slumped. *Lack* of transportation helped to save this building, but the return of good transportation in the form of the SeaBus and the redevelopment boom on the Vancouver-area waterfront has revitalized Lower Lonsdale. In the past decade, impressive new apartment and office blocks have been erected along the Esplanade around the Lonsdale Quay development, casting a figurative shadow over the older commercial, industrial, and residential buildings of the original settlers.

It is still possible to see, within a few blocks of the corner of Lonsdale and the Esplanade, a representative slice of North Vancouver's early history. There is the Syndicate Block, just above the old ferry wharf; there are the wharf itself and Ferry Number Five, now doing stationary service as a restaurant, next to the present generation's ferry system; there are the Wallace shipyards on the Esplanade just east of Lonsdale, since 1906 one of the biggest shipbuilding and repairing operations on the west coast; there are the Aberdeen Block and the Bank of Hamilton Chambers on Lonsdale at 1st Street, fine brick commercial structures built in 1911 that demonstrate how much more prosperous the city had become in the few years since the construction of the Syndicate Block;[1] there is the 1908 Pybus cottage, just east of Lonsdale on

1 There is also Paine Hardware in the Aberdeen Block, a classic hardware store in a well-preserved storefront.

OOT OF LONSDALE

M.KLUCKNER 1990

1st Avenue (see overleaf), a prefabricated dwelling erected by a land speculator during the first great North Vancouver development boom; and a few blocks east along 1st Avenue, there are the 1904 house and gardener's cottage of one of the city's most significant property owners (see page 180). This is only a partial list of the interesting and significant historical buildings and "connections" within a stone's throw of the ferry wharf. No other part of Greater Vancouver has such a range of historical components, which together form a "map" of the layers of European settlement, preserved in such a compact area.[2]

The use of the word "preserved" is not really justified — the buildings are simply there, and although recognized as part of North Vancouver's heritage, have no designation or protection. Their survival is no more than an historical accident: if the dreams of the speculators and developers of the original city had materialized, North Vancouver would have remained prosperous through the decades and this legacy of early development would likely have been long since demolished.

Looking south on Lonsdale to the Esplanade, with the old ferry wharf and the City of Vancouver in the distance. The ochre-coloured wooden building on the right is the Syndicate Block, built in 1903 — not just the oldest surviving commercial building in North Vancouver, but actually the first one built.

2 It is comparable to the few blocks around James Bay in Victoria, where the elements of the city's early history are reflected in buildings still standing in their original locations.

CAPTAIN PYBUS

Captain Henry Pybus, in his Royal Navy Reserve uniform.

From the time of the first rumours in the early 1880s that Canada's transcontinental railway was to terminate at Burrard Inlet, land speculation and real estate have been the most common preoccupations of the residents. The railway and its associated ocean commerce were such powerful economic forces that Vancouver and its adjoining municipalities were literally invented overnight, and built with the capital of investors from as far away as Eastern Canada and Europe. There was always another prospective purchaser of land moving west to the new boomtown, and before long everyone became involved in the real-estate mania — even Rudyard Kipling, on his visit to the young city, bought a few lots. Many of these hopefuls lost money in the 1893-94 depression, an eastern stock-market crash that was exacerbated locally by severe flooding in the Fraser Valley. But when the economy began to grow at the end of the century, the little investors became speculators again, and jumped back into the real-estate market. A speculative bubble grew in the years before the 1913-14 crash, when prices fell so hard and so far that many individuals were ruined. Prices in many areas did not reach their 1912 levels again until the 1950s. The lessons of the past are not easily learned — in the current Vancouver market, the boom-and-bust cycle seems to run about every seven or eight years, with recent peaks in 1973-74, 1980-81, and 1989-90.

The little prefabricated bungalow at 147 East 1st Street in North Vancouver is a monument to the folly of one Vancouver speculator of the years before 1913. Captain Henry Pybus was in command of the Canadian Pacific Railway's legendary *Empress of China* on its sea trials, and later of the *Empress of Japan*; he was first officer of the former on its maiden voyage to Vancouver via Hong Kong late in 1891, and ten years later became permanent commander of the latter, whose figurehead (actually, a reproduction thereof) is still a fixture in Stanley Park. Pybus (1850-1938) had been born in the Cape Colony, South Africa, the son of a man who had made a fortune in the early part of the century in the opium trade.[1] Foregoing a college education, Henry Pybus went to sea at sixteen, worked in the Chinese coastal trade as a river pilot on the Yangtse Kiang, and in the 1880s received training in the Royal Navy Reserve. Following several more years at sea, he joined the CPR's newly formed steamship line, whose ocean liners connected Asian ports with the transcontinental railway's terminus at Vancouver.

Pybus established himself and raised his family in Vancouver, living first in a house on Hornby Street downtown, and later in one on Jervis Street. In his spare time, he was so active and successful as a real-estate speculator in the years after 1908 that he felt wealthy enough to retire in 1911. His notes and journals detail pieces of property scattered throughout the Lower Mainland; he believed that Main Street had an excellent commercial future and owned many lots there, as well as lots throughout the east end and this little lot on East First in North Vancouver, upon which he erected the prefabricated bungalow. His empire crashed in 1913-14, and pieces of property such as this one had to be abandoned for taxes; suddenly impoverished, the Pybus family abandoned their long-held plans to retire to South Africa. Remaining in Vancouver, Pybus became active with the Art, Historical and Scientific Association, serving as its president from 1921 to 1927 and pursuing his interests in genealogy. Following his death in 1938, his ashes were committed to the sea from the new *Empress of Japan*. His two daughters married members of the locally prominent Bell-Irving family; his eldest grandson, Henry Pybus Bell-Irving, was a lieutenant-governor of the province.[2]

1 The story of Joseph Pybus and his brother is documented in *The Opium Clippers*, by Basil Lubbock.

2 Information and photograph from Elizabeth O'Kiely, Pybus's granddaughter.

The bungalow at 147 East 1st Street in North Vancouver, painted in the summer of 1989.

The cottage erected by the speculator Henry Pybus on East 1st Street in North Vancouver bears witness to the stagnant North Vancouver real-estate market, having survived within a block of the city's old commercial centre for more than eight decades. Erected in 1908, it is a prefabricated "Model J" from the B.C. Mills, Timber & Trading Company (see page 19) — a kit, floated across the inlet from Vancouver and erected on Pybus's lot.

The watercolour, painted in July, shows what happens to a neglected property in Vancouver: it quickly reverts to a "natural landscape," consisting mainly of blackberry and morning glory (the common bindweed), with the addition sometimes of the five-foot-tall, pink-plumed hardhack (*Spiraea douglasii*) and lesser weeds such as dandelion and the look-alike summer-blooming Hairy Cat's Ear (*hypochaeris radicata*). Blackberry and morning glory, such as the ones in front of this property, grow with exceptional speed, quickly forming impenetrable, thorny thickets that with support can reach heights of more than ten feet. The house stands almost on a "platform" of high land — behind it and beside it is a wasteland of old lumber and abandoned cars. In the background are the Versatile Pacific shipyards, established in 1906, two years before Pybus erected his little house. In recent years, the house achieved a certain celebrity status, due to its occupancy by Richard the Troll, the leader of the Rhinoceros Party.

1 Foundation Group, *City of North Vancouver Heritage Inventory*, page 19.

The gardener's cottage on the Hamersley estate, at 364 East 1st Street in North Vancouver.

That ultimate rarity in middle-class Vancouver — the purpose-built servants' dwelling — survives on East 1st Street in North Vancouver, separated by a block of apartment buildings from the master's house on East 2nd Street. The former was built in 1904 as the gardener's cottage for the estate of Alfred St. George Hamersley, which occupied the land bounded by the waterfront and 3rd Street between St. Andrews and St. Patricks; the master's house, "Langton Lodge," is now the restaurant called Forster's at Emerald Park at 350 East 2nd Street. Hamersley (1850-1929) was an aristocratic Englishman who, following the Maori wars in New Zealand, came to Vancouver in 1888 and served as its first solicitor. Shortly after the turn of the century, he became interested in North Vancouver real estate, developed the ferry system to ensure the community's prosperity, and moved there himself. Hamersley soon lost interest in life in North Vancouver and returned to England where he served as a Conservative member of parliament from 1910 to 1918.

"Langton Lodge" is a solid, beautifully built structure, with granite foundations and brick and concrete walls in some places nineteen inches thick.[1] Shingle siding and decorative brackets give it a woodsy look appropriate to North Vancouver. The gardener's cottage is a modest structure with a wraparound porch and a few rooms; its only decorative touch is the carved brackets on porch posts. To its west (the left of the painting) is a small park of berms and evergreens, a style of landscape design unlikely to have found favour with Hamersley and his gardener. Although the City of North Vancouver owns the cottage, it is not especially well maintained; there is a plaque at the front gate, but the cottage is not a designated heritage building.

WEST VANCOUVER

Recent redevelopments in West Vancouver have removed many of the little cottages and properties that were reminiscent of the municipality's rustic beginnings. Many of these cottages looked like the retirement homes of wanderers, calling to mind the last lines of Robert Louis Stevenson's "Requiem": "Home is the sailor, home from the sea, And the hunter home from the hill."

One of the last of the old rural properties was "Tower Hill," at the top of 29th Avenue. It occupied six picturesque, rambling acres, a few of which were meadow and old orchard, while the balance was a woodlot, on the hillside above Rogers Creek. The tower of "Tower Hill" was a water-storage tower that stood on the highest point of the property and was filled by creek water pumped up the hill by a hydraulic ram set into the creek. This complicated arrangement was installed by the property's first owner and the namesake of the creek, an engineer named William J. Rogers. He settled there in 1919, and built a modest Swiss Cottage-style bungalow, partially visible on the extreme right of the watercolour on the next two pages. A formal garden occupied the grounds immediately in front of the house; below was a long, rhododendron-lined driveway descending to the corner of 29th and Rosebery, then a view through the treetops to English Bay, Point Grey and beyond. The property was sold and subdivided into eleven lots in the spring of 1990.

"Tower Hill" was on the outskirts of the old West Vancouver municipality of numbered and named streets. Much of the North Shore, especially those parts developed before the Second World War, is gently sloping rather than hilly; to create a "settled" look, property owners often filled in small gullies and clearcut the lots, and surveyors located the roadways to conform to the dreary grid system common elsewhere in the region.

By contrast, Caulfeild is the one real-estate development of the early years of the North Shore that uses the area's topography as an asset. "This beautiful property," said its 1909 promotional brochure, "has been laid out with the special object of preserving the natural beauties of the site, and thus giving opportunities for pleasant homes among unusually picturesque surroundings." One of the community's founders, Henry A. Stone, made the comment that the result is "visible proof that town planning falls far short of nature's planning."[1] It was, and is, the idealized English countryside transferred and adapted to the rocky, lush, west coast of North America.

Francis Caulfeild (1844-1934) was an Englishman on a tour of Canada with his daughter when he visited the Vancouver area in 1899. During a boat trip, he saw the land around what was then known as Skunk Cove; smitten, he purchased the area, changed the cove's name to his own, and over the next decade laid out roads and parks and established a water supply.[2] In 1909, he built for himself the house at 4768 Pilot House Road, later used as a store and post office for the area.[3]

Before the opening of Marine Drive in 1915, Caulfeild was accessible either by the Union Steamships or by the Pacific Great Eastern Railway's train service between Horseshoe Bay and the North Vancouver ferry terminal.[4] It was probably a good thing that it took the municipality and the province so long to establish road access, as Caulfeild laid out his community with reference to the water, rather than to an automobile throughway, and the difficulty of access discouraged speculation. But although it was a comparatively remote location, residents could commute to and from the city without too much difficulty. They were a mixed lot who moved there — from businessmen to writers, retirees, and the independently wealthy — but they shared the desire to maintain Caulfeild's appearance as a "poetical commonwealth" of rustic houses and rambling gardens in a rural setting. Their efforts have survived more or less intact to the present.

Of the "artistic" individuals who moved to Caulfeild in the early years, the most significant was Henry Athelstan Stone, the president of the Gault Brothers dry-goods firm. Born in 1861 within the sound of Bow Bells in London, he came to Canada in 1882 and worked for Gault

1 Quoted in an article by "A.C.B.," "Caulfeild Has Unique Story, Now Unfolded," *Sun*, August 22, 1939.

2 Stone, *A Short History of Caulfeild Village*, 1939.

3 Foundation Group Designs, *West Vancouver Heritage Inventory*, page 54.

4 Sanford, *The Pictorial History of Railroading in British Columbia*, page 72. As a condition of securing its right-of-way through West Vancouver, the PGE (now B.C. Rail) had guaranteed to maintain passenger service through the area. At the end of 1928, at a point when many of the railway's trestles through West Vancouver needed replacement, the company cancelled service and abandoned the line.

THE LAST APRIL OF TOWER HILL, WEST VANCOUVER.

Brothers in Montreal for twenty years, before moving to Vancouver to establish a branch of the firm. In the city, he is best known as the prime mover behind the founding of the Vancouver Art Gallery in the 1920s. He was the first purchaser, in 1909, of a Caulfield lot, and moved in 1918 to his newly completed house, called "Stonehaven," at 4648 Piccadilly Road South. Although he remained president of Gault Brothers until a month before his death, he had no difficulty allotting time to his artistic interests.[5] He was a talented watercolourist — the show commemorating the tenth anniversary of the founding of the Vancouver Art Gallery featured his work — and also designed the original part of St. Francis in the Wood church and its lychgate.[6] These constitute the ultimate expression in Vancouver of "old-country" village Anglicanism and the "little Cornish town" envisioned by both Stone and Caulfeild; almost everything about the church and its landscaping pays homage to the Arts and Crafts Movement and the beliefs and backgrounds of the community's founders, including the 1920s stained-glass windows by the William Morris Company, and the late 1930s ones commemorating notable Caulfeild residents Julia Henshaw and her husband, Charles.

The Henshaws lived in the blue wooden house near the bus stop at the corner of Piccadilly and Marine Drive. Julia Henshaw was a noted botanist and writer, whose alpine garden at

5 Information about H.A. Stone from clippings in the J.S. Matthews collection, CVA. Obituaries published in Vancouver newspapers on June 26, 1943.

6 Foundation Group Designs, *West Vancouver Heritage Inventory*, pages 26-27.

The view towards English Bay from the top of ''Tower Hill,'' the six-acre William J. Rogers property at the top of 29th Avenue, shortly before its subdivision in the summer of 1990. The gateway to the property is visible at the bottom of the driveway in the middle distance.

Caulfeild was known around the city; during the 1920s and 1930s, the period when she lived there, she was the arts writer for the *Vancouver Sun*. Another like-minded resident was Miss Dorothy Constance Dashwood, daughter of a baronet. A canteen worker in France and supervisor of women munitions workers in England during the First World War,[7] and subsequently a volunteer social service worker in London, she moved to British Columbia and eventually settled at 5037 Howe Sound Lane, where she painted and gardened.[8]

Two of the wealthy businessmen who moved to the area built large houses on Piccadilly Road South, the entrance into Caulfeild from Marine Drive. "Greystones," at number 4670, was erected in 1927 by former Vancouver mayor Frederick Buscombe (who had previously owned "Fairacres," see page 168), the one-time owner of a successful plumbing business called Skinner's, whom Alfred St. George Hamersley described as "a mere purveyor of chamber pots."[9] At number 4732 lived Stuart Cameron, the president of the Cameron contracting firm, and vice-president of Armstrong Morrison & Company. His firm's undertakings included the municipal power plant at Nelson, the New Westminster grain elevator, the B.C. Electric's Ruskin power plant, and a power plant at Stillwater for the Powell River (forestry) Company. In the late 1930s, it built the foundations at the north end of the Lions Gate Bridge.[10]

7 It is quite likely that she met Julia Henshaw through her war service, and heard about Caulfeild from her.

8 *Who's Who in British Columbia*, 1944-46 edition, page 63. Obituary in *Province*, November 15, 1950.

9 From a column by Roy Brown dated November 13, 1953, "A Twisted Tongue Turned the Trick," in J.S. Matthews news clippings, file "Hamersley," CVA.

10 *Who's Who in Canada*, 1930-31 edition, page 65.

THE LEFEAUX HOUSE

2250 BELLEVUE, WEST VANCOUVER

The early 1960s decision of West Vancouver municipal council to allow apartments along the Bellevue Avenue waterfront between Ambleside and Dundarave doomed the immaculate Lefeaux house at 2258 Bellevue Avenue. The land on which it stood eventually became simply too valuable for single-family use. As the house and garden were an inseparable unit, it would have been pointless to subdivide the property in order to try to keep the house; in any case, it was not on West Vancouver's heritage inventory.

Built in 1939 for Wallis Walter and Effie Lefeaux, the house was a rambling, clapboard structure of indeterminate parentage, subservient to its garden, in keeping with all the west-coast residential-design ideals dating back to the California Bungalow. The interior had a carved oak staircase and wooden ceiling beams, all in original condition, as subsequent residents had maintained both the house and the garden. The latter was especially picturesque, with its clipped box hedges and camellias; at the top of the steep bank above the B.C. Rail tracks and seawall, past the left-hand edge of the watercolour, was a screen of mature cedars, and a shake-roofed gazebo entwined with wisteria; the garden was terraced down the steep bank to the level of the railway tracks and seawall. The watercolour does not convey the complete effect of the sweep of the garden, which continues to the left for some distance; at the back of the house, there was a formal garden, with camellias around a reflecting pool. Out of the picture on the right was a garage, echoing the style of the house, with a gate and hedge along the roadway.

W. W. Lefeaux was born in London in 1881, and worked as a clerk, bookkeeper, and commercial traveller in England before immigrating to Canada in 1901. Over the next dozen years, he worked as a fur trader, grocer, store proprietor, and real-estate agent, while completing his training in law. He gravitated towards socialism, first as a defender of objectors to military

M.KLUCKNER 1989

The Lefeaux house at 2258 Bellevue Avenue in West Vancouver, painted in February, 1989. The watercolour looks west, towards the distant Caulfeild headland, on a cold, sunny day, with a dusting of snow and hard frost on the lawns.

training during the First World War, and secondly in Winnipeg in 1919 as advocate for the leaders of the Winnipeg General Strike. The following year he visited Russia, and returned again in 1936. In the early 1930s, he became well known as an organizer of the Cooperative Commonwealth Federation, and ran for provincial and federal office in 1933, 1935 and 1940. In the 1941 provincial election, he won the Vancouver Centre seat for the CCF, and during the war was often in the news explaining and defending his party's views, and countering charges from the likes of Vancouver Mayor Gerry McGeer that the CCF was allied to the Russian government.[1]

In 1962, when Lefeaux's property taxes shot up from $800 to $2,300, he successfully challenged the property assessment system that required him to pay an inflated, apartment-scale rate although he was using his property for single-family purposes. However, the original assessment was upheld on appeal to the B.C. Supreme Court, when Mr. Justice J.G.A. Hutcheson agreed that property should be assessed on its potential value and suggested that home-owners such as Lefeaux were standing in the way of the community's development.[2] Lefeaux died in 1972[3] and the property later passed out of his family's hands, but remarkably, the house and garden remained intact through almost three decades of apartment zoning.

The property came on the market in 1988 and was quickly sold to a development group. At a rezoning hearing that December, council approved the construction of a "fourteen-storey luxury residential apartment tower." Many of the shrubs from the garden were donated to the municipality. The house was purchased by a man named Cameron Keddy, who wanted to use it on Bowen Island as a bed-and-breakfast inn. On a morning in August, 1989, it was jacked off its foundations, moved to the foot of 18th Street, loaded onto a barge, and floated away.[4]

1 See the *News-Herald*, March 6, 1940; a number of news clippings on Lefeaux's career are collected in the J.S. Matthews news clippings in CVA.

2 *Sun*, November 2, 1962.

3 Obituaries published in local newspapers on November 25, 1972.

4 *North Shore News*, August 25, 1989, page 4. The house at 1591 South West Marine Drive also took a boat trip; see page 142.

RICHMOND

BURKEVILLE, SEA ISLAND

The first settler west of New Westminster was the farmer Hugh McRoberts, who purchased 1,600 acres on both sides of the North Arm of the Fraser River in 1860-61, and built a home called "Richmond" on the Sea Island riverbank in 1862.[1] McRoberts's nephews were Fitzgerald and Samuel McCleery, who worked on McRoberts's government road-construction contract — the North Arm Trail, later River Road and now Marine Drive.

In recent decades, suburban sprawl has eliminated most of the evidence of the area's agricultural beginnings. The historic fishing community of Steveston has fared better; some of its old commercial centre and canneries have been restored. Less lucky were the historic farming area north of the Vancouver International Airport on Sea Island and the old Grauer store — the last relic of the Eburne Village — which was levelled in the 1970s.

Burkeville, the only surviving residential community on Sea Island, is the best example in the Lower Mainland of a 1940s workers' housing community. It was developed at the end of 1943, on the former mushroom farm of Thomas Aspin, to provide housing for the families of 300 workers at the nearby Boeing Air Company of Canada plant. In its September, 1943, issue, the *Boeing Beam* employees' magazine offered a $25 cash prize for the best name for the new subdivision; three shrewd employees submitted the winning name Burkeville, after the company's president, Stanley Burke, and split the money.

Looking southwest along Catalina Crescent in Burkeville. The main east-west runway approach to the airport is at right angles to Catalina Crescent in the middle distance.

The 300 houses were thrown together by the National Wartime Housing Corporation after Aspin took his autumn crop off the fields. Most were bungalows on fifty-foot lots, featuring a living room, two bedrooms, a bathroom, and a kitchen. Construction techniques were basic and sometimes slipshod — a fire caused by a short circuit in the ceiling wiring damaged one a few months after it was built. All the streets were named for aircraft, including Catalina Crescent, after the flying boats that the workers were building nearby. An old barn on the edge of the property became the community's social hall.[2] The first residents of Burkeville were the fitter B.M. Neville, and his wife and three children, who moved into the cottage at 300 Lancaster Avenue in December. Neville was a survivor of the torpedoing of the ship *Athenia* in the North Atlantic in 1942.[3]

In the ensuing decades, the airport has expanded to a hitherto inconceivable size, but Burkeville has so far managed to avoid demolition. Burkeville's character is now gradually being eroded, as the little cottages are expanded, refinished, rebuilt, and in some cases removed altogether, in the ongoing process of adapting them and their rather noisy locale to current needs. However, it is still a quaint and charming little community — children play on the almost traffic-free streets, there are no sidewalks, and open ditches separate the houses from the roadway.

1 Ross, *Richmond, Child of the Fraser*, pages 26-27.

2 "Things Happening Fast in Burkeville," *News-Herald*, November 6, 1943.

3 "First Family Moves Into New-Built Burkeville," *Sun*, December 12, 1943.

While the modern Vancouver International Airport has expanded across Sea Island and obliterated most of the evidence of the historic farming community there, the modern suburban expansion of the Municipality of Richmond has obliterated all traces of the original Vancouver airport. Evidence of this original airport are the photographs above, taken about 1930 by A.E. "Ted" Hinchcliffe, showing the operations of the Aero Club of B.C. Their airstrip occupied about forty acres of pastureland west of Garden City Road and south of Alexandra Road, on what was then usually called Lulu Island, and had been established in 1919 by Billy Stark "to teach the rudiments and pleasures of flying."[1] In 1928, B.C. Airways started from this field the first scheduled flights in British Columbia: a Vancouver-Victoria service using a twelve-passenger tri-motor Ford. In the background of the photographs are the tell-tale double poles of the Vancouver-Steveston interurban railway. The gabled house in the distance, built about 1910, still stands at 4600 Garden City Road.[2] This airfield was superseded by the modern airport on Sea Island, which opened in July, 1931.

1 Ross, *Richmond, Child of the Fraser,* page 88.
2 Information and photographs from Ken Young, Richmond archivist.

THE KITZEL FARM

A photograph looking north from the corner of 2nd Avenue and 184th Street (Hall's Prairie Road) in the Hall's Prairie area of South Surrey, about 1910, showing David Kitzel and two of his children.

Since the end of the Second World War, the population of Greater Vancouver has expanded at an ever-increasing rate. As elsewhere in the industrialized world, the universal availability of the automobile has allowed erstwhile city dwellers to live far outside the city; personal transportation has meant that the densities of suburban communities no longer need to be high enough to support public transit, and so the farmland and countryside surrounding the Lower Mainland's urban centres has been systematically paved and suburbanized. It is fair to surmise that, throughout the hundred or so years of urban development in the Greater Vancouver area, most people wanted to escape the congestion of the city for as much of their time as possible, but it took until the 1950s for prosperity and technology to make it a reality. The result, in the Lower Mainland and the Fraser Valley, has been the loss of much fertile farmland, and an automobile-inflicted air pollution problem among the worst in Canada. The most striking visible evidence of this dependence on the automobile is the double garage built onto the front of a high proportion of suburban houses and dominating their front façades.

As described elsewhere, the City of Vancouver was "invented" in the mid-1880s by the Canadian Pacific Railway, and is something of a late arrival among the communities of the Lower Mainland. Fort Langley, and the proposed colonial capital of Derby, date from the 1850s and earlier; New Westminster was founded in 1859; settlement began in South Vancouver along the Fraser River and on Sea Island in the 1860s; Richmond was founded in 1879, and Surrey had numerous farmers by the early 1880s. The catalyst for all of this settlement was the Cariboo gold rush of the late 1850s, and the subsequent desire of some of the disillusioned goldseekers to settle on the fertile lands of the Fraser River delta. Their old farmhouses and properties have by and large disappeared, swallowed up by the expanding metropolis.

As the potential commuting range of urban workers expands, and the traffic patterns around the Lower Mainland get more complex, old properties that used to be "way out in the country" have become vulnerable to modernization, meaning in most cases subdivision, defacement, or outright redevelopment. One such place is the old Kitzel farm, one of the best heritage properties left in the Hall's Prairie area of south Surrey, almost on the American border just east of White Rock.

THE KITZEL FARMHOUSE, HALL'S PRAIRIE

The Kitzel farm dates from the mid-1890s. David Kitzel was German, born in the Rhineland in 1858. With his wife, Katherine, he left Germany and landed in New York in 1882. Over the next several years, they migrated slowly westward across the United States, eventually homesteading a quarter-section near Blaine, Washington, where they were joined by David's brother Nicholas. Reversing the pattern of many migrants to western North America, they decided to leave the United States, and moved north into Canada about 1895. Both brothers settled near the junction of Hall's Prairie Road and Campbell River Road — the modern intersection of 184th Street and 8th Avenue, about a mile northeast of the Douglas border-crossing. A 1903 map of Surrey property owners shows Nicholas Kitzel occupying land to the southwest of the corner — the site today of the Hazelmere Golf Course — and David Kitzel to the northeast of the corner of 2nd Avenue and 184th Street. David Kitzel was a farmer, and his specialty was sauerkraut, which he packed in barrels and hauled by wagon to market in New Westminster, crossing the Fraser River there on the ferry called the "K de K" before the railway and traffic bridge was completed in 1904. Katherine Kitzel died around the turn of the century; David Kitzel died in 1935.

Local records do not say when the house and its outbuildings were erected. The photograph on these pages was probably taken sometime around 1910-12, and shows David Kitzel standing at the corner of 2nd Avenue and 184th Street, probably with two of his children from his second

M.KLUCKNER 1989

The Kitzel farm, looking south along 184th Street to 2nd Avenue (at the crest of the hill), in the autumn of 1989. The grouping of old buildings, all dating from about the turn of the century and including the farmhouse, root house and barn, is one of the oldest in that part of the Lower Mainland.

marriage in 1903 to Amelia Seeling. According to one story,[1] Kitzel built the house, with the assistance of a carpenter named Mr. Craig, immediately after moving to Hall's Prairie, about 1895-96: it seems more likely that what they built at the time is the old house that now stands behind the main one (on the right of the main house in the photograph and the left of it in the watercolour), as it is of cruder, simpler construction. The old house was perhaps retained as dwelling space for farm help. The main house, with its symmetrical window placement, wall dormer and off-centre portico on the front porch, is more typical of a style that began to be built around the turn of the century,[2] and was perhaps built by Kitzel when he remarried. Kitzel also built the root house (visible in the left foreground of the watercolour), with its foundation made of rocks gathered on the property. The barn, visible in both the photograph and the watercolour, was evidently built about 1904.[3]

An application to subdivide the ten-acre property was approved in the summer of 1989, and the new owner of the portion containing the farm buildings proposed to bulldoze them and the remains of the orchard, and erect his dream home in their place. He actually moved a large backhoe on the property, and began to clear the land, but inexplicably he changed his mind, and put the property back onto the market, at which time Sharon Fownes and Terry Lemieux, the real-estate agents who had been handling the subdivision and sale of the property, decided to buy it themselves, repair it and modernize it.

1 Background paper presented to Surrey council by Ald. Stanley McKinnon, August 9, 1989.

2 It looks like a variation on the Edwardian Builder style, see pages 18 through 21. The off-centre portico on the front porch is very typical of Kitsilano builders' houses, such as the ones on Macdonald Street just north of 7th Avenue on the east side of the street.

3 Interview with Ron Kitzel, March 8, 1976, Surrey Archives.

BOWEN ISLAND

MRS. E.H. GUDEWILL

"Fairweather," under construction in the spring of 1930.

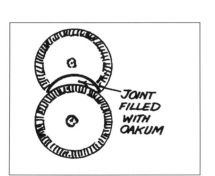

JOINT
FILLED
WITH
OAKUM

Detail of log construction at "Fairweather," redrawn from the original plans by B.C. Palmer in January, 1930.

1 Proposal for "Cowan's Point Resort:" by the Praxis Group, with land supplied by Ernest Rogers's sons John and Ted and grandson Joe, in association with Arthur Erickson architects and others, December, 1989. See "Residents Resisting Bowen Development," *Sun*, May 4, 1990.

2 *Who's Who in Canada*, 1930-31 edition, page 1883.

3 Howard, *Bowen Island 1872-1972*, page 60.

Technology and population pressure are beginning to make Bowen Island a "bedroom community" for Vancouverites. People's attitudes to how much time they are willing to spend commuting are changing as the city grows and people move here from places like Toronto, where an hour and a half or more spent travelling in each direction each day is commonplace. Thus, Bowen Island's arcadian isolation is slowly vanishing — the morning and afternoon ferries between Snug Cove and Horseshoe Bay are packed with worker-commuters, and proposed new developments, such as the Cowan's Point Resort, include plans for high-speed water connections with downtown Vancouver.[1]

With each passing year, more of the old-timers on Bowen Island, and their rustic properties and "island" philosophies, succumb to the march of progress. The old properties are generally primitive by contemporary standards; however, current city standards for houses, such as size and water use, do not translate *philosophically* into the island lifestyle. So many of the new houses in new subdivisions on Bowen Island, and in developments such as those at Fairweather Point and proposed for Cowan's Point, are not "getting away from it all," at all. They are city houses — in some cases far larger than anything that can be built in the city — on erstwhile remote island property.

The wealth and ostentation of some of the residents, and their willingness to endure lengthy commuting time, is negating the distinctiveness and rustic quality of Bowen Island. Ranked in opposition are the people — mainly those who are already established on Bowen — who want to keep it the same and thus stall the island's impending population explosion. Occupying the figurative middle ground are those who can accept the inevitability of new development but wonder why so much of it has to be so lavish and place such demands on the island's natural water supply and rural environment.

• • •

The earliest significant settler on the southeastern end of Bowen Island — the side of the island that faces downtown Vancouver across English Bay — was George Cowan,[2] a lawyer who, beginning in 1899, bought over 1,000 acres in the area that became known as Cowan's Point. Remnants of Cowan's property still survive and retain the bucolic ambience of the early years of this century: his shingle-covered "Swiss cottage" on a meadow near the beach, the Malkin cottage illustrated on page 196, and the quiet up-hill-and-down-dale dirt roads winding among the cedars and arbutus trees near Seymour Bay.

However, Cowan's dreams for a "poetical commonwealth"[3] on his Bowen Island estate never amounted to much. He was a lawyer with impeccable Conservative credentials in an era dominated by the Liberal governments of Sir Wilfrid Laurier and William Lyon Mackenzie King; he retains the dubious distinction of being made a Queen's Counsel by the Mackenzie Bowell Conservative government in 1896, and having it cancelled by the Laurier administration when it assumed power. Although a source to him and his wife of great pleasure, and the site for generations of carefree summertime frolicking by his descendants and friends, his Cowan's Point

The interior of "Fairweather" on Bowen Island.

property was also a source of continual financial grief, as he struggled to make mortgage and tax payments. The result of one crisis, immediately following the Wall Street stock-market crash of 1929, resulted in the creation of "Fairweather."

In the summer of 1922, Cowan's daughter Irene married Ernest Rogers, the second (but eldest surviving) son of the late B.C. Sugar Refinery owner. As a wedding present to them, Cowan drew "some lines on the map of his Bowen Island property," dividing off a piece of land on which Ernest built a cabin called "Peterout." The nickname for Ernest's cabin came from the feeling in the family that his enthusiasm would "peter out";[4] however, several years later, Ernest Rogers was still enthusiastic about his summer cottage. Late in the autumn of 1929, Cowan's mortgage on his Bowen Island property, held personally by the Canadian Pacific Railway president Edward Beatty, was called, and Cowan had no money to pay it.[5]

Ernest's mother, the widow Mrs. B.T. Rogers, had little interest in rural property in general, or in Bowen Island in particular, but, after some lobbying by members of her family, Mrs. Rogers wrote in her diary on December 10, 1929: "I decided to buy the Cowan Point property, and change the name from Winnipeg to Fairweather Bay."[6] She bought the land — 234 acres on the western end of Cowan's waterfront holdings, sight unseen — for the value of the outstanding mortgage.[7] "Fairweather" was her mother's maiden name.

Four days after deciding to buy the property, she engaged the architect Bernard Charles Palmer, with whom she had worked on the interior decoration of "Shannon" (page 137), to design a summer house for the new property. Within weeks, Palmer developed plans for a log house, sited dramatically on the steep slope above Fairweather Bay, and surrounded by old-growth cedars and Douglas fir. Mrs. Rogers engaged Dominion Construction, which had previously converted "Gabriola" and built "Shannon" for her, to build the house there. It is

4 Private diaries, cited in *M.I. Rogers*, page 134.

5 Letter from Forrest Rogers, 1987.

6 Private diaries, cited in *M.I.Rogers*, page 135.

7 Letter from Forrest Rogers, 1987.

"FAIRWEATHER" + BORNEO CHAIRS

unlikely she had any impression of how precipitous the site is, for she did not visit "Fairweather" until March 1, 1930, when she noted in her diary that the logs were all in place for the first storey.[8]

"Fairweather" is a nine-bedroom family lodge, probably unique in the province both for its design and its purpose. It is the type of "family compound" that exists in places such as Hyannisport — jointly held, and visited by numbers of relatives during the season. There are other properties on Bowen Island, including several in the Cowan's Point area, where the individual members of families each have a cottage around a common meadow or beach, but "Fairweather" is unique in that it is a single house. Mrs. Rogers transferred its ownership to her second daughter Elspeth and son-in-law Jan Cherniavsky; they handed it down to their children, Peter Cherniavsky and Janey Gudewill, who have since arranged to pass it on to the next generation. Thus, it will soon be in its fourth generation of ownership by one family — something of a record in itself for the Vancouver area.

The house was built of logs floated to Bowen Island from the Roberts Creek area and hauled up the steep slope from the beach by a steam-powered donkey engine — the skid road up the slope still exists, and is used by the property's caretaker to salvage beach logs for firewood. The main floor of the house is true log construction, as indicated in the drawing on page 192, but the upper floor and gable are frame construction, covered with a log veneer. The foundation is stone-faced concrete. The house is about forty-nine feet wide and forty-five feet deep, including

8 It appears that Mrs. Rogers bought this particular property primarily to come to the rescue of her son's father-in-law. The idea of building a log house probably was the architect's; the house plans, dated January, 1930, still exist. Information and opinions from Mrs. E.H. Gudewill, a granddaughter.

The view from the swimming pool towards "Fairweather." The pool is built into and blasted from a natural depression in the rocks about a hundred yards to the west of the main house. Below the concrete pool edge on the left of the watercolour, the land drops away steeply to a small, rocky beach.

a ten-foot-deep porch across the front façade. Inside is a massive fireplace and hearth faced with Haddington Island stone; there are three bedrooms on the main floor, with another six upstairs, reached by cantilevered gallery walkways on each side of the open-ceilinged living room. The living room, shown in the watercolour on page 193, measures twenty-eight feet by twenty-three feet.

Over the decades since the house was completed, family members have spent summers terracing the steep slope and insetting stone walls, developing the garden, and erecting and maintaining the outbuildings. A garage, diesel-generator house, and caretakers' cottage were built during the 1930s in picturesque fashion, faced with beach stone and finished with rough lumber, by the property's caretaker, a former farmer from the prairies by the name of George German, with the help of his family and various able-bodied Rogers family members. The swimming pool, an enhanced natural depression in the rocks on the headland east of the main house, was created by another caretaker, Mr. Lindekilde, who lived on the property in the years around 1950.

The house's original water supply — an open pipe running down the hill from a spring — and its old diesel generator, were superseded in the late 1970s when the family divided off 180 acres to the west of the house for the "Fairweather Point" development; "Fairweather Point" financed a modern water system and brought power lines to that part of the island.[9]

9 Conversations with Mrs. E.H. Gudewill.

THE MALKIN COTTAGE

MALKIN COTTAGE, BOWEN ISLAND

Nothing expresses the historic and pastoral quality of the old, vanishing Bowen Island better than the cottage near Seymour Bay built by J.P.D. Malkin for his mother.[1] Its rear section, a portion of which is visible on the right of the watercolour, is a B.C. Mills, Timber & Trading Company prefabricated cabin,[2] erected about 1906 on a fifteen-acre property purchased from George Cowan.[3] The front wing and porch, which form a "T" at the front of the prefab and from which there is a splendid view of English Bay and downtown Vancouver, were added in 1918 by Dominion Construction.

In the lifetime since, the cottage has sat quietly on its little meadow, without electricity or piped water or television or stereo or any of the other modern conveniences considered essential elsewhere on Bowen Island. For most of that time, in the summer season, it has been occupied by J.P.D. Malkin's daughter Ursula and her companion Jean Russell. Although the cottage is in perfect harmony with the ideals of Bowen Island's original cottagers, it has become an anachronism. The enormous ferries on the Horseshoe Bay-Nanaimo run skirt the shoreline, their profiles almost filling the little bay; seaplanes fly low along the shoreline, and occasionally

M. KLUCKNER 1989

there is the sound of recorded music from a passing boat, or thumping through the trees from a distant house.

Not only is this the quintessential summer cottage of old Bowen Island, but there is much about it that is archetypal of Vancouver, for it is a picturesque shack with a million-dollar view. New generations of Vancouverites, whether they are natives or immigrants, fail to appreciate the quirky and picturesque nature of so much of the Lower Mainland's past. Whereas it is possible to adapt the grand old buildings of the city — or of any city — to contemporary uses, a building such as this one *must be adapted to*, because its essence is its modesty, its well-worn primitiveness, and its comparative rusticity. It conveys the impression that it is growing out of the landscape. So much of Vancouver's heritage lies in buildings such as this, and in other comparatively small houses like California Bungalows that capture the spirit of a philosophical movement, and a moment in the city's past. Unless the city as a whole can grasp this fact, Vancouver's distinctive residential heritage, which new generations now feel must make way for them, will be demolished and forgotten.

2 See page 19; the only surviving catalogue from that firm shows no gabled cabins, so either this was a discontinued model or else it has been modified at some point in the eighty-five years of its existence.

3 These fifteen acres, and the 234 sold to Mrs. B.T. Rogers for "Fairweather," were the only parts of Cowan's estate disbursed during his lifetime. See Howard, *Bowen Island 1872-1972*, page 61.

APPENDIX I: WHAT'S THERE NOW

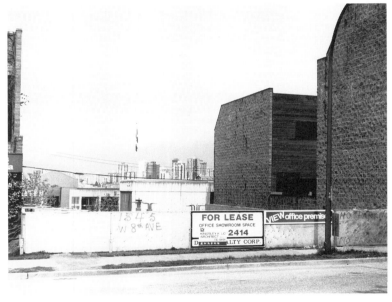

Photographs taken in May, 1990.

(Top left) Page 2: the corner of 16th and Laurel. (Middle left) Page 34: the site of the house at 1545 West 8th Avenue. (Above) Page 46: the "pipe-organ" façade re-erected on the Pacific Centre. (Bottom left) Page 87: 451 East Pender Street, standing alone after the fire.

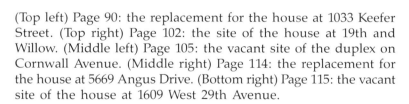

(Top left) Page 90: the replacement for the house at 1033 Keefer Street. (Top right) Page 102: the site of the house at 19th and Willow. (Middle left) Page 105: the vacant site of the duplex on Cornwall Avenue. (Middle right) Page 114: the replacement for the house at 5669 Angus Drive. (Bottom right) Page 115: the vacant site of the house at 1609 West 29th Avenue.

(Top left) Page 116: the replacement for the house at 1308 West 47th Avenue. (Top right) Page 121: the site of the Kerrisdale Grocery, with the doomed Magee High School in the background. (Middle left) Page 123: the replacement for the house at 1701 West 49th Avenue. (Middle right) Page 125: on the right, the Tudor Revival house being reconstructed following its movement to one side of the lot. (Bottom left) Page 142: the replacements for the house at 1591 South West Marine Drive.

(Top left) Page 149: new commercial buildings on the site of the farmhouse at 8220 St. George Street. (Top right) Page 155: the replacements on the site of the house at 4707 Trafalgar Street. (Middle left) Page 156: the replacements on the site of the house at 2880 West 28th Avenue. (Middle right) Page 160: the replacements on the site of the house at 3517 West 30th Avenue. (Bottom right) Page 165: the site of the house at 3556 Victoria Drive.

APPENDIX II: GLOSSARY OF ARCHITECTURAL TERMS

ART DECO. Also known as Zigzag Moderne; the name art deco comes from the 1925 Paris exposition of *arts décoratifs*. A style mainly used in large buildings of the 1920s and 1930s, art deco often employs a central tower whose summit recedes in a stepped pattern, as in the Marine Building and the Georgia Medical-Dental Building (pages 49 and 51). Ornamentation is zigzags, chevrons, sunbursts and stylized, geometrical motifs. The style metamorphosed into the Streamline Moderne, an outgrowth of the machine aesthetic of the time.

ARTS AND CRAFTS STYLE. The large, picturesque houses inspired by Tudor manor houses of England, and in Vancouver and Victoria usually associated with the pre-First-World-War work of the architect Samuel Maclure. See the Hunter house on page 99, and the houses on pages 169 and 170. The Tudor Revival buildings of the 1920s and 1930s are usually more modest in size, and are picturesque façades by comparison with the big prewar Tudors.

BATTENS. The narrow vertical strips covering the joints of horizontal boards that provide the siding for a building. In Vancouver, they were a feature of the BCMT&T prefabricated houses (see page 19).

BEAUX ARTS STYLE. In the United States, it is also known as City Beautiful Classicism. The style is a more baroque version of neoclassicism, as seen in the Federal Building, now the Sinclair Centre (page 40). "Shannon" (page 137) is an example of the style in a residence, using a classical portico, bracketed window crowns, an arched entranceway and barrel-vaulted main hallway, and an interior designed as an interconnected sequence of spaces.

BELLCAST EAVES. A pitched roof that curves outward at its projecting lower edges (the eaves) like a bell. An example is the roof of the farmhouse at 41st and Wales (page 153).

BRACKET. A horizontal supporting member. Examples are the brackets between the vertical porch posts and the porch roof on the house on page 20, and the triangular brackets between the wall and the eaves of Craftsman houses, such as the house on page 156.

BUILDERS' BOX. See VANCOUVER BOX.

CALIFORNIA BUNGALOW. The small, box-like houses with low-pitched roofs, porches, and understated second storeys built between about 1905 and 1925. They were inspired by the so-called "Pasadena lifestyle," and the simple, garden-oriented, unfettered suburbia of southern California; in their use of materials and their reflection of a social aesthetic, they are part of the Craftsman Style. At the time of their construction, the terms California Bungalow Style and Craftsman Style were used interchangeably, but this book refers specifically to the houses on pages 28-29 and 129 as California Bungalows.

CAPE COD STYLE. A breezy, informal house style inspired by the domestic architecture of the American Atlantic seaboard, and ideally featuring white bevelled clapboard siding, wooden mullioned (divided into small panes) windows, and dormers set into a steeply pitched roof. The few good examples in the city were built in the 1930s, including the house on page 117.

COLONIAL REVIVAL STYLE. Large, square, two- or two-and-one-half-storey houses, usually symmetrical, with broad, full-width front porches held up by columns, bay windows, a central dormer set into a low-pitched hipped roof, and either clapboard siding or shingles. A round window is a typical decorative element, as in the house on page 142. The Cape Cod Style is sometimes referred to as a later variant of the Colonial Revival Style.

CRAFTSMAN STYLE. The most popular housing style, in all its variations, between 1910 and 1925. Typical features are prominent, sheltering roofs, exposed brackets and rafter ends, and in the best examples, rough brick or stone for chimneys, foundations, and porch piers. Siding is usually shingles, giving the buildings an overwhelmingly wooden look. The style is the outgrowth of the Craftsman aesthetic developed in the nineteenth-century writings of John Ruskin and William Morris; it is a synthesis of influences from the English Arts and Crafts Movement (especially the cottages, designed by M.H. Baillie Scott and Charles F.A. Voysey, inspired by medieval English rural architecture), the collaboration of the architect Edwin Lutyens and the garden designer Gertrude Jekyll, and the traditional architecture of Japan and Switzerland. See pages 17, 21-29, and the houses on pages 80, 99, 101, 102, 103, 123, 129, 130, 131, 155, and 156.

DORMER. A window projecting from a pitched roof.

DUTCH COLONIAL REVIVAL STYLE. Reviving features of Dutch Colonial architecture in the United States, this style has as its main feature a double-pitched mansard roof (the lower pitch being steeper than the upper one), often referred to as a Dutch Gable.

EASTLAKE STYLE. A concept that developed from the drawings and writings of the English architect Charles Eastlake (who denied he had anything to do with it), the pure Eastlake Style was popular in the eastern United States, but few pure examples were built on the west coast. Some of its stylistic features, dating from the 1850s and 1860s, were grouped together by the historian Vincent Scully as the Stick Style. In the Lower Mainland, a few houses — 449 East Pender Street (page 87), the Shaw house (page 98), and the Galbraith house (page 171) — contain elements of the style, most notably in their verticality, their division of surface areas into panels defined by board moulding and containing diagonal siding, their profusion of jigsaw work, and their use of projecting turned knobs as repeated decoration.

EDWARDIAN BUILDER STYLE. See VANCOUVER BOX.

FRENCH NORMAN STYLE. A picturesque style built occasionally in the 1920s and 1930s, inspired by the farm houses and small manor houses of Normandy and Brittany. See the house on page 116.

GABLE. The triangular piece of wall beneath the end of a pitched roof.

GABLED ROOF. A roof that slopes on two sides.

GEORGIAN REVIVAL STYLE. A formal, symmetrical, box-like house type, built in Vancouver mainly during the 1920s and 1930s. The larger and more elaborate examples often have side gables and and attic dormers. More common are the hipped-roof examples built in the Second Shaughnessy and Kerrisdale districts, such as the houses on pages 114 and 134. Walls are usually stucco, and the best examples have restrained wooden ornamentation around the entranceways, windows, and rooflines, and a finely proportioned balance between windows and walls.

GINGERBREAD. The decorative wooden ornament on houses of the late nineteenth century. Most of the gingerbread on Vancouver houses is porch brackets and gable ornaments. See the houses on page 87, 98, 149, 165, and 171.

GOTHIC REVIVAL STYLE. A style that uses the pointed arches, ornamentation, and buttresses of the church architecture of the Middle Ages. In houses, the stylistic elements are steep-pitched roofs, pointed windows, and the use of wall dormers; in Vancouver, elements of the style appear in the Strathcona area, where it is often mixed with elements of the Queen Anne style.

HALF-TIMBER. The mixture of plaster, stucco or masonry set between the gaps in the wooden frame of a Tudor house; both the timber and the complementary material are visible.

HIPPED ROOF. A roof that slopes on four sides.

LINTEL. A beam set directly above a door or window to support the weight of the structure above.

NEOCLASSICAL REVIVAL STYLE. A symmetrical, grand style, restrained in ornament and using classical Greek design models. The style's typical feature, as seen in the Vancouver Art Gallery and "The Hollies" (page 108), is the full-height portico with classical columns.

PORTE-COCHÈRE. A drive-through entrance porch for vehicles.

PORTICO. A covered porch, usually consisting of a triangular pediment atop columns.

QUEEN ANNE STYLE. The picturesque housing style of the years before the First World War, featuring an irregular and asymmetrical plan, steeply pitched and complex rooflines, bay windows and, often, wraparound porches and a turret. Typically, in the simple examples built by builders, surfaces were covered in combinations of decorative wooden textures, especially fish-scale shingles placed within the gables. See the houses on pages 75, 76, 87, 90, 94, 98, 110, 165, and 171.

ROMANESQUE STYLE. Based on Imperial Roman design and the churches of the pre-Gothic Middle Ages, the style features very heavy rounded arches and uses massive, rough-cut stone to achieve a solid, weathered look. See the Innes-Thompson Building on page 54.

SIDING. The weatherproof facing on the outside of a wood-framed building. The common materials of old Vancouver were shingles, clapboard (bevelled boards laid horizontally with a slight overlap), and tongue-and-groove shiplap (which was in addition used to sheath the frame before shingles were added). Later types of siding, either used in new construction or to renovate deteriorating old buildings, include asphalt and asbestos shingles and "boards" of vinyl or aluminum. Stucco — a weatherproof plaster sometimes mixed with rock and glass particles and applied to a netting attached to the house's frame — became a popular finishing material in the 1920s.

SKYSCRAPER GOTHIC STYLE. Ornamentation derived from Gothic churches and applied to office buildings, beginning with the Woolworth Building in New York just before the First World War. See the Weart Building on pages 54-56.

SPANISH COLONIAL REVIVAL STYLE. Hearkening back to the buildings of Spanish Colonial California, the style features white stucco walls, round-topped windows, arches, and tile roofs, and began to appear in Vancouver in the late 1920s.

STICK STYLE. Highly ornamented and related to the Eastlake style, it emphasizes delicate surface detail, and was most often mixed with Queen Anne elements, such as the profusion of jigsaw and lath work seen in the house on page 171.

SWISS COTTAGE STYLE. Also sometimes called the Chalet style, it is based on the picturesque Swiss vernacular architecture that was one of the stylistic influences on the Craftsman movement. Craftsman houses with side gables, such as the ones illustrated on pages 8, 24 (left), 25 (left), 31, 34, 79, and 102, are often called Swiss Cottages.

TERRA COTTA. Clay shaped in a mould and fired, then sometimes glazed, and used for ornament on buildings such as the Georgia Medical-Dental (page 49) and the Convent of the Sacred Heart (page 158).

TUDOR REVIVAL STYLE. One of the revival styles especially popular in Vancouver during the 1920s and 1930s (and less often in the decades since), seen most often in Shaughnessy and Kerrisdale. It revives the picturesque architecture of Tudor England, including the half-timbering and steep-pitched roofs, and its best examples have diamond-mullioned leaded-glass windows, irregular profiles, curving rooflines, black timbers and white plaster, and are set into overgrown English gardens. See pages 15, 67, and 125.

VANCOUVER BOX. The style of builders' house, subject to infinite variation, erected throughout the city in the first decade of the century. All Vancouver Boxes are relatively simple, symmetrical shapes; some were superb examples of craftsmanship and contained elaborate leaded glass, bay windows, and classically inspired wooden ornamentation, while others were poorly built with few amenities and little detailing. They often contain features of other styles, including Queen Anne and Craftsman. Most were built by carpenters, who took their original inspiration from the plan books that sired "builders' boxes" all over North America. The two most common variations of the Vancouver Box are the hipped-roof house with an attic dormer (pages 18-19), and the gabled house (pages 20-21). Other Vancouver Boxes are illustrated on pages 69, 77, 85, 90, 94, 97, 107, 162, 165, 179 and 190.

VANCOUVER SPECIAL. The most common speculative-builders' house style since the mid-1950s. The classic "Special" is relentlessly rectangular, with a low-pitched, tarred roof, a brick-veneered lower storey, and a stucco upper storey with sliding glass doors opening onto a narrow, metal-railinged balcony. Their popularity stems from their inexpensive construction; usually, the bedrooms are on the ground floor and the living area is upstairs.

VICTORIAN STYLE. Although there were once examples of the various Victorian residential styles, especially the High Victorian Italianate, in the Lower Mainland, they have been demolished. The Victorian Italianate style survives in commercial buildings from circa 1890 in the Gastown area, such as the Horne Block at 311 West Cordova Street. There are a number of Victorian Italianate houses still surviving in the city of Victoria.

BIBLIOGRAPHY

GENERAL HISTORY

Bayley, Charles M. *The Kerrisdale Story*. Vancouver: Kerrisdale Courier, 1955.

Boris, Eileen. *Art and Labor: Ruskin, Morris, and the Craftsman Ideal in America*. Philadelphia: Temple University Press, 1986.

Burkinshaw, Robert K. *False Creek*. City of Vancouver Archives Occasional Paper No. 2, 1984.

Carter, S. Maurice, ed. *Who's Who in British Columbia*. Vancouver: Published by S. Maurice Carter, 1944-46 edition (author's collection)

Ewert, Henry. *The Story of the B.C. Electric Railway Company*. Vancouver: Whitecap Books, 1986.

Greene, B.M., ed. *Who's Who and Why*. Toronto: International Press Limited, 1913 edition (collection of Metro Toronto Reference Library).

Greene, B.M., ed. *Who's Who and Why*. Toronto: International Press Limited, 1921 edition (author's collection).

Greene, B.M., ed. *Who's Who and Why*. Toronto: International Press Limited, 1930-31 edition (author's collection).

Hopkins, John Castell. *Canadian Annual Review of Public Affairs*. Toronto: Review Publishing Company, 1916, 1917, and 1921 editions.

Howard, Irene. *Bowen Island 1872-1972*. Bowen Island Historians, 1973.

Howay, F.W. and Scholefield, E.O.S. *British Columbia From The Earliest Times to The Present*, 4 volumes. Toronto: S.J. Clarke Publishing Ltd., 1914.

Kluckner, Michael. *M.I, Rogers*. Victoria: privately published limited edition, 1987.

Kluckner, Michael. *Vancouver The Way It Was*. Vancouver: Whitecap Books, 1984.

Kluckner, Michael. *Victoria The Way It Was*. Vancouver: Whitecap Books, 1986.

Ormsby, Margaret A. *British Columbia: A History*. Toronto: Macmillan, 1958.

Ross, Leslie J. *Richmond, Child of the Fraser*. Richmond '79 Centennial Society, 1979.

Schreiner, John. *The Refiners*. Vancouver: Douglas & McIntyre, 1989.

Steele, Richard M. *The Stanley Park Explorer*. Vancouver: Whitecap Books, 1985.

ARCHITECTURAL HISTORY

Allan Parker & Associates. *Vancouver Heritage Inventory*. Summary Report, B.C. Heritage Trust, 1986.

City of Vancouver Planning Department. *Vancouver Heritage Inventory*, amended 1988.

Foundation Group Designs. *The Ambitious City — City of North Vancouver Heritage Inventory*. City of North Vancouver, 1988.

Foundation Group Designs. *West Vancouver Heritage Inventory*. District of West Vancouver, 1988.

Gebhard, David and Winter, Robert. *Architecture in Los Angeles*. Salt Lake City: Gibbs M. Smith, Inc. Peregrine Smith Books, 1985.

Gebhard, David and Winter, Robert. *Architecture in San Francisco and Northern California*. Salt Lake City: Gibbs M. Smith, Inc. Peregrine Smith Books, 1985.

HRH The Prince of Wales. *A Vision of Britain: A Personal View of Architecture*. London: Doubleday, 1989.

Kalman, Harold. *Exploring Vancouver 2*. Vancouver: University of British Columbia Press, 1978.

Scott, Jack. *Once in the Royal City*. Vancouver: Whitecap Books, 1985.

PLAN BOOKS

Dustman, U.M. *Dustman's Book of Plans and Building Construction*. Charles C. Thompson Company, 1909 (collection of Metro Toronto Reference Library).

Pedersen, Jens. *Practical Homes* (Fourth Edition). Saint Paul, Minnesota: Brown-Blodgett Company, 1927 (author's collection).

Stillwell, E.J., and Company. *Representative California Homes*. Los Angeles: 1912 (pamphlet number 1912-13, City of Vancouver Archives).

Von Holst, H.V. *Modern American Homes*. Chicago: American Technical Society, 1912 (collection of Metro Toronto Reference Library).

Yoho & Merritt. *Craftsman Bungalows*. Seattle: 1920 (pamphlet number 1920-13, City of Vancouver Archives).

MAPS

Goad's Atlas of Vancouver, 1912 (collection of City of Vancouver Archives).

Insurance Plan of Vancouver, 14 volumes, 1955 (collection of Metro Toronto Reference Library, FO.912.13681 I56 No. 28).

ACKNOWLEDGEMENTS

I was busy with the watercolours in this book during a period when, no matter where I went in Vancouver, the topics of conversation were invariably the disappearance of the old city, monster houses, whether or not the Georgia Medical-Dental Building should be saved, and spiralling house prices and apartment rental costs. Almost everyone had an opinion or a piece of information, such as the impending demolition of the last old house on a block, or the behaviour of a contractor, or the price that so-and-so got for his little bungalow, or the impossibility of raising the down payment or affording the mortgage for a piece of the Vancouver dream, or the latest bells and whistles that someone had seen in a new house. As has been the case for most of the past century, We-the-Vancouver-Residents are obsessed with real estate. I am reminded of a comment that I first heard or read sometime around 1970, which I considered at the time to be the ultimate in commercialism and philistinism: real-estate agents have the real stake in the community, because the average home-owner moves every four years or so.

The great source of information on what was happening in residential Vancouver was the *Real Estate Weekly*, in all its Lower Mainland editions, published by the Elty Sales company. I dutifully combed through it week after week, looking for interesting old houses and properties that were being sold for their location and lot value. Without the *Real Estate Weekly*, this book would have been very difficult to write and illustrate, and many of the houses recorded here would have been lost to everything except the memories of a few; perhaps it is churlish to say that without the success of the *Real Estate Weekly* and the enthusiasm for redevelopment of some of the agents who placed advertisements in it, this book might have been unnecessary, too. I must also acknowledge the contribution to my militancy made by the treatment of the house at 4707 Trafalgar Street (page 155), whose agent was so certain that prospective purchasers were only interested in the land on which the house stood that he had not bothered to prepare any information on the house itself.

The information from which I wrote the text came from a number of sources, including: the City of Vancouver archives, whose director Sue Baptie and dedicated staff, especially Anna Sumpton, are a credit to this city; the Vancouver Public Library, especially its historical photographs division; Jackie Murfitt, the City of Vancouver's heritage planner, and Marco D'Agostini, planning assistant; the University of British Columbia library newspaper collection; the archives of the Municipality of Richmond, and its director Ken Young; the Surrey Museum and Archives, and its curator Jacqueline O'Donnell; provincial land titles director J.P. Malcolm McAvity; the Vancouver Land Titles Office, and assistant director Jim Small; and the Metro Toronto Reference Library, which has a unique and complete insurance atlas of the City of Vancouver and its suburbs in the early 1950s, from which I developed the maps. I also received the help and collaboration of the members of the heritage committee of the Community Arts Council of Vancouver, most notably Jo Scott-B., John Atkin, John Stuart, Anthony Norfolk, and Janet Bingham.

The following people contributed information and assistance for the project, including the purchase of the watercolours: Louise Adams, Joan Anderson, Rev. Val Anderson, Mr. and Mrs. Peter Cherniavsky, Diane Cope, the Davis family, Doris Dennison, Joyce Diggins, Dave Fairhall, Richard Fearn, Sharon Fownes, William J.L. Gibbons, Elizabeth Godley, Cliff Green, Janey Gudewill, the Gurney family, Betty Jarvis, Mrs. Alita King, Cora Lampman, A.L. Lazenby, Robert Lemon, Ray Lepovsky, John McIntyre, Carter Maitland, Ursula Malkin, Susan Mills, Bill Nesbitt, Elizabeth O'Kiely, Joan Paterson, Gary Penway, Gordon Price, Carol Ann Reynolds, Mr. and Mrs. Arthur Ross, Sean Rossiter, Jean Russell, Evelyn Salsberry, Jack Scott, Brian and Pat Stone, Bruce Stratton, Diane Sutherland, Carole Taylor, David Thomsett, June Thompson, Gerald Timleck, Eric Watt, Gordon and Alison Wyness, Rob Wyness, and Mr. and Mrs. Lawrence Young.

Christine Allen did a first edit of the manuscript, and ensured that it contained "the best words in their best order." Thanks also to the staff at Whitecap Books, especially Colleen MacMillan, and as always to Elaine Jones, who did a final edit on the manuscript and prepared it for publication.

INDEX